Comparative
Criminal Justice

Francis Pakes

WILLAN
PUBLISHING

To my wife Suzanne

Published by

Willan Publishing
Culmcott House
Mill Street, Uffculme
Cullompton, Devon
EX15 3AT, UK
Tel: +44(0)1884 840337
Fax: +44(0)1884 840251
e-mail: info@willanpublishing.co.uk
Website: www.willanpublishing.co.uk

Published simultaneously in the USA and Canada by

Willan Publishing
c/o ISBS, 920 NE 58th Ave, Suite 300,
Portland, Oregon 97213-3786, USA
Tel: +001(0)503 287 3093
Fax: +001(0)503 280 8832
e-mail: info@isbs.com
Website: www.isbs.com

First published 2004

ISBN 1-84392-031-X (paperback)
ISBN 1-84392-032-8 (hardback)

British Library Cataloguing-in-Publication Data

A catalogue record for this book is available from the British Library

Typeset by TW Typesetting, Plymouth, Devon
Project management by Deer Park Productions, Tavistock, Devon
Printed and bound by TJ International Ltd, Trecerus Industrial Estate, Padstow, Cornwall

Comparative Criminal Justice

Contents

List of boxes and tables

Boxes

Tables

Acknowledgements

Comparative criminal justice is an area so wide that when writing a book on the topic assistance from a variety of sources is a necessity. I am grateful to those who looked at drafts of chapters and provided thoughtful comments on them. Thanks to Mark Button, Nathan Hall, Marc Jacobs, Barry Loveday, Steve Savage, Daniel Silverstone and Tom Williamson for undertaking that chore. Particular thanks goes to Keith Soothill and an anonymous reviewer for exposing many a weakness in earlier drafts.

The book also owes something to students at the Institute for Criminal Justice Studies at the University of Portsmouth, who took my Comparative Criminal Justice unit and produced some excellent essays that challenged my thinking. It is encouraging to find that old truism of students educating their teachers is sometimes true indeed.

Thanks also go to colleagues at the Institute for Criminal Justice, University of Portsmouth for enough peace and quiet to allow me to make headway with this book. In particular, I would like to express my appreciation to Sam Poyser for acting as a protective shield in this regard.

Finally, I am much indebted to the love and patience of my wife Suzanne. I dedicate this book to her. Married, settled and published, I really feel I have it all.

Chapter 1

Comparative criminal justice: a timely enterprise

'In the Netherlands they don't have juries'; 'In Saudi Arabia they cut off your hand for stealing'; 'British judges wear wigs'; 'Police officers in China do people's laundry'. Such generalised statements about criminal justice in other countries are commonplace. In the news media, an interest in looking at criminal justice in far-away places invariably occurs when compatriots find themselves in trouble with the law abroad. Britons subjected to the death penalty in Singapore for drugs trafficking or to imprisonment in Greece for spying receive a great deal of coverage, and so do the criminal justice systems through which their cases are administered. But typically, when a case comes to an end, so does the interest in the criminal justice system of the country at issue.

Comparative criminal justice is the academic study of criminal justice arrangements at home and abroad. By means of documenting, analysing and contextualising criminal justice processes and institutions elsewhere and comparing them to more familiar settings a broader understanding of criminal justice can be gained. The other obvious advantage constitutes the acquisition of specific knowledge about arrangements in other jurisdictions.

Criminal justice forms part of the set of processes, bodies and institutions that aim to secure or restore social control. Social control is defined as 'the organised ways in which society responds to behaviour and people it regards as deviant, problematic, worrying, threatening, troublesome and undesirable' (Cohen, 1985: 1–2). In this book I take a broad perspective on criminal justice. It includes, therefore, a discussion on private policing, and also on extra-legal means of institutionalised social control, such as, for instance, those in place in remote areas of Alaska. The definition of criminal justice is therefore not restricted to bodies that directly represent the state in aiming to achieve social control.

Why study criminal justice comparatively?

There are theoretical as well as practical incentives to the comparative study of criminal justice. A good starting point is simply academic curiosity. Considering the opening example above you might wonder how the Dutch can manage to enact justice without the involvement of a jury anywhere in their criminal justice process. Such a state of affairs raises various questions. First of all, how exactly does this work? Comparative research would discover that it is professional judges (individual judges in case of minor offences and a panel of three judges for serious offences) who reach verdicts and impose sentences. That might raise the suspicion that seasoned judges are perhaps rather prone to convict defendant after defendant. This is an argument often heard in favour of the jury. Subsequently, we might wonder about how the jury-less state of Dutch criminal justice is perceived by defendants, the legal profession and by society at large (see Kelk, 1995; Tak, 1999).

In Britain, any attempt by the Home Secretary to tamper with the right to trial by jury is likely to be met with protests from the legal profession and civil liberty organisations alike (see Lloyd-Bostock and Thomas, 2001, on the state of the jury in England and Wales). There seems to be widespread agreement within these groups that the jury represents a pillar of the criminal justice system: the jury symbolises fairness and impartiality. It begs the question of whether similar opinions are held in the Netherlands and to what extent these opinions inform law and policy-making. That might lead to a better perspective on criminal justice in the Netherlands as well as on the value of the jury in various contexts and jurisdictions.

A similar argument can be applied to sentencing practices in Saudi Arabia (Souryal *et al.*, 1994). The lay impression is that these are harsh compared to many other countries, with frequent reports of executions and body mutilations. However, we need to know more about these practices before we can reach a balanced judgement with regard to their propriety. In Saudi Arabia, harsh punishment is justified by reference to the country's low crime rates, which are claimed as a sign of its success. When potential offenders realise that they might lose a hand as a result they might think twice before committing theft. The second argument to justify severe sentences carries even more weight. It relates to the fact that law in Saudi Arabia is, to a large extent, based on the Koran and therefore strongly dogmatic. The sentencing practices derived from the

Muslim holy book are considered just and proper, regardless of their effectiveness. Any discussion about their utility is not very meaningful in light of that, in the strongly religious state of Saudi Arabia (Souryal, 1987).

The academic endeavour of comparative criminal justice requires a certain degree of understanding of not just criminal justice processes but also the actors involved in it, and the society in which the system is set. Criminal justice arrangements need to be contextualised so that we can understand how they work in relation to each other, and how the nuts and bolts of arrangements fit together. We also need to find ways of deciding how criminal justice arrangements fit a country, a culture or a legal tradition. As Fairchild and Dammer put it, 'The fact is that a nation's way of administering justice often reflects deep-seated cultural, religious, economic, political, and historical realities. Learning about the reasons for these different practices can give us insight into the values, traditions, and cultures of other systems.' (Fairchild and Dammer, 2001: 9).

Acquiring such knowledge has the added benefit of preventing ethnocentrism from occurring. Ethnocentrism refers to sentiments that regard domestic arrangements as necessarily 'normal' and 'right', and other cultures or customs as 'weird' or 'wrong'. It occurs frequently in the spheres of culture and religion and is no stranger to criminal justice either.

The second impetus for comparative study is of a practical nature. Knowledge of systems in neighbouring countries has been vital in securing basic levels of cooperation. Longstanding agreements exist, for instance, between Belgium and its neighbouring countries with regard to limited cross-border powers. These have been in place with France since 1919, with Luxembourg since 1920 and with the Netherlands since 1949. Such arrangements are handy, for instance when dealing with bank robbers who manage to flee into a neighbouring country while being chased by the police. They ensure that police activity does not come to a complete stop when the border is reached (Geysel, 1990).

As transnational arrangements go, such arrangements are of a local nature. There exist more overarching arrangements, which include, for instance Europol, which is a cooperative body within the European Union (see Anderson et al., 1995) and Interpol, which is a policing organisation that is operative on a global scale.

There is no doubt that crime has increasingly become a global issue. This is particularly true for crimes such as terrorism and cyber-crime. However an increasing number of other crimes also have a transnational component. This is because offenders commit their crimes in more than one country, cross national borders themselves or reap the benefits of their crimes in another country. International cooperation is increasingly necessary in order for offenders to be apprehended, tried and convicted. Because officials of different systems cooperate with increasing frequency, a certain level of harmonisation of laws and procedures is beneficial. In order to achieve this, a certain level of understanding and appreciation of their similarities and differences is important. Harmonisation without understanding will always be very difficult indeed.

A further benefit of comparative research is to learn from the experience of others. For example, prior to the EURO 2000 tournament, the European Nations Football Championship, the co-hosting nations Belgium and the Netherlands passed legislation that would allow them to pro-actively arrest, detain and possibly deport suspected football hooligans. It has been alleged that these two nations used these and other policing powers in rather differing ways, with Dutch policing being more restrained and the Belgian forces using tear gas and water guns more readily (e.g. Adang, 2001). A discussion on how best to deal with travelling football hooligans ensued, not only in the context of international sports tournaments but also domestically. Debates in criminal justice are informed by, or even instigated by, developments abroad, and experiences gained elsewhere might serve to inform decision-making at home.

Criminal justice systems around the world are likely to face similar challenges. It might therefore be instructive to investigate how other systems tackle some of their problems, not just in major events, such as sports tournaments, but also with regard to more persistent issues. It is safe to assume that England and Wales are not the only jurisdiction whose race relations, in the context of criminal justice, have proved to be a challenge. It might be instructive to see what, for instance, the opinions in Australia are on the over-representation of Aboriginals in their criminal justice system. Is there recognition of 'institutionalised racism' in Australia? Perhaps lessons could be learned from there.

A further incentive for comparison relates to the question of 'Where do we stand?' In order to gain insight into states of affairs at home it might be helpful to examine matters abroad. Prison populations are a good example. In England and Wales the prison population is rising and has been for some time (see www.hmprisonservice.gov.uk for data and information). One way of making sense of prison populations is by taking a comparative perspective. The first and obvious place to look might be the so-called league tables that present detention ratios for various countries (e.g. Walmsley, 2002). These statistics invariably show that both the US and the Russian Federation have a lot more people incarcerated (as calculated over their total population) than the UK. It is equally obvious that there are many countries with smaller numbers of prisoners on, as well as outside, the European continent. Additionally, it is helpful to dispel the myth that prison rates in every Western country are on the rise. In Finland, in particular, prison rates have gone down for decades, a development that is attributed to the political determination to use incarceration sparingly (Törnudd, 1993). Such, possibly atypical, examples help to put the case across that not every country appears to be heading for a crime complex in which mass incarceration is the kneejerk reaction to growing public feelings of insecurity and fear of crime (Garland, 2001). As Garland himself emphasised, it does not necessarily have to be that way.

Statistical comparisons are not necessarily straightforward. A simple comparison of prison figures in isolation is not particularly informative as they can only say so much. For a proper comparison on, for instance, nations' tendencies to use imprisonment as a means of social control, more information is required than just prison rates. This information should at least include crime figures, but we might also wish to include information on the relative wealth of countries and the distribution of wealth in society. Unemployment rates and information about political stability might also be relevant in understanding comparative prison rates. The same is true for policing and sentencing practices. Do similar crimes attract similar sentences in different countries? What about the differences between sentences imposed and actually served? What alternatives to prison are there for sentencers to consider?

A further consideration is the extent to which these figures themselves are comparable. Do they include only convicts, or remand prisoners as well? Are those detained in mental hospitals incorporated in the figures? The comparison of criminal justice statistics across countries is fraught with difficulty, as any available data require a great deal of interpretation. That requires intimate knowledge about the acquisition of the data itself and a thorough understanding of the system and the society that produced them. We will explore these methodological issues further in Chapter 2.

Criminal justice systems are undoubtedly less self-contained than they have been in the past. Laws in England and Wales nowadays are strongly influenced by international treaties and by European legislation and rulings. Such supranational arrangements add a global element to criminal justice systems. Comparative criminal justice as an enterprise increasingly involves the study of such transnational and international arrangements. A good knowledge of the bodies and processes that make international law is therefore vital in order to understand how criminal justice is developing across the globe.

What this book is about

A text on comparative justice can be written from various perspectives. In these perspectives certain themes might receive emphasis possibly at the expense of others. First, it is important to note that this book emphasises *criminal justice* rather than crime. This of course does not mean that crime and its patterns and impact are ignored. However, this book particularly examines how criminal justice is enacted across the world rather than patterns of crime or any explanations of such patterns. In other words, this book is not about comparative criminology.

Second, this book focuses more on *procedural* aspects of justice than on substantive law. Thus, for instance, prosecution systems and the way trials are conducted are analysed in depth, but for example, the difference in legal definitions of murder and manslaughter in various jurisdictions is not discussed. Nevertheless, it would be nonsensical to adhere over-rigidly to such a distinction, and I have no intention of ignoring comparative matters of substantive law. Legal definitions of criminal behaviours are of particular interest in certain contexts. This includes, for example, the definition of genocide as adopted by the Yugoslav War Crimes Tribunal in The Hague in the Netherlands. Similarly, the way in which terrorism is defined by various national and international bodies is also a topic of discussion. Nevertheless, the emphasis remains on procedures.

Similarly a comparative book could primarily examine either criminal justice *structures* or criminal justice *processes*. Criminal courts can serve as an example here. A structural description would involve a description of higher and lower courts and their relative competencies. An emphasis on process would look at what actually happens inside these courts, and that is what will be discussed in Chapter 5.

A related distinction is often made between *law in the books* and *law in practice*. Law in the books is obviously how it is written up in codes, acts and constitutions. It would however be naive to assume that what it says in the law books is the sole determinant of how justice is actually administered. There are extra-legal arrangements that do not occur in statutes but which have, nevertheless, gained widespread acceptance within criminal justice systems. Similarly, any law book contains many a dead letter. These are laws or statutes that are no longer used and which therefore have lost their practical value. In the UK there are many local laws stemming from centuries back that are no more than inconsequential remnants of days past, even though they were never formally revoked.

Nevertheless, not every so-called dead letter should be considered meaningless. In many countries where the execution of convicts is no longer the practice the death penalty might still linger in the law books. While on the one hand it could be said that it is merely a harmless trace of a more punitive past, it could, on the other, be argued that such dead letters could be resurrected relatively easily, so that a reinstatement of the death penalty in such countries would be easier – and therefore possibly more likely – than in countries with no such traces left in the law books.

Additionally, the treatment of offenders receives more attention than that of victims in this book. This is arguably against the worldwide trend of securing a more prominent place for victims throughout the criminal justice process (see Zedner, 1997). However, an exhaustive review of comparative criminal justice is simply impossible. It is equally imposs-ible to include each and every development in all corners of the globe, which is why the choice is made for this more traditional emphasis on criminal justice with the perspective on the offender.

I have chosen a thematic approach, as opposed to a country-by-country approach, in which descriptions from a limited set of countries are utilised throughout the book. The rationale behind this choice is that I assume the reader to be more interested in general issues in criminal justice rather than in criminal justice in specific countries. Therefore, this book will use examples to fit the issue to be discussed, rather than exclusively focusing on a pre-determined set of countries. Whatever country can serve as a suitable example will be used as such. For that reason, Japan will feature in detail when we discuss policing styles. However, when it comes to prosecution, we will look more in depth at the state of affairs in the Netherlands. Suitable examples are often typical examples, although on occasion it makes sense to discuss the exception to the rule and use deviant cases instead, and the process of decarcer-ation in Finland serves as such a case. In other areas I have chosen to discuss the archetypical example, the example that bred a category. The jury in England and Wales constitutes one of those, as does the practice of zero-tolerance policing in New York City.

This thematic approach is carried out in what can be called a kaleidoscopic fashion. While some of the major criminal justice systems in the world receive extensive coverage, I have attempted not to stick to these. Australia, England and Wales, Japan, France, the Netherlands and the US do feature in various chapters. However, arrangements in many other countries have also been examined. In making such choices I have aimed to highlight the diversity found in criminal justice arrangements around the world. This is why the rise of the death penalty in Trinidad and Tobago, the gender balance of the judiciary in the Czech Republic, and police corruption in Hong Kong are all discussed.

Diversity is a key word in comparative criminal justice. The way in which justice is administered around the world is surprisingly diverse

7

and there is no need to travel far to encounter it. Not many people, even in England and Wales, might appreciate the substantial differences in arrangements between England and Wales, Northern Ireland, Scotland, the Isle of Man, and the Channel Islands of Jersey and Guernsey. This is true in particular when we look at the jury system. The composition of the jury in these places is spectacularly different, even though they are geographically and culturally very close to home, as we shall see in Chapter 6.

The same argument applies to the federal states of Australia and the US, where many arrangements are made at a local level, allowing for substantial differences across the country.

Federal and local law enforcement in the US

A circumstance that complicates foreign understanding of the US criminal justice system is the distinction between federal law enforcement, and state and local criminal justice. At one point in time, probably at least a century ago, this distinction was quite straightforward. The bread and butter of everyday law enforcement were local matters. Only when the position of US states was at issue in some shape or form, or when a crime was clearly transcending state borders, was there a reason for federal (roughly speaking, national) law enforcement to get involved. Counterfeiting, for instance, was seen as an offence of federal importance. The same was true for offences involving mail. These offences and their effects were likely to affect not simply individual states, but the US as a whole. The protection of the President also was a federal matter. However, the distinction between what is federal and what is local in terms of law enforcement is no longer sharply defined:

> Explaining the boundary that separates Federal enforcement concerns from state and local is a daunting task indeed. The more one knows, the harder it gets. Federal agents still seek out counterfeiters. But they also target violent gangs and gun-toting felons of all sorts, work drug cases against street sellers as well as international smugglers, investigative corruption and abuse of authority at every level of government, prosecute insider trading, and pursue terrorists. Until recently, about the only area of criminal enforcement that seemed immune from Federal activity was domestic violence. (Richmond, 2000: 82)

The areas of federal involvement have tremendously increased and the Federal Bureau of Investigation (FBI) has grown accordingly. Federal legislation is now seen to supplement local legislation in many areas, so that crime can be dealt with more effectively.

This state of affairs regularly raises issues relating to competence on one hand and to the harmonisation of local and federal rules of procedure on the other hand. There is certainly room for tactical decision-making about whether to deal with a crime as a local or a federal matter. Laws of evidence and resource allocations are not necessarily identical so that practical considerations might be decisive in the determination of whether an offence should be dealt with by the local or the federal law enforcement machinery.

Richmond (2000) argued that the increased federal involvement in criminal justice is the result of a shifting of the balance of power between the states and the federal government. Over the last century, this balance has shifted toward the federal government along with the realisation that crime, law and order are national, if not international, issues.

Shifts of power from local to national and vice versa occur regularly in most criminal justice systems. A movement towards localisation is often motivated by the intention to better serve local communities' needs. A shift towards centralisation might occur because of central government's desire to control criminal justice matters more tightly. That desire for control might originate from the wish to enhance the extent to which the criminal justice system serves the interests of the state, or might stem from tendencies to secure a more uniform treatment of offenders and offences throughout the country.

Throughout this book, case studies such as the one in Box 1.1 serve as examples. In many instances they pertain particularly to the issues described in the main text. Sometimes, however, case studies are included for illustration purposes. An example is the one on the history of foreign influences on Japanese legal procedures in Chapter 5. They cover issues that are less pertinent to the chapter in which they are placed, but are included for general interest purposes.

Depending on the issues concerned the comparative approach is sometimes quantitative and sometimes qualitative in nature. A discussion about policing styles and principles is almost inevitably qualitative, as they require a deeper understanding of the contexts in which they are applied. I have therefore chosen to conduct a limited number of in-depth case studies and focused comparisons, to illustrate styles of policing in the context of different societies.

In other areas a more quantitative approach was the appropriate choice. A discussion regarding detention is likely to feature detention ratios as a starting point. However, it is important to reiterate that the collection of such numerical information does not usually suffice to answer any question. Nevertheless, such figures do provide for a foundation on which meaningful comparisons can be made. The discussion of the differences in pre-trial detention rates between Finland and Estonia serves as an example.

Box 1.1 Differences between the criminal justice systems of
Scotland and England & Wales

People outside the United Kingdom could perhaps be forgiven for
assuming that criminal justice in Scotland is identical to that in England
and Wales; but it is not. Whereas England and Wales constitute one
criminal justice system, Scotland has a separate system with its own
characteristics. Whereas Wales does not have a separate police service,
court or prison system, Scotland has, and they have evolved quite
separately from those of its southern neighbours. Scottish scholars tend to
argue that there is an additional difference in criminal justice culture.
Scottish criminal justice is often said to be less adversarial, less punitive,
and more welfare-oriented (see Duff and Hutton, 1999). A number of
specific differences between both systems can easily be identified.

In Scotland, a jury can return three verdicts: guilty, not guilty or *not
proven*. Guilty and not guilty are essentially the same as elsewhere, but
the third category, of not proven is probably unique to Scotland. The not
proven verdict is returned quite frequently and it results in the acquittal
of the accused, so that it is by virtually all intents and purposes identical
to a verdict of not guilty. The answer to why this verdict exists lies in
history. There was a time that the only verdicts a jury could return were
proven or not proven. While the verdict of proven has long since been
replaced, that of not proven has survived the test of time.

The suggestion is that when a jury returns a not proven verdict instead
of a not guilty one, they might nevertheless feel that the accused actually
committed the offence but that there is insufficient evidence to justify a
conviction. A not guilty verdict could then be taken to mean *really*, or
factually not guilty. But it has been argued that the 'not proven' verdict
is only confusing. Proponents, however, stress the purity of the not
proven verdict. After all, the role of the jury is not to decide on guilt but
on whether the prosecution has proven the charge beyond reasonable
doubt. A verdict of not proven might more accurately reflect the actual
decision that jurors are asked to make (Duff, 1999b, 2001).

Whereas in England and Wales there are 12 jurors, in Scotland a jury
consists of 15 members. They are randomly pulled from the voters'
register in the jurisdiction of the court where the accused stands trial.
Until recently, both prosecution and defence had the right to peremptory
challenge. Nowadays, however, prospective jurors cannot be removed
easily before trial and this action requires both parties' agreement. In
Scotland there is no need for a unanimous verdict. For a guilty verdict a
simple majority of eight versus seven will suffice. Because there is a choice
of three verdicts, it could, for instance, happen that seven jurors favour a
guilty verdict, five a verdict of not guilty, and three a verdict of not
proven. If this is the case a not guilty verdict should be returned. An
accused is not convicted unless at least eight jurors find him or her guilty

(Maher, 1988). In England and Wales a unanimous verdict is preferred but a 10:2 majority is possible. The Scottish simple-majority verdict is not uncontroversial. Observers have argued that when 7 of the 15 jurors are not prepared to render a guilty verdict, that by itself might constitute reasonable doubt (see Duff, 2001).

Unlike in England and Wales, a prosecution service that receives cases from the police has been the state of affairs in Scotland for a long time. The head of the service is the Lord Advocate, who is a government minister. His deputy, the Solicitor General, is also a government appointee. Most prosecutions take place in sheriff's courts or district courts through local prosecuting officials called Procurators Fiscal. The term 'Fiscal' relates to their past function, to do with the collection of tax revenue (Moody and Tombs, 1982; Duff, 1993, 1999a). The Procurator Fiscal is wholly independent. That protects the service against pressure from outside, but it also means that it is almost impossible for victims to challenge a decision made by the Procurator Fiscal.

There are other differences between England/Wales and Scotland that deserve brief mention. The accused in Scotland does not have a say in the mode of trial decisions, unlike suspects in England and Wales for the middle range of offences. In Scotland, mode of trial is always a decision for the prosecution. Finally, lawyers in Scottish courts (those who are called barristers in England and Wales) are called advocates in Scotland, and do not make opening statements.

The source of many of the differences between Scottish criminal justice and criminal justice in England and Wales is historical. Scotland became part of the United Kingdom in 1707. A separate criminal justice system existed before that, and while it has been kept separate ever since, the subsequent laws for Scotland were made by the UK parliament in Westminster, London. The 1707 union was the start of a long period in which the similarities between both systems increased. Arguably, at this moment there might be more scope for divergence than there has been for centuries. Scottish devolution and the instigation of a Scottish Parliament in Edinburgh, which can pass laws on criminal justice matters, gives Scotland opportunities for taking matters in their own hands in a way not possible for almost 300 years (Duff and Hutton, 1999).

Finally, it must be said that a single-author text on comparative criminal justice does require the author to attempt to be a bit of an expert on everything. This obviously can never be fully achieved (Mawby, 1999b). It is therefore inevitable that I rely mostly on jurisdictions with which I am familiar, and my experience and knowledge inevitably have coloured this book.

To conclude this chapter, it is worth emphasising that since crime has become a global problem, and many crimes are essentially transnational or international in nature, comparative study has received a new impetus. Traditionally, comparative research was perhaps a luxury, to broaden one's horizons and to see if elsewhere there might be success stories in criminal justice worth adopting at home. Today, comparative research is a necessity. Crime poses a global threat. The only way to effectively prevent and combat crime on the world stage is via the harmonisation and the coordination of national and international efforts. That requires up-to-date and intimate knowledge of criminal justice arrangements abroad. And with that comes, one hopes, an appreciation of meaningful and valuable differences, stemming from culture, history and social discourse, which help shape criminal justice arrangements in places quite different to our own.

Chapter 2

Aims and methods of comparative research

Going abroad has universal appeal. Travelling has been regarded as one of life's formative endeavours for centuries. Seeing different cultures broadens one's horizons and yields a fresh perspective on local affairs. For upper-class Britons in the 18th century, embarking on the so-called Grand Tour of the European continent, in order to appreciate the cultural splendour of France or Italy, was particularly in vogue (Chard, 1999). Comparative criminal justice is its contemporary academic counterpart. The principal questions addressed in this chapter concern, on the one hand, what can be learned from looking abroad, and on the other, methodology. Most important in answering these is defining what it is that we aim to achieve.

The aims of comparison

The potential benefits of comparative research are numerous (Cole *et al.*, 1987). A distinction can be made between the aims of *seeking to understand* and of *seeking to change*. Although any change without understanding is obviously hazardous there is a difference between the two. A further, possibly more modest, aim is that of classification. Cole and colleagues classify criminal justice systems as follows. First, there are so called common-law or adversarial systems. The three examples they mention are England and Wales, the US and Nigeria. Originating from the British Isles, they are found in all English-speaking countries, with the possible exceptions of Scotland and South Africa. Second, there are civil law or inquisitorial systems. These originate in continental Europe, although Japan, to an extent, can also be viewed as possesing such a system. The third group consists of socialist law systems. Cole *et al.* describe the systems of the former USSR and Poland. Their book was published in 1987, two years before the fall of the Berlin Wall, and is obviously dated in some respects. In this book we do not discuss socialist law systems, although it would be wrong to assume that this legal tradition has died out completely. (In Cuba, the legal system still has a strong socialist orientation.) However, in place of these we discuss Islamic legal systems, which are of increasing interest globally.

Different philosophies tend to underlie the research that is geared towards understanding and that which is aimed towards achieving reform. The *relativist approach* that we will discuss first is better suited for research aimed at understanding. The *positivist approach* is more often associated with research involving an agenda of change.

Relativist and positivist approaches

Perhaps the oldest academic endeavours involving comparative research come from anthropology. Anthropology is the science of humanity, or more specifically the scientific study of the origin, the behaviour, and the physical, social, and cultural development of human beings. In the first half of this century many anthropologists studied exotic communities, often on sunny islands far away from Europe. The most famous exponent is probably American anthropologist Margaret Mead. She spent a great deal of time in the South Pacific islands to study civilisations in this area. During her career she conducted field studies on islands such as New Guinea, Bali, and Samoa (Mead, 1928, 1935).

An anthropologist is particularly concerned with understanding human behaviour in the context of history, culture and social structure. Anthropology endeavours to illuminate dissimilarities and to sharpen contrasts, and that focus can be applied to the study of criminal justice as well. Immersion in one's own criminal justice system tends, inevitably, to solidify assumptions and blunt critical faculties. Laws appear 'natural', modes of implementation 'inevitable' and relationships between criminal justice agencies 'necessary'. The anthropological-research approach guards against such tendencies and emphasises the fact that everything in social reality is relative.

Such research therefore represents a *relativist* philosophy. The way societies are organised does not correspond to certain templates or principles but is rather a function of the environment. The arrangements in place therefore depend on habits, culture and history. Thus, because society in the UK works in a certain way that does not mean that other societies would even remotely work in the same fashion. After having learned how societies are organised abroad, one can look on one's own society with a new perspective and realise that the way society is organised is not necessarily the best possible way, and certainly not cast in stone.

The equivalent to relativism in comparative criminal justice research has been called the *interpretivist* method of study. Nelken (1994) defined this as aiming to show how crime and criminal justice are embedded within changing local and international, and historical and cultural contexts. Such studies examine criminal justice or a certain aspect of it, and seek to understand how that aspect has come into existence and why it seems to work in the way that it does. It relies heavily on fieldwork and on spending a considerable amount of time in the country of interest (Hodgson, 2000). The aim of this type of research has been summarised by Dixon, not without a hint of pathos, as the attempt to 'maximise understanding of alien cultures by honest-to-God field work, moral charity, intellectual humility and a determination of the taken-for-granted assumptions of both his own and others' cultural milieu' (Dixon, 1977: 76).

In summary the objective underlying comparative research from a relativist perspective is to gain understanding of criminal justice in a foreign system. In order to acquire such knowledge it is important to understand the context of the society and culture in which it operates.

In contrast stands the positivist approach. The philosophy underlying this approach is that criminal justice can be best understood by focusing on the communalities that criminal justice systems share. The assumption is that, at a certain level, criminal justice is a universal phenomenon. Social control is a phenomenon that occurs in any society, so that, consequently, criminal justice systems can be understood in general terms. The main aim of positivist comparative research is identifying the core set of principles underlying criminal justice and distinguishing them from those traits that are merely external features.

In the positivistic approach the more straightforward questions tend to be addressed, and it is fair to say that the bulk of comparative research falls under this heading. Such comparative projects tend to be more practical and inspired by current issues. Often there is a domestic problem identified in need of scrutiny, which might involve looking elsewhere for ideas as to how the tackle the problem. In these research projects, arrangements elsewhere are given meaning in relation to domestic arrangements. The relativist position, in contrast, would be that arrangements should be given meaning in their own context.

Finally, there are countless publications that effectively have the theme 'let me tell you what the state of affairs is concerning a certain aspect of criminal justice in my country'. You could argue that these case studies are not truly comparative. However, they usually aim to facilitate understanding and comparison, and therefore can be said to be of a comparative nature anyway.

Understanding comparative research

Comparative research can take place using a range of methods. In this section we will be discussing some of these. It has been argued that methodology in comparative criminal justice is underdeveloped, and the following outline borrows therefore from methodologies in comparative politics (e.g. Hague *et al.*, 1998). The research methods in this area are to a large extent valid for studies in comparative criminal justice as well. In turn, I will address case studies, focused comparisons, truth tables and statistical analysis.

Case studies

As noted before it is perfectly feasible to carry out a comparative study that treats only one country or jurisdiction in depth. In order for such a case study to be meaningful, the case should be picked carefully. The key is to ensure that it should represent a wider category. For instance, when a researcher is interested in examining suspects' rights in inquisitorial criminal justice systems, picking 'any old inquisitorial system' is not sufficient. Such a choice has to be justified. Following Hague *et al.* (1998) I distinguish four types of cases to be selected for a case study. They are *representative cases*, *prototypical cases*, *deviant cases* and *archetypical cases*.

A *representative case* is a typical example of a wider category. It is the bread and butter of comparative research. A comparative study involving a country with a low crime rate may choose to focus on Japan, well known (at least until fairly recently) to have a low rate (see, e.g., Komiya, 1999). Similarly, a study involving high rates of imprisonment may consider the US for much the same reason.

Prototypical cases are cases that might be expected to become representative cases in the future. Prototypical cases are often frontrunners with regard to particular developments. In certain countries decriminalisation of euthanasia might be at an advanced stage of development. These countries may serve as examples and lead the way for others as to how to go about decriminalising medical life-ending conduct. Study of such prototypical cases might yield valuable insight for policy makers in countries tending in the same direction but which have not quite proceeded as far.

Deviant cases are selected to yield insight into the atypical or unconventional. They can shed light on causal relations, or the lack of them.

For instance, it is often thought that crime rates cause rates of imprisonment, so that when crime rates go up one would assume that prison rates would follow. The study of what seemingly is an atypical case, such as the Netherlands between 1950 and 1975, might show that this relationship is not one of causality, as prison rates in this period went down while the crime rate consistently went up (Downes, 1988).

Archetypical cases are cases that generate a category. The French inquisitorial system of criminal procedure is a good example: all other European inquisitorial systems are more or less derived from it. Thus, when studying inquisitorial modes of justice, the French one would be an appropriate choice, as it can be said to be the quintessential inquisitorial system. Similarly, England and Wales could be said to be the archetypical adversarial system of justice.

Focused comparisons

Focused comparisons are like case studies, but include more than one case. Most often the number of countries compared is two or three. As with case studies, the key question is how to select jurisdictions for study. We will discuss two techniques, the 'most-similar' and the 'most-different' design. Hague *et al.* (1998) defined them as follows:

> A most similar design takes similar countries for comparison on the assumption that the more similar the units being compared, the more possible it should be to isolate the factors responsible for differences between them. By contrast, the most different design seeks to show the robustness of a relationship by demonstrating its validity in a range of contrasting settings. (Hague *et al.*, 1998: 281)

Most-similar designs tend to be easier to achieve. They often involve neighbouring countries or countries in which the same language is spoken. Most-similar designs can involve former colonies as well. Most-different designs are often more difficult to carry out, as they tend to involve a selection of at least one jurisdiction that is alien to the researcher, with all the associated problems of familiarising oneself with such a system and all its intricacies. Leishman (1999) called such problems the 'gang of four' because they often co-occur: problems with gaining meaningful access, cultural literacy, ethnocentric bias and problems of language.

Truth tables

A more quantitative form of analysis can occur by means of truth tables. The use of truth tables represents an intriguing method, which can help the researcher establish causal relationships by looking at a large number of criminal justice systems.

It must be noted that truth tables tend to be particularly useful when the variables are dichotomous: when their value is, for instance, either 'yes' or 'no', or 'present' or 'absent'. This makes the inspection of such tables more straightforward. Truth tables can be used as a meta-study instrument: they can be used to integrate the findings of a large number of case studies and produce conclusions of a more general nature. We could, for example, examine the legalisation of cannabis in a number of countries, and assess whether certain results occurred or not in these jurisdictions. These results could include an increase in self-report cannabis use (yes/no); an increase in use of other drugs (yes/no), an increase in organised criminal activity (yes/no) and so on.

Statistical analysis

Statistics may occur in any comparative study. The description of crime rates in any country will probably involve at least descriptive statistics to describe the prevalence of various forms of crime. In this context, however, statistical analysis is meant to mean statistical testing as a main research methodology. The aim of such analysis is to explore the relation between two or more variables, which can be measured quantitatively. An example might feature the size of a country's police service (in terms of personnel) and its prison rates. That might help us decide whether more police would lead to more arrests being made, and ultimately more people in prison. Consider Table 2.1. As this is for illustrative purposes only, we will look at only a few countries.

Table 2.1 Police numbers and prisoner numbers (both per 100,000 inhabitants) in four European countries

Country	Police rate	Prison rate
Austria	420	101
Denmark	265	64
France	403	110
Netherlands	254	83

Sources: Walmsley, 2002; Den Boer (forthcoming).

This comparison would suggest that police rates and prison rates do seem to be related. The two countries with more police officers, Austria and France, do seem to have more people imprisoned as well. Both other countries score lower on police numbers as well as on prisoner numbers.

For two reasons this evidence is inconclusive in deciding that the two factors are meaningfully related. First, the number of countries considered is very low. A statistical analysis of four countries is not enough to allow for conclusions of a general nature to be drawn. Second, we should examine other variables as well. Crime rates would obviously help in explaining both figures. Prison capacity in each country would be useful to know, as would sentencing practices.

Via statistical means insight can be gained into the relationship between such variables in a range of jurisdictions. It must, however, be borne in mind that the existence of a statistical relation does not necessarily mean that there is a causal one. Other factors may be at work behind the scenes that actually cause the effect to occur. A relation that seems to imply a causal relationship but actually does not is called 'spurious'.

Examples of spurious correlations are plentiful. For instance, the more surgeons in an operation theatre, the more likely it is that the patient dies. This is an actual statistical relationship. However, this obviously does not mean that these surgeons would actually cause the patient to die. The mediating factor is of course the seriousness of the patient's condition. In criminal justice the positive relation between public approval ratings of the police and reported crimes is argued to be spurious. When the public have high confidence in the police they might be more willing to report crimes because they feel confident that the police will be able to do something about it. The inference that the relation between the two might be causal, that a more positively rated police service causes crime rates to increase is obviously not valid.

One particular kind of statistical analysis is called 'meta-analysis' (Rosenthal, 1991). It aims at integrating research findings from a large number of empirical studies in a statistical fashion. The procedure is for researchers to collect a large amount of experimental data on a particular subject, such as the effectiveness of prison sentences as compared to community sentences when measured by rates of recidivism. When the data is reported in sufficient detail, these results can be statistically combined and different outcomes might be explained by differences in certain characteristics of the various studies. In comparative criminal justice, meta-analysis studies have been influential in the theoretical underpinning of effective programmes for working with offenders (Lipsey, 1995).

Using criminal justice statistics comparatively

The use of statistics in criminal justice is fraught with difficulty. While these difficulties are commonly acknowledged, it is worth emphasising that many of them get amplified in comparative research.

We know that official statistics will not, and cannot, tell the whole story of the extent of crime in society. A main reason for this is underreporting. There are many reasons why crimes are not always reported to the police. In order for a victim to go to the police a number of criteria have to be met. The victim must realise he/she is a victim of a crime; victims might not notice items lost that have been stolen, or might not realise that what has happened to them constitutes a crime.

Victims (or witnesses) usually take the step of reporting only when they feel that there is a certain benefit to be gained from it. Such benefits are obvious in the case of an insurance claim, but often a victim may feel that the authorities might not be able or willing to do anything about the crime, let alone solve it. The extent to which the police are judged to be capable of doing something about crime differs considerably among countries. As an illustration, see Table 2.2, below, on the percentage that think the police do a good job, based on International Crime Victimization Survey data (Van Kesteren *et al.*, 2001).

Table 2.2 Percentage of people that think the police do a good job in controlling crime in their area

Country	Percentage %
USA	89
Canada	87
Scotland	77
Australia	76
England and Wales	72
Denmark	71
Finland	70
Northern Ireland	67
Switzerland	67
France	65
Belgium	64
Sweden	61
Netherlands	52
Poland	46

Source: Van Kesteren *et al.*, 2001.

After a crime is reported the police might, for various reasons, decide not to record it. When a crime is recorded, that does not mean that is it recorded properly, which does not automatically mean that it will be investigated, or that a suspect will be identified. An identified suspect might not be found or apprehended; his/her case might be discontinued because of lack of evidence or for other reasons. And when cases come to trial, they might not result in a conviction. Thus, crimes are filtered out of the criminal justice system at various stages, whereas a significant number of crimes never enter the system, and hence the statistics, in the first place.

The extent to which crimes are underreported also depends on the crime itself. According to the 2000 British Crime Survey, theft of (motor) vehicles is reported in 95 per cent of cases. Bicycle theft, however, is reported in only about 54 per cent of cases. The findings from the 2000 International Crime Victimisation Survey (Van Kesteren *et al.*, 2001) showed differences in the extent to which citizens are reporting crimes to the police. In the European category, people in Denmark and Sweden tended to report crimes relatively often. In Finland and Portugal there was a higher level of underreporting. For certain crimes, the differences in reporting were quite large. Sexual crimes, for instance, seemed to be much more readily reported in Scotland than they were in Finland. Table 2.3 ranks across-the-board crime-reporting rates for 17 jurisdictions, and for two types of crime in particular, bicycle theft and sexual incidents.

Table 2.3 Reporting percentages for all crimes, bicycle theft and sexual incidents in 17 countries

Country	All crimes %	Bicycle theft %	Sexual incidents %
Denmark	60	67	12
Sweden	59	61	12
Northern Ireland	59	64	22
Netherlands	58	66	17
Belgium	56	70	11
England and Wales	55	69	14
Switzerland	53	80	10
France	52	35	26
Scotland	52	78	23
USA	50	63	18
Australia	49	63	15
Canada	47	50	19
Finland	46	54	1
Poland	38	50	18
Catalonia (Spain)	37	39	13
Japan	37	36	13
Portugal	32	32	16

Source: Van Kesteren *et al.*, 2001.

The functioning of any criminal justice agency depends partly on its workload. This is affected significantly by crime rates and by the extent to which the public report crimes to the police. The performance of these agencies has to be viewed in the context of such indicators. For many countries, those indicators are available. For many others they are not.

The selective reporting of crimes probably happens everywhere. The crux is, however, that it is often very difficult to tell whether this happens at the same points in the system, for the same reasons and to the same extent in the different jurisdictions. Thus, whilst dealing with official figures is hazardous in the first place, it is doubly so in a comparative context.

Even when official figures are available and reliable that does not mean that comparison necessarily becomes straightforward. Take the following example. In higher courts in France the conviction rate is extremely high: in total, 90 per cent or more of all defendants appearing before these courts are found guilty (Hodgson, 2001). In comparison to England and Wales this proportion seems staggeringly high. Based on the Judicial Statistics in 2001, only 39 per cent of Crown Court cases ended in a conviction; 36 per cent were discharged or acquitted by the judge, whereas 25 per cent led to a jury verdict of not guilty (Home Office, 2001). This difference, when taken at face value, should raise questions about the treatment of defendants in French courts who seemingly stand a poor chance of acquittal.

The key question here relates to what these figures represent. An examination of trial procedures in France and England reveals important differences that put these figures into context. In France there are no separate procedures for defendants who do not protest their innocence. There is no such thing as a guilty plea. That certainly helps explaining the high conviction rate.

A further explanation might be found in the role and functioning of police and prosecution in France as compared to England and Wales, discussed in later chapters. But there are additional areas worth investigating in order to make sense of the French conviction rate. We may have to consider the role and functioning of jury trials, which are more common in England and Wales than in France. Perhaps we would also need to look at the different rules of evidence in the two systems. Thus, in order to compare statistics, we need to know how these figures came about and what they represent. Simply comparing figures on an assumption of like-for-like may give an impression of accuracy and precision that might well prove to be deceptive.

Methodological hazards

Zedner (1995) noted the following risks involved in comparative research. The first is what she called 'criminological tourism'. This is a trap into which it is relatively easy to fall. Going abroad often occurs in a positive frame of mind. We feel free of the worries and commitments of everyday life and are set to enjoy ourselves. It is then easy to find the locals friendly, helpful and hospitable without realising that our own positive attitude (not too mention our tourist money) might bring that about such feelings. Zedner warns of the possibility of misreading or simplifying local customs and regarding exotic arrangements uncritically. In particular, when reading reports on countries that traditionally receive praise, a critical attitude is necessary. That includes policing in Japan as well as the soft drugs policy in the Netherlands, where at times particularly rosy accounts have been provided by foreign observers, sometimes vehemently protested by native scholars (e.g. Franke, 1990).

The second caveat relates to linguistic difficulties, one of the aforementioned pitfalls cited by Leishman (1999). Zedner (1995) took the position that anything less than complete fluency leaves one vulnerable to misinterpretation. This, however, has not stopped many a prominent scholar from writing books about foreign systems without having mastered the native language. In countries where most people speak English as a second language the English-speaking researcher is probably in less of a vulnerable position than in countries where the researcher's language is not widely spoken. Thus, although the advantages of speaking the indigenous language are obvious, an inability to do so should not automatically disqualify anyone from engaging in comparative research.

The third difficulty relates to what might be called 'touching base'. It relates to questions such as Who do you talk to? What do you read? What do you observe? Many aspects of criminal justice worth looking into are controversial. It is therefore important to try to assess both sides of any argument and not limit oneself to talking to a restricted range of people with a shared set of opinions and knowledge. This need is closely related to what Leishman called 'meaningful' access (Leishman, 1999). The touching-base caveat becomes more poignant as a function of the intensity of contact with the people and culture that is being investigated. Participant observation carries its own set of risks, including that of going native, that is the over-identification with the population studied at the expense of one's critical faculties (Bruyn, 1996; Jorgenson, 1993).

There are sceptics who argue that the entire enterprise of the comparative analysis of foreign criminal justice systems is flawed.

Stephen argued in relation to comparing the systems of France and England and Wales that:

> The whole temper and spirit of the French and the English differ so widely, that it would be rash for an Englishman to speak of trials in France as they actually are. We can think of the system only as it would work if transplanted into England. It may well be that it not only looks, but is a very different thing in France. (Stephen, in Vogler *et al.* 1996: 17–18)

Similarly, Vogler emphasises that comparative research involves 'many attempts to translate the untranslatable and to introduce concepts completely alien to English lawyers' (Vogler, 1996: 18). It might well be impossible to reach a complete understanding of foreign systems, just as it might be impossible to understand completely another person. But that should not stop us from attempting to get to know others, and learning from their experiences. The same is true for the study of foreign criminal justice systems.

Conclusion

People look at other countries and contexts for differing reasons. Generally, it is the case that broadening one's horizon will always be a learning experience. However, to avoid the pitfalls of 'tourism', the purpose of the comparison should always be made clear. The risk for anthropological research is that one gets too engrossed in the new, the exciting and the exotic. The risk of positivistic research is that there will be too little actual immersion. As with so much, it is about striking a balance. Zedner (1995) describes the reality of comparative criminal justice research as follows:

> Doing comparative research rarely entails selling one's own home and tearing up one's passport, forever to live among the drug dealers of Delhi or the detectives of Düsseldorf. Neither can one, with credibility at any rate, write about continental criminal procedure without stepping outside the ivy-clad walls of an Oxford college. Rather the research process entails developing a general theoretical (but distant) understanding at home-base, punctuated by a series of forays (often of increasing duration) into the terrain of study. This itinerary is matched by an intellectual journey which takes one from the perspective of global structures to the minutiae of local detail and back and forth over the course of the research in

'a sort of intellectual perpetual motion' (Geertz, 1983, p. 235). While periods of fieldwork provide for immersion in local culture (the court, the prison, the police station), the journeys between make possible an intellectual distancing. Once more library-bound, the researcher can engage in the detached reflections and distanced evaluation which are the very stuff of comparison. (Zedner, 1995: 19)

Finally, a word of caution is in order. The field of comparative criminal justice is not known for its methodological rigour. Choices of methodology and selection of criminal justice systems to include in any study are often made for reasons of convenience, or even of opportunism. Arguably there is no need to adopt too rigid a position with regard to methodological imperfections. In the area of comparative criminal justice, perfectionism is less important than a balanced assessment of the advantages and weaknesses of any method, so that any findings can be evaluated according to their merits.

Chapter 3

Comparative policing

Popular images of the police are commonplace in television and fiction. Police television series, from *The Streets of San Francisco* to *Miami Vice*, seem to have an enduring global popularity. The police intrigue the public, whether in fiction or in reality (see Reiner, 2000b, for an overview of police depictions in the media).

From a comparative perspective, two contrasting fictional portrayals of police officers are worth discussing here. British comedian Harry Enfield's depiction of Dutch cops is the first. In a typical sketch we see two cannabis-smoking police officers in a police car parked in the streets of the city of Amsterdam. With their feet on the dashboard, they happily witness the commission of crimes around them. 'Burglary? Oh, we legalised it', says one of them, officer Van der Hoogst Graacht. Harry Enfield's characters ridicule the stereotypical notion of Dutch tolerance in criminal justice matters, and they are portrayed as friendly but clueless softies.

At the other end of the fictional continuum lies Harvey Keitel's portrayal of the unnamed title character in the film *The Bad Lieutenant* (1992). This thoroughly corrupt police officer harasses members of the public, steals and sells drugs, and is as bad, if not worse, than the criminals he is supposed to protect the public from. He meets a tragic end, when killed because of gambling debts.

These examples make a useful contrast. The Dutch cops, utterly uninterested in law enforcement, seem nevertheless to blend into their environment. The same can be said for the Bad Lieutenant, who is as criminal as the people who surround him. Both are more similar to those they police than one might expect. That brings us handily to the first point of this chapter: policing must fit those 'to-be-policed'. Therefore, a comparative analysis of policing requires a great deal of knowledge regarding the context in which it operates, which makes case-studies and focused comparisons appropriate methods of analysis.

Unfortunately, examples where police forces do not quite fit the community they police are nevertheless plentiful. Colonial police forces around the world often had the interests of the motherland at heart primarily (see Cole, 1999, for an overview). The same is true for police forces in dictatorial or authoritarian states, whose main objective is usually to ensure a tyrannical regime stays in power. Their style and organisation are often of a military nature, and orientated against the citizens who are seen to constitute a constant threat. In such contexts, community concerns come second place at best. New democracies often face the challenge of transforming a police force that traditionally operated against the people into one that actually serves them. Needless to say, such new identities are not achieved overnight. The police force in Argentina, for instance, is still regarded by many as heavy handed and the state continues to be seen as authoritarian: even though the country has been a democracy for some time there remains considerable distrust of those in power (Ebbe and De Olano, 2000). Ebbe has argued that in such countries as Argentina, Nigeria and Brazil the police continue to be viewed as instruments of repression, antagonistic to the general public and estranged from the communities in which they operate (Ebbe, 2000a).

Police and policing

It is important to distinguish between *police* and *policing* (Reiner, 2000a). *Policing* implies a set of processes with specific social functions. Reiner (2000a) describes policing as the attempt to maintain security through surveillance and the threat of sanction. Policing is a relatively broad concept, which encompasses a wide range of activities and personnel. Teachers, parents, and sports referees can all be said to engage in kinds of policing.

Police refers to the institution – the force or the service. The police are the modern specialised body of people who carry out much of the policing function in today's society. The police assume a unique position within criminal justice. They face pressures unlike any other criminal justice agency, as they form the primary interface between the public and the criminal justice system. Police officers on a daily basis face a myriad of difficult tasks and situations. Compare this to the role of judges: the number and types of defendants in front of them may vary widely, but the format in which they deal with those defendants is highly scripted.

Police officers on patrol enjoy no such structure. They have to take each situation as it comes.

The present chapter will focus largely on the police; but we should bear in mind that the police are rarely the only official body engaged in policing in any society. Later in the chapter, I will examine briefly private policing as well.

Police numbers and policing tasks

The sentiment seems to be the same whenever citizens are asked about the size of their police force. They want more police officers on patrol, or, as the phrase is in the UK, more 'Bobbies on the beat'. The rationale for the sentiment is obviously that more police officers on patrol will make for safer streets.

The number of police officers per 100,000 population for 15 countries is shown below:

Table 3.1 Number of police officers per 100,000 population in 15 countries

Country	Police officers per 100,000 population
Austria	420
Denmark	265
England and Wales	347
France	349
Germany	311
Hong Kong	476
India	140
Italy	477
Japan	207
Netherlands	254
Singapore	288
Spain	488
Sri Lanka	175
Sweden	309
United States	300

Sources: Den Boer (forthcoming), Fairchild and Dammer (2001), and US Department of Justice (2001).

It seems that in most Western modern states the number of police officers ranges somewhere between 200 and 500 officers per 100,000 population. Japan's rate is relatively low, but that in India and Sri Lanka is lower still.

The traditional activity for a police officer is to be 'on the beat'. Police officers walk the streets and deal with problem situations as and when they encounter them. Bayley (1991) found that in many countries the majority of a police officer's time is indeed spent patrolling. Police presence is regarded as a deterrent for the commission of crimes and other disturbances, and police officers on the beat can deal with any crisis situations swiftly. Such police presence should, therefore, be a potent reducer of crime rates. However this is 'a neat idea, but unfortunately not one that corresponds to reality' (Waddington, 1999: 6).

Research from the US helps to illustrate this point. In the 1970s, in Kansas City, an experiment was carried out in which the patrolling time was systematically varied. Odd as it may seem, it did not have an effect on crime levels. Although there were some methodological issues raised, the experiment did provide evidence for the fact that levels of patrolling might actually not make much of a difference to levels of crime (Kelling *et al.*, 1998). Greater numbers of police on the streets, as the academic consensus seems to be, do not reduce crime. This lack of effectiveness raises questions as to how the police ought to go about their business and indeed what their core business actually is. Various classifications of police tasks or policing functions exist, but the distinction between the *maintenance of public order*, and investigating crimes, or more broadly *crime control*, is probably most important (Waddington, 1999, 2000).

Waddington has stressed the fact that first and foremost the police are the agents that enforce the power of the state over its citizens. When investigating crimes the police, in the first instance, represent the state: a theft is therefore not just an issue between victim and offender; it is also, and perhaps primarily, an issue between the state (embodied in institutions such as the police, prosecution office and courts) and the offender. The argument for this arrangement is that an offence is not only an offence against the victim but also a violation of society's legal and social order. In that light, crime control is a particular type of public-order maintenance (Waddington, 1999). When the state has certain aspirations with regard to issues of crime or social control it looks primarily to the police.

McKenzie and Gallagher (1989) argued that a key difference between the police services of England and Wales and the US reflects a difference in the traditional emphasis on crime control on the one hand and public order on the other. English 'Bobbies' are there traditionally to keep the peace. In the US the police came into existence with an emphasis on crime control. Public-order maintenance could too easily clash with the American ideal of the freedom of the individual and would therefore constitute insufficient *raison d'être* for the US police.

The conceptual distinction between crime control and public order maintenance is important because of their varying political potency. The authority of the state is much more easily threatened by riots and mass protests than it is by criminal activity. Crimes generally do not overthrow governments, but riots and protests can and do. States, therefore, have a vested interest in suppressing mass dissent. In doing so, the police are one of their most powerful tools.

A riot could be characterised as a battle between the two sides – rioters and police – both of whom are willing to use violence for what they each regard as a good cause (King and Brearley, 1996; Waddington, 2000). This makes public-order policing morally ambiguous, as it cannot *a priori* be assumed that the police are in the right and the protesters in the wrong. The policing of riots and mass disturbances is where one of the dilemmas of police services across the globe becomes most pertinent. Whom do the police serve? In totalitarian regimes, the police will normally serve the interests of those in power. Any public-order disturbances will be dealt with swiftly and harshly without too much concern over civil-liberty issues. The scenes at Tiananmen Square in Beijing, in 1989, were testament to that. In democracies, however, the situation is often less clear-cut. The police will have to balance the rights of the protesters (to protest peacefully) against public-order considerations.

Wright (2002a) has distinguished four models of public order policing, depending on how the relationship between the police, the state and the military is given shape. The first is the civil police model, in which the police and the military are completely separate in terms of organisation and objectives. The police deal with crime and are meant to keep the peace, whereas the role of the military is to protect the country from external aggression. Their differing roles require different types of organisation, with the military being organised along hierarchical lines with a high level of centralisation. The police on the other hand tend to be decentralised, with high levels of discretion. Wright mentioned England and Wales and the Netherlands as examples of countries with a civil police model.

The second model is the state police model, in which the influence of the state is stronger and the police and military are separated to a lesser extent. It therefore allows for the military to get involved in public-order operations and for the police to deploy so-called paramilitary methods somewhat more readily than is possible to do under the civil police model. Wright defined paramilitary action as police units using military-style deployments with tactical coordination and rules of deployment. This might include the use of special equipment, such as weapons and shields. Paramilitary action is characterised additionally by a lack of the discretion normally associated with everyday policing. Wright (2002a) used Germany and France as examples where, to an extent, the state police model is followed. In France, one of the two main forces, the Gendarmerie Nationale, is accountable to the Ministry of Justice. As is the case with the military, they are not allowed to be unionised (Monjardet, 1995).

The third model is the quasi-military police model, associated with contexts in which the state has seized a great deal of control over the police, which primarily serves its interests. Police and military are closely associated and personnel are to a considerable extent interchangeable. Most Eastern European states used to correspond to this model before the transformation following the fall of the Berlin Wall.

Finally, there is the martial law model, which is the stronger version of the quasi-military police model. In this case there is no separation of police and military forces. Both are under the same command and control. Wright argued that an implementation of pure martial law, in which soldiers are police officers and vice versa, does not often occur in the long term; rather, it is particularly associated with law-and-order programmes in the context of war and civil unrest. Instances, however, have been seen in Britain's colonial past, for example, whereas Indonesia's law-and-order programme in East Timor quite recently also corresponded relatively closely to the martial law model (Wright, 2002a).

Policing styles and crime control

Though the extent to which the police are instrumental in reducing crime can be questioned, this remains one of their main responsibilities. That is so in spite of strong statements made by academics such as Bayley (1994), who argued that reducing crime is a promise that the police are unable to keep. Nevertheless, the police can go about their business in various ways that may not only be more or less conducive to reducing crime, but also to increasing public confidence and maintaining public order. These can be termed policing styles, and I shall discuss community policing, zero tolerance policing and intelligence-led or proactive policing. The assumptions underlying these styles differ considerably with regard to the type of crimes to be targeted, the types of communities in which they fit, and the nature of the relationship between police and local communities. Certain contexts are no doubt better suited to certain styles than others, which makes them useful territory for comparative analysis.

Community policing

The principles of community policing can be identified as follows. First, it relies on the consent and support of local communities: policing by consent. It requires regular interactions between the police and the public with regard to what policing priorities should be, and how the

Box 3.1 Trouble in paradise: the policing of riots on the island of Mauritius

About 1,500 miles east of southern Africa's mainland in the Indian Ocean, we find the island of Mauritius. It was ruled consecutively by the Portuguese (who found it uninhabited), the Dutch, the French and the English before gaining independence in 1968. The Mauritian police force is modelled after that of England and Wales, and it polices a truly multicultural society. The majority of the population (just over 1 million in total) is of Indian origin (68 per cent). The descendants of the African slave population who used to work on sugar plantations are called Creoles, and make 27 up per cent of the population. 'Orientals' make up about 3 per cent of the population, and the remaining 2 per cent are White.

There is similar diversity in terms of religion, with 52 per cent Hindu, 28 per cent Christian and 16 per cent of the population Muslim. Finally, apart from ethnicity and religion, there is diversity in terms of languages spoken. While English is the official language, the unofficial language spoken most widely is called Creole, which is a Creole variety of French. Most people are proficient in Creole, but also in English, French or both. Hindi is widely spoken as well.

While the official Mauritius web site (www.maurinet.com) says that these different groups live together in peace, and normally they do, public order disturbances occurring in 1999 did show that below the surface there is no lack of ethnic tension. Based on the official inquiry into the disturbances, the events of that year are as follows (Matadeen, 2000).

It started with a death in custody. Joseph Reginald Topize, better known as popular local musical artist Kaya, died in a prison cell in Line Barracks, police headquarters in the nation's capital, Port Louis, on 21 February 1999. He was arrested during a music festival for smoking gandia, a cannabis derivative strongly prohibited by law but socially acceptable in large portions of the Creole population. The news of the singer's death spread like wildfire, as did rumours that Kaya had been killed by the police.

Kaya's death sparked riots across the island. Police headquarters and many local police stations were under siege, primarily but not exclusively from Creoles. One local police station opened fire on the crowd. Two individuals died, which only served to escalate the situation across the island. Although the police were the prime targets of the rioters, a fair amount of vandalism and looting of commercial properties took place as well. The riots went on for several days, and the country experienced an unprecedented level of violence and chaos.

The Mauritian police force, about 8,000 strong and ethnically predominantly Indian, found itself in the middle of the controversy. The first reason was the death in custody of a folk hero. The outspoken and, according to some provocative, gandia supporter Kaya might have served as the ideal martyr for those opposed to its prohibition. The fact that it remained unclear for some considerable period of time whether he was actually killed or not only made matters worse. Although autopsy results later showed that he was not, by that time the hue and cry had become unstoppable. Additionally, it has been alleged that the police, in their reaction to the violence, overreacted initially (particularly in answering the siege with gunfire), and in the subsequent phase were paralysed because of what had already happened.

We know from this and other case studies that the stages of development of riots does correspond to certain patterns (Smelser, 1962). First of all, there must be *structural strain*. This term is used to describe conditions where aspects of the social, economic and political system are 'out of joint'. In this case, the level of social exclusion of the Creole population, and the criminalisation of behaviours that to them are not morally wrong can be argued to have induced that strain. Second, there must be *precipitating events*. The death of Kaya and the rumours about the cause of death were such events. Subsequently, there must be a *mobilisation of a crowd*. Creoles in Mauritius do tend to live much of their lives in the open air, which is a favourable condition for mobilisation; and here there was mobilisation in the first place, because of the music festival. Finally there must be *a lack of effective control*. This undoubtedly was the case, with the subsequent over- and under-reaction of the police force across the island.

Riots do seem to follow a certain pattern wherever they occur. That is good to know when analysing public order policing in such circumstances in other countries. Waddington however, argues that Smelser's analysis misses crucial points: his theory is silent on the moral character of riots. Protest, at least in theory, is principled action. Protesters, even though they may frequently be breaking the law, are not automatically morally reprehensible as what they protest about may well have merit (Waddington, 1999, 2000).

police should go about tackling those priorities. The police should be aware of their community's special characteristics and preferences and be sensitive to them.

Community policing requires a localised police force. Only locally established units are able to maintain links with communities so that they can respond to local needs properly. The nature of community policing is that the police need to ask the locals what they want from them, and that should inform their policy-making, and thus they engage the community in taking joint responsibility for social control within that community. Alderson called this a 'social contract' between police and community (Alderson, 1979).

Japan is perhaps the best example of successful community policing. Japanese policing is traditionally characterised by the police and local communities working closely together (Leishman, 1999). It is a tradition for local police officers to spend a relatively large amount of their time dealing with respectable members of the community instead of chasing suspects (Bayley, 1991) and there is considerable emphasis on this non-law-enforcement aspect of their work. In comparing US and Japanese policing traditions, consider Bayley's distinction: 'An American policeman is like a fireman – he responds when he must. A Japanese policeman is more like a postman – he has a daily round of low-key activities that relate him to the lives of the people among whom he works' (Bayley, 1991: 86).

In order to serve local communities properly, the Japanese have low-level police posts called *koban*. They are a mix between a police station and a post of general assistance. The scope of general assistance is wide. *Koban* officers advise on addresses, lend out umbrellas, may act as a lost and found office, and often run various community activities. Such activities might involve the production and distribution of local newsletters and the running of classes in self-defence or sports for locals (Leishman, 1999).

A normal sized *koban* consists of about a dozen officers. The unit is typically housed in a two-story building, recognisable by the traditional red lamp. *Koban* officers typically do not drive around in patrol cars, but are often on foot. This encourages frequent interactions with the community, where issues of crime are not necessarily to the fore. Apart from many daily informal contacts with members of the community, the *koban* also administer surveys. Twice each year, uniformed officers visit every home in their area and ask the residents various questions, to do with age, occupation and relations. Most people seem to be willing to answer such questions and to provide useful background information as well.

It has been argued that the *koban* system of policing helps to explain the famously low crime rate in Japan (Reichel, 1999). It must also be appreciated that this system emerged apparently naturally in Japan, and that it seems to fit the country's social fabric very well. Much is made of Japan's special cultural character. For example, the country is ethnically very homogeneous, as well as inclusive though there are exceptions, such as the historically outcast *burakumin* (Upham, 1987). Apart from the ethnic homogeneity, there is a supposed unity in social norms. Japanese culture places considerable value on the importance of harmony. This is certainly conducive to a community-oriented policing style (Castberg, 1990).

Leishman (1999), however, has argued that Western observers have perhaps been too keen to uncritically accept the *koban* model of policing as the reason why Japan's crime rate has been so low. There is no doubt that crime has risen considerably since the 1980s and that the community-oriented style of policing is now seeking to adapt itself to a changing society. Changing family and work patterns and increased social mobility and levels of anonymity have arguably led to a slackening of the social cohesion on which traditional policing strongly relies. Reform measures aimed to enhance levels of communication with the community have resulted in the establishment of *Koban* Liaison Councils. Additionally, measures are taken in an attempt to raise the profile of *koban* policing and to make community policing more attractive to young officers who might find the battles against terrorism and organised crime more exciting career prospects (Leishman, 1999).

Despite these more recent developments, the friendliness and harmony associated with Japanese policing has generated a widespread appeal. It is therefore not surprising that the example has been followed in other countries. One of these is the city-state of Singapore. In order to serve its multicultural society of various Asian communities, a total of 91 neighbourhood police posts were introduced in 1981 at the expense of other police units, such as the motor patrol. These posts are very much modelled after the Japanese *koban* stations and are claimed to be successful too (Fairchild and Dammer, 2001). The success of community policing in Singapore is of interest because of the diversity of its population. Whereas the population in Japan is quite homogeneous, in Singapore the opposite is the case. It could, however, be argued that perhaps both cultures share a lower level of individualism than we find more commonly in Western societies.

England and Wales are considered to be good examples of community policing in the Western world. Community-policing elements are, for instance, embodied in the Crime and Disorder Act 1998. It arranges for the administration of crime surveys to establish local priorities with regard to crime and disorder. The English tradition of high levels of discretion and decentralisation of the police service also fit a community-oriented policing style. Community policing is also in operation, albeit sometimes seemingly in disguise, in Sweden, Norway and the Netherlands. When introduced in Western societies it often means that a shift is made towards either more local efforts on crime prevention, a reprioritisation of non-emergency services, increased public accountability, or a decentralisation of decision-making on policing (Skolnick and Bayley, 1988).

In the US, recent efforts have been made to introduce community policing up and down the country. Skogan (1995) evaluated a number of these initiatives. The Chicago Alternative Policing Strategy (CAPS), in operation since the early 1990s, is a good example (Skogan *et al.*, 1999).

CAPS includes elements of community problem-solving and an enhancement of beat-community contacts. Although its evaluation has been positive it is important to consider the differences between community policing in Chicago and in Japan. First of all there is the fact that in Chicago it is a recently introduced and borrowed concept. Second, there is the fact that it is deployed in communities not necessarily characterised by homogeneity and harmony. Community policing would probably reflect less of a way of life in Chicago as compared to Japan. At the present time of writing, CAPS seems to be at crossroads. While the programme is positively evaluated, the evaluation seemed to concern primarily its implementation and has not removed all doubts as to whether community policing in any pure sense can work in deprived and non-cohesive communities (Skogan *et al.*, 1999).

Criticisms levelled at community policing tend to focus on the role of the community. Community policing might assume too great a degree of harmony within communities. Many communities are, in fact, utterly divided among variables such as class or race. In such situations, the police might be unduly influenced by those sections of the community that do actively engage in communication with the authorities at the expense of those who choose not to. That might lead to unequal policing, which might deteriorate into unfair policing.

The second point of caution relates to perceptions of the police and of their role. Police officers seem to have a great deal of respect in Japan, and *koban* officers are generally proud of their neighbourhood and the work they do. Needless to say, in many countries around the globe this is not quite the case. Lack of trust between police and citizens will make effective community policing almost impossible.

Finally, community policing does not sit easily with an authoritarian police-role orientation. When the police serve the interests of the state rather than those of the community, then community policing as a concept seems rather pointless.

Zero tolerance policing

Zero tolerance policing is a generic term for a policing style that is proactive, confident and assertive (Hopkins Burke, 1998). While American theorist James Q. Wilson described the viewpoints that were subsequently to be labelled as 'zero tolerance' policing, not all of its proponents have actually adopted the term. It is fair to say that the term 'zero tolerance' has found a life of its own, and it is applied freely to many an initiative in criminal justice that might well be rather remote to the original idea.

Wilson and Kelling's (1982) so-called broken-windows theory underpins the zero tolerance philosophy. If the first broken window in a building is not repaired, then people will assume that no one cares. That lowers the threshold for others to also break windows. More and more windows will be broken and soon the building will have no windows. A quick reaction to the first broken window is therefore imperative: it needs to be fixed as soon as possible. That is the idea behind zero tolerance policing, and it is in opposition to the notion that when crime is rife, the police should focus on only the most serious crimes. Zero tolerance policing is about making an effort to tackle minor crimes and misdemeanours. In that way a sense of law and order can be regained, which will serve as a deterrent with regard to more serious crimes. Signs of improvement on the law-and-order front will allow the local community to gain confidence in the police as well as in the community itself (Wilson and Kelling, 1982).

In the philosophy of zero tolerance policing, its relation to the community rests on a different footing from community policing. Whereas in the Japanese example, communities care and communicate, Wilson and Kelling (1982) described the American experience as one in which communities can be careless and cynical. An experimental study by Zimbardo in 1973 seems to prove the point they made. Two cars were left without licence plates and with their hoods raised, one in the Bronx, New York City, and one in Palo Alto, California.

The car in the Bronx was attacked by vandals within ten minutes. First of all a family – father, mother and a son – removed the radiator and the battery. Within twenty-four hours, virtually anything of value had disappeared. Then random destruction took place. The car in Palo Alto, on the other hand, was left untouched for more than a week. Then Zimbardo himself decided to do a bit of damage to it. That led to an avalanche of vandalism. Within hours the car was utterly destroyed. Vandalism does seem to beget vandalism.

Zero tolerance policing has been particularly successful in New York City. Under the leadership of Mayor Guiliani and Police Commissioner Bratton, a policing style with zero tolerance features was introduced with the main objective of claiming back the streets. A particular focus was the so-called 'quality of life' crimes. These included graffiti, vagrancy, begging, illegal vending, street-level drug dealing and street prostitution. These offences were pursued to regain and demonstrate control of the streets. Bratton had previously been chief of the New York Transit Police and there embarked on a 'quality of life' policing programme, which saw large numbers of arrests for fare evasion (Bratton, 1997).

During the initial period of zero tolerance policing, between 1993 and 1996, arrests for misdemeanours rose by 40 per cent and arrests for minor drug offences rose by 97 per cent. By way of contrast, arrests for more serious offences (felonies) rose only by 5 per cent during the same period. Interestingly, it was the number of reported incidents of serious crimes that went down spectacularly as they fell by 44 per cent. There was a 60-per-cent drop in murders, a 12-per-cent drop in rapes, a 48-per-cent drop in robberies and a 46-per-cent drop in burglaries (Dwyer, 2001). It appeared to be a case of 'take care of the pennies and the pounds (or dollars) take care of themselves'. It also must be noted, however, that the size of the New York City police force was increased with an injection of 7,000 extra police officers on top of the 30,000 already there.

Despite protests from various interests groups, who complained about police heavy-handedness, it seems that the zero tolerance approach has been a success. Although other major cities have seen reductions in crime in the same time period, the New York City data are quite remarkable. Equally remarkable is the way in which the NYPD collects crime data, and use them to devise localised crime-fighting strategies. Crime statistics are collected with rigour and precision. Local police chiefs are held accountable for their local statistics in so-called CompStat meetings. If, in a particular area, reductions in crime are not achieved, questions will be asked.

The success of zero tolerance policing might tell us something about the communities to which it is applied. In order for it to be successful, it would seem that the situation before zero tolerance must be quite bad in terms of crime rates and public confidence. When a neighbourhood is struck by fear; when people do not dare to leave their houses after dark, and are afraid to be alone on the streets, then something drastic might be called for. In such communities, a zero tolerance approach might be the best, or perhaps the only, answer.

Compare this to the communities described in the Japanese model. They are almost opposites. In Japanese communities, characterised by cohesion and openness, zero tolerance policing would probably destroy more than it ever could repair. It is for this reason that zero tolerance policing might well be successful in certain contexts only. These contextual factors will probably include a poor situation to begin with, so that there is little, if anything, to lose in terms of the relation between community and police. The second requirement is likely to be a strong financial commitment, so that the police can afford to be consistent and convincing in their attack on all crimes, big and small.

Zero tolerance policing in Australia

In Chapter 2 I explained the focused comparison as a method of conducting comparative research, i.e. looking at a phenomenon in one context, and then considering its applicability in another set of circumstances. Zero tolerance serves as a good example for such a comparison, given that its success might depend very much on the community to which it is applied, and the way in which it is implemented.

Because of the success of the technique in New York City, and the fact that this success have been well advertised, combined with the fact that New York City is quite an attractive travel destination, the NYPD has enjoyed countless visits from police officers and policy-makers from all over the world. Those seeking to claim back the streets in their own communities have looked for ideas on how to achieve similar success in their domestic jurisdictions. Some of those visitors have been from Australia.

Australia is a federal state. It has one police force for each of its six states as well as for the Northern Territory. There is also a Common-wealth agency known as the Australian Federal Police, which provides police services for the Australian Capital Territory and is involved in preventing and investigating crimes committed against the Common-wealth. Consequently, there are eight separate police forces. The number of police personnel for the year 1991–92 for the eight forces is as depicted in Table 3.2.

Table 3.2 Strength of the police service in the states of Australia (Biles, 1991)

State	Police numbers (total)	Population (× 1,000,000)	Population per police officer
New South Wales	16,017	6.5	404
Victoria	11,794	4.8	406
Queensland	6,271	3.6	574
Western Australia	4,129	1.9	460
South Australia	5,749	1.5	260
Tasmania	1,014	0.47	463
Northern Territory	224	0.19	428
Federal Police	3,079	n/a	n/a

Obviously, the introduction of zero tolerance policing in one of Australia's major cities would be a different issue from in, for instance, rural Tasmania. In Tasmania, the area covered by its police force is very large as compared to the number of police officers, even though the police officer density in terms of population is similar to the rest of Australia.

Wadham (1998) has identified five issues in relation to zero tolerance policing from a civil liberties standpoint, which will help focus our comparison. Zero tolerance enforcement involves a prioritisation of what are minor crimes but major nuisances; it inevitably shifts resources away from other types of crimes. Second, it focuses on *street crime*, at the possible expense of crimes such as fraud, and domestic violence. The third issue is that zero tolerance emphasises *criminalisation*: whereas community-policing strategies would focus on problem-solving, zero tolerance policing would instead focus on making arrests, with the likely result of more people ending up with a criminal record. Fourth, there is the issue of *discrimination*: it tends to be the poor and socially excluded, and sometimes in particular minority groups, who are out on the streets more often and who are disproportionately associated with crime; the marginalisation of these minority groups might be amplified by employing zero tolerance techniques. Finally, the issue of *accountability* must be mentioned: with the potentially dramatic impact this policing style might have, public accountability is vital.

One of the acknowledged challenges to Australian criminal justice lies in its treatment of its indigenous population, which has a troubled history over 200 years. This population consists of Aboriginals and the Torres Strait Islander population. The following quotation provides a cutting summary of the problems involved in policing Australia's indigenous population:

> Most of the conflict with Aboriginals arises from police endeavours to enforce street offences legislation. That legislation arguably seeks to impose on Aboriginals the views of the European culture about the appropriate use of public space. While sections of the Aboriginal population have adopted the values of the dominant community on these issues, the values are in many places constantly challenged by groups of Aboriginals who do not conform to ideas about public drinking, noisiness, language, dress and general decorum. It is thus the constant effort of police to subordinate to the standards of the white society Aboriginal conduct which reflects cultural differences. No doubt police seldom think of their role as maintaining the subordination of Aboriginal people, nor are they the only institution in Australian society that act to do so. Indeed, it is often the relationship with other institutions that is crucial, as for example, with local government or hospitals or the media or hotel owners or schools. Nevertheless, the routine nature of much of police involvement with Aboriginal people means that their day to day practices act to entrench the subordination of Aboriginal people and, with it, racist attitudes in the dominant society (Wootten, 1991: 287).

Given this state of affairs it is not surprising that the indigenous population is overrepresented in the criminal justice system. The rate of imprisonment for indigenous adult persons is 1,755 per 100,000 (Australian Bureau of Statistics, 1995). That is about 15 times the rate of the general population. Nationally, the reason for being placed in police custody for 31 per cent of indigenous people was intoxication in public. Nearly half (48.2 per cent) of all people throughout Australia placed in police cells for public-order offences were Aboriginal or Torres Strait Islander, which is an enormous overrepresentation (Carcach and McDonald, 1997).

Any policing strategy that increases arrest rates for these types of offences is likely to therefore have a dramatic and discriminatory effect on the Aboriginal and Torres Strait Islander people. This increase will flow throughout the criminal justice system, with increases in court appearances, imprisonment and possibly deaths in custody. These sensitivities involving the indigenous population provide for a strong argument against the introduction of zero tolerance policing in Australia. You could say that whereas what needed to be fixed in New York city was a general state of lawlessness, in Australia it is rather the treatment by the criminal justice system and society at large of the indigenous population: zero tolerance policing provides no answer to that.

Proactive policing

Proactive policing refers to a collection of methods employed to gather intelligence on what is typically regarded as serious and organised crime. Where traditional policing often starts only with the report of a crime to the police, proactive policing has the potential offender in its view. The word 'view' can sometimes be taken rather literally, as much intelligence-led or proactive policing is to do with observation. Surveillance in various forms is perhaps the core business of intelligence-led policing. Much of it is covert and includes bugs, telephone taps and tracking devices or the installation of closed circuit television (CCT). As subjects tend to move around, mobile surveillance is another proactive technique. This is colloquially called 'shadowing', and is a very labour-intensive police method. Maguire and John (1995) estimated that the running of a dedicated surveillance team costs in the order of £400,000 per year.

Other proactive methods involve the use of intelligence. Important sources for intelligence are *informants* or *infiltrants*. Informants are individuals who happen to have specific knowledge about subjects and their activities; infiltrants are often police officers who enter the lives of organised criminals in order to gather information.

It is in the very nature of proactive policing that much of it is done in secret. The effectiveness of informants and infiltrants relies on the fact that their true motives are not known to those around them. That raises issues with regard to the invasion of privacy, and there are also issues in relation to possible entrapment. It is therefore no wonder that such methods are subject to much debate. The idea of policing serving its citizens is at odds with the notion of the police spying on them.

Under totalitarian regimes, the secretive gathering of information, performed either by specialist bodies or by the police service, is one of the pillars of control. The extent to which the *Stasi*, the secret service in the former German Democratic Republic (East Germany) spied on its citizens, for instance, is now well-known. Proactive policing in such a context is thus yet another instance of covert operations on the behalf of the state against its citizens. You would expect this technique to be in vogue in countries where the state is traditionally strong. France provides a good example: it is a country where the state is traditionally powerful, and where proactive policing indeed is a longstanding tradition (Monjardet and Lévy, 1995).

There are two police forces in France. The Gendarmerie polices rural areas whereas the Police Nationale is responsible for urban policing. As mentioned earlier, the Gendarmerie is controlled by a director-general who is part of the Ministry of Defence. The Police Nationale on the other hand, falls under the Ministry of the Interior. Such a dual mode of police forces is not uncommon on the European continent.

Horton (1995) has described the advantages of having two separate police forces as follows. First, the state can employ a 'divide and rule' strategy when the quality or loyalty of one of the forces is in question. Second, there is the possibility of transferring investigations from one force to the other, for instance in case of procedural errors or for the investigation of complaints. When both forces police each other, there is a better chance of guaranteeing civil liberties. However, in Belgium, which has three police forces, issues of competencies and bad relations between the forces have actually threatened the quality of policing. This became particularly acute in the Dutroux scandal in the late 1990s. Michel Dutroux was accused of abducting, abusing and murdering a number of teenage girls. The investigation of the crimes prior to and after his arrest has given rise to grave doubts about the Belgian police's competence in investigating major crimes requiring a great deal of inter-force cooperation.

Covert policing in France is often performed by the Police Nationale, sometimes in conjunction with the Customs service. Such operations are always performed under the formal supervision of a prosecutor and regularly a *juge d'instruction*, a member of the judiciary, as well (see Chapter 4 for a discussion of such arrangements). Particularly when the trafficking of drugs is at issue the investigative powers are substantial, and they might involve infiltration and the controlled transit of drugs. Issues of entrapment and of the infiltrants themselves committing crimes are pertinent. When the latter happens, the admissibility of the evidence is not often at issue: it usually will be allowed. The more pertinent issue is whether the infiltrant should be prosecuted. In France, rejection of evidence is not used as a means to control police behaviour (Field *et al.*, 1995). The evidence of anonymous witnesses, often informants and infiltrants, is relatively easily admissible as well. There is hardly a law of evidence as in England and Wales but there is case law to the effect that a conviction solely on the basis of anonymous witnesses cannot stand. On the other hand, an anonymous tip can be enough for judicial chambers to approve measures such as telephone tapping.

Scandals in both Belgium and the Netherlands have showed how easily undercover policing can get out of control. Separate controversies involving police wrongdoing in proactive policing have led to a state of crisis in both countries. In the Netherlands this led to the Van Traa parliamentary inquiry, after which two government ministers lost their job (see Van Traa, 1997). New legislation on proactive policing was subsequently developed (see Chapter 4). In Belgium an inquiry published a damning report in 1990, after the police failed to bring the infamous so-called 'warehouse murderers' to justice (Fijnaut and Verbruggen, 1995). These guidelines have enhanced centralised control over undercover and other policing operations. Legislation and guidelines in these countries now ensure control exercised by prosecution and judiciary, and the specification of instances and situations in which proactive policing methods may be used. Guidelines now specify that police infiltration may only occur in the short term, and it must never lead to an officer committing a serious offence. European legislation and case law on privacy, fair trial and entrapment inform such laws in Belgium and the Netherlands as they do across the rest of Europe (Clareboets, 1997).

To what extent proactive policing is appropriate depends on the nature of the perceived crisis or problem that it is supposed to address. When organised crime is seen to threaten the fabric of society, and when it is felt that traditional policing methods fall short an investment in intelligence-led policing might be seen as necessary. But when community relations are at issue, proactive policing is not the best way forward.

Policing corruption

Although police corruption might occur anywhere in police organisations there are certain danger areas. Many of these have to do with undercover policing (see Newburn, 1999). Corruption may be defined as: 'The misuse of authority by a police officer in a manner designed to produce personal gain for the officer or for others' (Goldstein, 1977: 188).

Punch (1985) distinguished four forms of corruption. They are: *straightforward corruption*, which is the action (or inaction) for a reward; *strategic corruption*, where a police officer actively stimulates crime and extorts money or goods; *combative corruption*, where the police use illegal or unethical means to strengthen their case; and finally *corruption as perverting justice*, where the motivation is either revenge or avoiding prosecution.

Strategies against corruption can be classified as either internal or external. Internal controls rest within the police. External controls rely on other bodies. Both the UK's and US's anti-corruption strategies are dominated by internal controls. They take the form of codes of ethics, integrity testing and internal-affairs departments. UK police corruption is said to be 'under control', but that does not mean that it is non-existent. In 1999 there were over 100 police officers facing charges of dishonesty (Wright, 2002b). In situations where corruption is feared to be more widespread and deeply ingrained within police culture, there often is a need for external control bodies with sufficient powers and resources to overcome it.

A compelling example of successful external control is to be found in Hong Kong. Hong Kong, is a special administrative region of the People's Republic of China with an estimated population of 6.7 million. It was under British rule from 1842 until 1997. On 1 July 1997, Britain handed Hong Kong back to China and it was agreed that the capitalist economic system of Hong Kong would be maintained for another 50 years. In order to ensure this within the socialist system of the People's Republic, Hong Kong enjoys high levels of autonomy, which is why it is sensible to regard Hong Kong as a separate entity for comparative criminal justice purposes.

While crime in general is perhaps not very high on Hong Kong's agenda, the fight against corruption has taken centre stage since the 1990s (Wing Lo, 2000). A separate office is in charge of fighting government corruption. The Independent Commission Against Corruption (ICAC) was set up in 1994, and has a staff of more than 1,200. That makes it one of the largest dedicated anti-corruption bodies in the world (see www.icac.org.hk).

The ICAC was initially given rather wide-ranging investigative powers. Subsequently, the reviewing role of the judiciary has been enhanced to curtail the Commission's use of arrest and detention, and an independent complaints commission has been established as well.

The ICAC's size and powers show the preoccupation Hong Kong has with corruption, which was said to be rife at time of its instigation. The Commission, effectively a separate police force, has been hailed a success, and the fact that the relative extent of non-anonymous reporting of corruption has increased is taken is as a sign of public confidence. What is more, the Commission claims to have eradicated large-scale police corruption, so that what remains tends to be isolated cases. Governmental corruption also seems to have declined, whereas corruption in the private sector takes up more and more of the Commission's time.

The ICAC utilises a so-called three-pronged approach. The first tier is effective enforcement. The second is education and prevention, whereas the third is to do with community relations. International cooperation in combating fraud and other forms of organised crime is high on the agenda as well (ICAC, 2001).

The example set by Hong Kong has been followed elsewhere. Similar commissions exist, for instance, in Australia and in some parts of Africa and South America. They are characterised by an investment in the investigation of corruption, often coupled with an increase in sentencing powers against crimes of corruption (Urquhart, 1998).

Corruption is thought to influence virtually every social sphere in the Baltic state of Lithuania (Pakstaitis, 2002), even though there are reports to suggest that the level of corruption is perhaps not as high compared to other states of the former Soviet Union (see Vaitiekus, 2001). The battle against corruption is a recurrent theme in the development of the criminal justice system, which is undergoing change after change since Lithuania gained its independence in 1990. There has been an emphasis on specialised internal controls, and a new police body called the Special Investigations Service was established in 1997.

In the newly written Criminal Code several forms of corruption are specified under the heading of crimes against the civil service. The code specifies passive bribery (acceptance of a bribe), active bribery (paying a bribe), abuse of office, illegal participation of a public official in commercial activities, exceeding of official powers, non-performance of official duties and forgery in office. They all carry prison sentences. Over the recent five years however, only some 50–60 people were convicted for any of these offences (Pakstaitis, 2002). This number is tiny compared to the assumed widespread level of corruption. According to a recent survey, about one in three individuals in Lithuania recently paid a bribe to a government official (Vaitiekus, 2001).

Several reasons for corruption being woven into the fabric of society are given by Pakstaitis (2002). The first relates to the formation of a new civil service since gaining independence: poorly qualified people, brought up in a communist style civil service, were required to give shape to a civil service with new aims and objectives and a new service-oriented culture. This continues to prove a challenge. Second, the transitional period was, and continues to be, characterised by economic strain: salaries of civil servants are low, and the police service is no exception. Additionally, there is the wider historical and cultural legacy of the Soviet era. During Soviet times, abuse of office was a fact of life and almost a symbol of status: those in powerful positions were often expected to abuse their offices in order to help friends and family (see Shelley, 1999, on the colonial legacy of the Soviet era).

It remains instilled into the minds of many Lithuanians that if you want to receive proper service from any authority, the best way to achieve that is by paying extra via a bribe. It is probably at this level where the fight against corruption will be won or lost. While top-down initiatives are necessary, the main battlefield will be in the minds of those used to small-time corruption and who regard it not so much as an evil but rather as an inevitable inconvenience of life. As long as corruption is regarded a useful tool for a state official to supplement wages, and a handy means to fast-track any official procedure, new anti-corruption legislation will probably struggle to have an impact.

It is generally accepted that no one type of measure can be a foolproof guarantee against corruption. Wright (2002b), however, has argued that the following points carry a certain degree of universality.

- There is a link between police corruption and the prevailing social, economic and cultural conditions;

- There are at least two levels of corruption, namely low level mooching and a more serious level, which tends to be related to drugs and vice;

- Recruitment and selection and human resource management is of crucial importance;

- Integrity testing and monitoring of 'at risk' individuals is necessary;

- Defusing corruption involves breaking the code of silence whilst maintaining the team ethos.

Tackling widespread corruption thus might require substantial changes to police education, training and police culture and management. As the case of Lithuania shows, public perceptions of corruption will have to change along with it.

Whether private or public, centralised or decentralised, overt or covert, strategies and arrangements conducive to securing ethical policing are increasingly necessary. Ethical policing is seen to be the way out of the conundrum of the moral ambiguity of policing described by Waddington (2000) and the point made by Bayley (1994) and Wright (2002a) that police effectiveness is not to be found in the reduction of crime rates. Neyroud and Beckley (2001) argue that policing should be guided by four ethical principles:

The first is *legality*. Police officers should uphold and comply with the law. The legality requirement places a burden on the law-making process as well. Laws should be transparent and accessible, and created in a democratically accountable way, through parliament.

The second principle relates to *proportionality*. Police officers should ensure that any action is proportionate to the legitimate aim pursued. It should be considered whether a less intrusive or coercive action is available to achieve the same end and the decision-making concerning such actions should be fair and transparent.

The third guiding principle is that of *necessity*. This principle particularly relates to the use of force by the police. The test whether a pressing social need is being addressed must be considered. In a broader sense, adherence to this principle aims to ensure that the police is tolerant and broadminded.

Finally, the fourth principle is *accountability*. This is often taken to mean external accountability, such as civilian involvement in complaints procedures and independent investigations into serious police wrong-doing.

Criminal justice's quiet revolution: the rise of private policing

Policing is not necessarily always the job of the police. Particularly in private spaces, such as nightclubs and shopping centres, this function is often performed by the private-security sector. Private-security personnel do not have police powers but nevertheless are vital in the maintenance of public order and crime prevention.

The private-security industry consists of an eclectic range of sectors offering services and products. Button (1999) has divided them into:

- The manned guarding sector. This includes in-house guarding, door supervision and bodyguard style services;

- Private sector detention services such as private, or perhaps more precisely contracted out prisons;

- Professional security services, such as private investigators;

- Security storage and destruction services;

- Security products such as the designers, producers, installers and maintainers of security equipment such as alarm systems or closed circuit television systems;

- Marginal sectors in which we include gamekeepers.

One thing to notice about the private-security industry is its rapidly increasing size (De Waard, 1999). Within the European Union, the industry is biggest in Great Britain where approximately 160,000 people are employed within it. That is quite close to the number of police officers, which is around 185,000. A few southern European countries known for their relatively high police rates, such as Spain and Italy, have in contrast a relatively small private-security sector. In Italy, the private-security sector is six times smaller than the police force. In Spain it is almost four times smaller, whereas in Greece, the proportion is only 5 per cent of the police numbers (De Waard, 1999). In the Scandinavian countries the size of police service is somewhat smaller but the private-security industry has expanded much further. In Finland, in particular, the ratio of private security personnel to police is 4:5, so with police officers maintaining a slight majority. In Sweden the ratio is three private-security personnel per five police officers. A smaller police force tends therefore to coincide with a larger private-security industry, at least in certain European countries.

The private-security industry is particularly large in several countries outside Europe. In the US there are almost twice as many private security officers as there are police officers. In South Africa, private-security personnel also outnumber the police by almost 200 per cent. High crime rates and sentiments regarding police incompetence help explain this state of affairs. It is expected that in transitional Eastern European states much of the policing function will be carried out by private firms in the future. In Bulgaria, the industry is already quite large, and estimates indicate that it may already be very large indeed in the Russian Federation as well (De Waard, 1999).

It is, of course, debatable whether people with criminal convictions should be allowed to be door supervisors at nightclubs, or stewards at a professional football club. In many countries there are therefore movements towards formal regulation of the industry, including compulsory vetting. Regulation might set standards for private-security personnel as well as for their education and training. Another issue is to what extent, and in what manner, the industry should be held accountable. While accountability structures for the police are hotly debated, accountability for private-security staff is considered in much less detail. The scale of the private-security sector urges us to rethink the very nature of policing and accordingly the role of the state in maintaining law and order in society (see also Jones and Newburn, 1998; Johnston, 2000; Button 2002).

Conclusion

Diversity characterises police origins and their role in various countries. That diversity is particularly apparent in the way police forces are organised. Taking one dimension, police forces can be more or less centralised. The US police service is particularly decentralised, for example. A US state may have dozens of forces: for each county and for bigger municipalities as well as for the state as a whole; and there are at least 63 supra-state forces, such as the Federal Bureau of Investigation (FBI) and the Drug Enforcement Agency (DEA) (Ebbe, 2000a). Diversity is also the name of the game in Europe's police organisations, to which the following quotation is a testament:

> Parts of the EC have single forces, organised nationally, for example, Denmark, Greece, Ireland and Luxembourg. Germany has a system in which responsibilities are divided between state and federal levels. Belgium has three forces, with conflicts over jurisdiction and competence. Portugal has several, whilst Italy has five separate, but mutually integrated, police organisations. France has two highly centralised forces, whilst Spain has two national ones. In the UK there are 52 semi-autonomous forces, and in the Netherlands a new system has recently been established of 25 regional forces and one new national force. There is no basic uniformity or pattern to the organisation of European police forces. (Benyon *et al.*, 1994: 48)

It is therefore suitable to focus on policing functions over police organisational structures despite the fact that there is plenty of diversity as to the policing function as well (Mawby, 1999a, 2000).

Comparative research helps us gain a deeper understanding of the various types of relationship that exist between the police, the state and the people. It illustrates that policing may constitute both a promise and a threat, depending on the nature of these relations – to be protected from crime and disorder or more generally 'looked after' by benign servants of the people, or, on the other hand to be singled out for persecution, to be harassed or oppressed.

Chapter 4

Prosecution and pre-trial justice

The importance of the pre-trial stage in criminal justice proceedings can hardly be overestimated. Whatever the legal system, much of the justice process takes place prior to trial, in arrangements and practices that are less transparent than trials and often less carefully regulated. Baldwin (1985) started the first chapter of his book *Pre-Trial Justice* as follows:

> Contrary to the popular view, the crucial decisions in most criminal cases are not made in open court but in discussions that take place in private beforehand. In these cases the court represent no more than the final stage in a lengthy series of exchanges involving police officers, lawyers, court officials and the defendant himself. The pre-trial stages of the criminal process have proved curiously impenetrable to outside observers, despite the fact that this is the time when the vulnerability of defendants might most easily be exploited. (Baldwin, 1985: 1)

Baldwin emphasised the caveats involved in pre-trial justice. Far-reaching decisions are often made in settings that are not public, and sometimes without the suspect having legal representation. Decisions made against the defendant in this phase are often less open to review. Ironically, the same is often true for decisions that favour suspects. In many jurisdictions decisions made by the prosecuting authority that involve the termination of a case before it goes to trial are often difficult to challenge. Thus, when considering both the suspects' rights and the interests of victims, the relative secrecy of pre-trial proceedings raises issues of accountability.

The relative importance attached to pre-trial justice differs considerably between countries with adversarial and inquisitorial legal traditions. In inquisitorial justice, examples of which we find across the European continent, great emphasis is placed on information in the case file. That case file, or *dossier*, contains all the relevant information obtained in the investigative phase. It is usually available to the courts, which might base much of their decision-making on its contents, thus making the pre-trial phase crucial. Adversarial systems place greater emphasis on orally presented evidence at trial, which is seen to work as a safeguard against courts placing too much trust in police investigations as the main provider of evidence.

In this chapter I will consider two main areas in relation to pre-trial justice. The first is prosecution. Who is to decide whether a case should go to trial? How are such decisions made, and who is to review the processes? When looking at overarching prosecution policies, at one end of the continuum we find systems that incorporate the *principle of legality*. This means that, in principle, any case of sufficient strength should be put before a court of law. In contrast, there are systems that embody the *principle of opportunity*, where prosecutions should only be brought if they serve the public interest. In practice, this distinction has faded. In many countries where traditionally the principle of legality informed prosecution policy there are mechanisms in place to divert trivial or otherwise unsuitable cases away from court. Similarly, in systems with a policy informed by the principle of opportunity there is many a case that is forwarded as a matter of cause without much reflection about the public interest. However, use of discretion has a different footing under each principle. Under the former, discretion is used to determine *not* to prosecute a case; under the latter the opposite is the case (Brandts and Field, 1995; Fionda, 1995).

The second area to be considered relates to pre-trial custody. As pre-trial custody is, by definition, the incarceration of a person presumed innocent the practice of locking people up until the day of their trial is a business that, in the interests of justice, needs to be regulated and monitored closely. The extent to which jurisdictions make use of pre-trial custody can be indicative of how those in authority relate to their citizens. Widespread use of this measure would give rise to suspicions of an emphasis not on crime control but on controlling (segments of) the population at large. Rules and practices regarding the use of pre-trial custody are an important indicator for the 'state of justice' in any given country.

I will discuss prosecution and pre-trial custody in separate sections. That might suggest that it is appropriate or even feasible for the two to be considered in isolation, but in reality, this is not quite as straightforward. The processes of investigation, prosecution and remand are often intermingled, and on the European continent often even more so than in England and Wales.

Finally, I shall discuss pre-trial diversion, the process of dealing with offending behaviour without the direct involvement of the court system. Sometimes these processes tend to be relatively informal and take place in relative obscurity. In other cases, such as New Zealand, such measures have taken centre stage, in particular with regard to youth justice.

Prosecution

In England and Wales, prosecution was historically a matter for the police. The police would conduct their own prosecutions in the lower courts where they would present cases themselves. In higher courts the police instructed counsel (i.e. a barrister) to present the case in court. The Director of Public Prosecutions would only deal with particularly difficult or sensitive cases.

The Royal Commission on Criminal Procedure produced what is colloquially known as the Philips Report in 1981. It concluded that it was undesirable for the police to both investigate and prosecute. The commission also noted that substantial differences in prosecution practises around the country existed, which it regarded as undesirable. It therefore concluded that a locally based prosecution service with some national features was needed (Philips, 1981).

In 1985 the Crown Prosecution Service (CPS) was created and it came into operation in 1986. Arguably, the CPS was inspired by considerations to do with the quality of justice: investigation and prosecution should be separated in order to reduce the probability of overzealous police prosecutions. Additionally, the emergence of a national prosecution service would make it easier for national guidelines to be issued and implemented. That would help to ensure that similar cases were being dealt with in similar ways across the country.

In England and Wales the days of police prosecutions have gone but in many other countries this is not quite the case. In particular, former British colonies in which an England and Wales-type judicial system was introduced often still rely on police prosecutions to a large extent, such as Nigeria (Ebbe, 2000b). The Director of Public Prosecutions in Nigeria prosecutes only serious cases, such as murder, armed robbery and narcotics trafficking. This is particularly telling because these are the crimes for which the death penalty can be imposed. The police tend to prosecute most other cases on their own accord.

The CPS in England and Wales is a relatively new institution, squeezed between two much older and well-established bodies, the courts and the police. It is perhaps not surprising that the CPS lacks a certain amount of visibility and clout as it is 'sandwiched virtually to vanishing point' (Uglow, 2002: 193). In most countries on Europe's mainland the situation is rather different. In these jurisdictions the public prosecutor is by tradition, by law and by practice in a much stronger position. There are not many countries where the prosecution service is as strong as in the Netherlands (Corstens, 1999), which is why I devote considerable attention to the Dutch arrangements. If you compared and contrasted arrangements in England and Wales with those in the Netherlands, that would be a *most different design* (see Pakes, 1999) as the differences between both jurisdictions are substantial. Subsequently I shall look at prosecution arrangements in Scotland, which, although differing in interesting ways from those in England and Wales, could be called a *most similar design* (see Chapter 2).

Prosecution in the Netherlands

Like many other European criminal justice systems, the Dutch system has been modelled after the French. This is particularly discernible as far as both prosecution services are concerned. Both organisations are large, influential and governed by the Ministry of Justice. Dutch prosecutors are magistrates and trained in a way that is very similar to the training of judges. To highlight the fact that both judges and prosecutors belong to the same corporate body, prosecutors are called 'standing magistrates' because they stand up in court to present and argue cases whereas judges are called 'sitting magistrates'. To exemplify the strong French heritage the prosecution offices in the Netherlands are called virtually the same as those in France. The French term *Ministère Publique* is translated literally into *Openbaar Ministerie* (or OM) in the Netherlands, whereas their offices are called *parquet* and *parket*, respectively.

The role of the Dutch public prosecution service is to direct the investigation of criminal offences, to prosecute the perpetrators of criminal offences, and to execute the decisions rendered by the courts. It is in the first core task where the Dutch prosecution service differs most from the CPS in England and Wales. In serious cases, Dutch prosecutors can and do guide and direct police investigations. In doing so they have the law on their side. The Dutch Code of Criminal Procedure specifies that police officers wishing to take particular investigative actions require a public prosecutor's approval before those actions can be carried out. This applies to arrests, remands in custody, and in most situations also to actions such as telephone tapping, house searches and seizures. Basically, police officers cannot do too much in an investigation without a prosecutor knowing about it, and expecting to be informed about the results of that action (Fionda, 1995).

53

This is a system of oversight or *review*: the police carry out the investigation, subject to continuous review by a public prosecution officer. This officer is invariably a lawyer. In systems of review, prosecutors exercise a dual role. On the one hand they are partners with the police. Together they fight crime and carry out investigations. On the other hand they are the supervisors of the police and exist to ensure that suspects' rights are respected. An investigative or examining judge oversees and reviews the behaviour of the prosecution, and might get involved directly in the more complex police investigations, so that the magistrate serves as an added layer of review on top of the prosecution service (Pakes, 1999).

The second task of the Dutch OM, the actual prosecution, is similar to that of the CPS, but there remain important differences. In the Netherlands the prosecution service decides on charges and discontinuations. It also presents all cases in court, whatever that court should be. Choice of court is also the privilege of the prosecution: defendants do not have a say, although judges in lower courts may direct cases to a higher court either because the case is deemed too complex for a single sitting judge or because the sentencing powers of the lower courts might be insufficient. Because prosecutors are physically present and argue their case in court one could say that public prosecutors in the Netherlands are their own barristers. In order to appreciate this practice, it is important to understand the nature of trials in the Netherlands and other inquisitorial systems and the role that prosecutors play in that system. I shall, however, postpone that discussion until the next chapter.

The prosecution service considers itself primarily accountable to the courts, which perhaps is not surprising given that prosecutors are part of the judiciary. This is illustrated by their rather pompous name, *Officier van Justitie*, which translates as Officer of Justice and serves as a reminder of the traditional orientation of these magistrates, in which objectivity is highly valued. They aim at achieving justice rather than necessarily at achieving convictions, at least in theory. The service is politically accountable to the Minister of Justice, who is a member of government.

It is worth mentioning that the service enjoys a monopoly of prosecution. Private prosecutions or prosecutions brought by other agencies cannot occur. Dutch prosecutors are the sole keepers of the key to the courts. To balance this, there is a complaint procedure open to victims and other parties against a prosecutor's decision not to prosecute a particular case.

The power of Dutch public prosecutors is considerable, and their influence stretches throughout the criminal justice system, which is why they are sometimes called the spiders in the web of the criminal justice process (e.g. Pakes, 2001). In comparison, prosecutors in England and Wales serve more as a link in the chain of law-enforcement bodies: they receive their cases from the police and decide whether or not to pass them on to barristers. The prosecution's independence is judged to be valuable: independence is seen as a safeguard against undue influence of one law-enforcement agency over another. In the Netherlands, in contrast, the grip that prosecutors have on police investigations is supposed to be firm: they are assumed to be in a position of authority of the police. It is that overview that is seen as a safeguard against police wrongdoing.

However, the system of review does not come with a guarantee of police propriety. The aforementioned 1995 Dutch parliamentary inquiry (colloquially called the Van Traa committee, after its late chairman Labour MP Maarten van Traa) revealed that in some regions of the country police officers had developed a practice of performing large-scale investigative operations using very intrusive measures without any factual, prosecutorial supervision. In order to use the information thus obtained as legal evidence, the fashion in which it was obtained was either fabricated or left unclear. Thus, instead of admitting to unauthorised telephone tapping or the 'wiring' of premises, investigating officers produced reports in which it stated that they simply could not help overhearing elaborate and self-incriminating conversations between suspects. Telephones were, strikingly, often left off the hook, windows were handily left open just when police officers walked past, and drugs happened to be placed conveniently in sight and spotted through open doors and windows. Prosecutors quite often failed to pick up on such phrases in the dossier and the same was true for the sitting magistrates, the judges (see Punch, 1997; Van Traa, 1997).

The Van Traa inquiry concluded that criminal investigation was in crisis. It identified shortcomings in law in police practice and ethics and in the area of prosecution review and control of police activity. Certain prosecutors were identified as standing shoulder to shoulder with the police and becoming too immersed in the 'war against drugs', at the expense of the magistrate-like aspect of their position. Others who followed the letter of the law were left uninformed about what really went on in proactive investigations and lost track of the methods police officers covertly used.

While a certain amount of trust is necessary for the system of review to work, it is relatively easy for the police to hide much of what they are doing from the prosecutors, who are hardly ever physically present when such actions occur. However, too much trust may constitute a lack of review, so that this mechanism of quality control easily becomes based on something hardly more firm than quicksand (Field *et al.*, 1995).

Arguably, the Dutch system provides a compelling example of failure of the judicial review. However, the action taken in the Netherlands was not to abandon that system but to strengthen it. New legislation has been put into place to ensure that the prosecution service has a firmer grip on police investigations. Regulations concerning intrusive policing methods have established a review committee to authorise and monitor their use on a national basis.

The other mechanism to ensure national consistency concerns the operation of guidelines, of which there are many. They typically are issued by the Board of Procurators General, the formal head of the service that is in frequent contact with the Minister of Justice. This, interestingly, is in contrast to Germany, where guidelines are regarded with suspicion as a reminder of state influence on criminal justice during the Third Reich (Fionda, 1995).

The Scottish procurator fiscal

As in most jurisdictions in continental Europe, the prosecution service in Scotland prosecutes virtually all cases after having received reports from the police. Private prosecutions are very rare indeed (Duff, 1999a). The head of the prosecution service is the Lord Advocate, who is a government minister. His deputy is the Solicitor General. In the lower courts prosecutions are carried out by the Procurator Fiscal or left to assistant or deputy fiscals. The prosecution service is to a large extent independent and enjoys considerable discretionary powers. Prosecutions are brought only when considered in the public interest, which is rather a broad concept and has remained largely undefined. The service is not accountable to the police, courts or to individuals such as victims. It is politically answerable only to parliament through the Lord Advocate.

Apart from the actual prosecuting decision, the service also decides on the charge, and can drop or modify charges. The prosecutor decides on the trial venue in case of either way offences (i.e., those charges that may be tried by either judge or jury). This decision is, unlike in England and Wales, not left to the defendant. The service may also issue instructions to the police. These may be of a general nature but may also concern specific actions to be taken in a particular case.

The independence of the prosecution service is mediated by the fact that it relies on the police for information (Moody and Tombs, 1982). The police service has been shown to be very influential with regard to how cases progress by the way they present and argue cases. This relationship moderates the independence and power of the prosecution service considerably, a situation that is as true for Scotland as it is for many other prosecution services around the world.

There are various controls on the work of prosecutors in Scotland. The most important internal control is the use of guidelines. Guidelines are frequently issued by the Crown Office, with the objective of achieving consistency in prosecutors' decision-making. However, many of these guidelines are confidential, so that public scrutiny is difficult. The second method of control relates to the return of statistics from the 49 separate procurator fiscal offices. Any regional variation in prosecution practices may become visible through this method but these figures are not always in the public domain, so that both measures mentioned above must be said to be internal controls first and foremost.

An external control that does not exist in Scotland is for victims or other dissatisfied individuals to challenge in court a decision made by the prosecution service. The service is simply not accountable in such a direct way to individuals. As private prosecutions in such circumstances are virtually impossible, the options for 'outsiders' to challenge decisions by the service are limited.

Duff (1999a) concluded by saying that:

> ... given the absence of effective external control over the use by prosecutors of their very wide discretionary powers, considerable confidence must be placed in the competence, professionalism and incorruptibility of the prosecution service. It is fair to say that, at present, the Scottish public prosecutor is generally held in sufficiently high esteem, by both the general public and other participants in the criminal justice process, for the necessary trust to be granted. (Duff, 1999a: 129)

Lay review of prosecution: the American Grand Jury

The oversight often employed by investigative judges over prosecutors is, in some of the US states, a task for the grand jury. (See www.edayton.edu/ ~ grandjur for information on the grand jury system.) A grand jury is formed in a way similar to *petit juries*, juries that decide on guilt at trial. Such grand juries are not to be confused with Federal grand juries that often serve a different function, which is typically more 'watchdog'-like: these tend to be involved in investigations to monitor the performance of government and other public agencies.

Grand juries can be as large as 23 persons, for instance in Pennsylvania (see Savitt and Gottlieb, 1983), or as small as 5 or 7, as is the case in Virginia and Oregon, respectively. Grand juries generally serve to bring charges, to oversee investigations or some combination of the two. One way a person can be charged is for a prosecutor to seek an indictment from a grand jury by presenting evidence to it. The jury must decide whether there is probable cause, in which case they 'return the indictment', which is also called 'returning a true bill'.

The status of state grand juries differs widely among US states. In some, they can be bypassed only with difficulty, and in other states their function is largely inconsequential. Nevertheless, one could argue that a grand jury returning indictments is the US way of controlling the power of prosecutors. Where in continental Europe this review is a matter for a judge, in many US states it is, perhaps not surprisingly, a matter for 'the people'.

It is additionally noteworthy that a prosecutor in the US, the District Attorney, can exert considerable influence over police investigations. District Attorneys may have investigative teams attached to them and on occasion conduct special investigations. Noteworthy examples have included the Watergate allegations involving President Nixon, and the Monica Lewinsky affair during Bill Clinton's presidency (Uglow, 2002).

The core function of a prosecution service

Prosecution is about filtering out cases that should not go to court. That requires rules and guidelines to decide how cases should be processed once they have reached the stage of prosecution. Arrangements will often involve a certain level of discretion on behalf of the prosecuting authority. Levels of prosecutorial discretion are high in France, Belgium and the Netherlands, where the principle of opportunity holds. In these countries prosecutions are brought only if they are deemed to be in the public interest, although it is not always clearly defined what constitutes public interest, unlike in England and Wales where the relevant guidelines are a matter of public record. In other European countries the principle of legality, also known as the *ex officio principle*, is upheld (Fionda, 1995). Germany is an example (Tak, 1986). It means that prosecutions should be brought for every crime that comes to the attention of the prosecution office for which there is sufficient evidence. The former principle of opportunity fits better with the inquisitorial tradition, in which state officials enjoy greater levels of freedom to decide on the course of action they think is best.

When discussing prosecution from a comparative perspective we find that comparing like with like is virtually impossible. Prosecution in Scotland is already rather different from that in England and Wales, whereas prosecution in most countries on the European continent is very different altogether because the relation between police and prosecution has a wholly different footing. The role of the prosecutors in court differs as well, and cannot be understood without understanding how judges, jurors and defence counsels play their roles in court, which is a matter to which I shall return in the next chapter.

In inquisitorial systems the usual mechanism for quality control is review. In adversarial systems the safeguard is one of independence.

Generally, in whatever the system, the prosecution stands between the police and the courts. It sits there to ensure that the police cannot bring cases to court without merit. Sometimes the prosecution service comes into play only in cases that are particularly serious or delicate. This is the way in which the CPS used to operate and in various countries, such as Nigeria and Mauritius, still does. Similarly, in many countries where the prosecution service is mainly responsible for police investigation, there are measures in place for the police to deal with minor crimes directly and independently. This is usually performed for reasons of expedience and does not correspond to the philosophy that underpins the role of the prosecution service in such systems.

An important aspect of the role of the prosecution service is to protect suspects from an overzealous police. The philosophy about how this is best achieved differs. One approach favours the prosecution service guiding and controlling police investigations as they occur. Another advocates that such control can be established by way of an independent body that reviews the police case after the fact. While inquisitorial and adversarial systems have deployed rather different solutions to the problem of unfair or unnecessary prosecutions the problem they address is, nevertheless, essentially the same.

Pre-trial justice: the role of magistrates

It can be argued that the phase of pre-trial justice starts properly when a suspect is charged and makes an appearance before a judge. An independent magistrate is usually required to ensure that a suspect's detention is appropriate. It is indicative of the severity of the measure of detention that after a few days in a great many jurisdictions a judge is required to rule on it, usually having seen the suspect and having reviewed the evidence that is accumulated up to that point. As far as England and Wales are concerned, Section 38 of PACE allows detention only if:

- The suspect's name and address cannot be verified;
- They are considered unlikely to appear in court;
- They are likely to interfere with witnesses or further investigations;
- They are likely to commit further crimes.

When defendants are granted bail they are allowed to go 'free'. In England and Wales the question of bail can arise at various stages. First, the police have the power to bail people before charge, so that further inquiries can be carried out and the suspect can be compelled to reappear at the police station at a specified point in time. The police can also make bail decisions subsequent to the charge. When cases are adjourned to a later date, it is a court that makes the bail decision. Conditional bail, where the suspect is free to go as long as he/she complies with certain conditions, such as not visiting certain places or individuals, is also a possibility (Hucklesby, 2002). The Bail Act 1976 specified the conditions under which bail can be refused. Defendants need not be granted bail if there are substantial grounds for believing that they will:

- fail to return to court when they should;

- commit an office while on bail;

- interfere with witnesses or otherwise obstruct the course of justice.

Additionally, bail may be refused when deemed to be in the interests of the defendant's own protection or when there is insufficient information available to make a decision (Hucklesby, 2002). Hucklesby has argued that the bail decision is a difficult one because of the balancing of competing rights. On the one hand there is the individual's right to liberty but on the other there is the public's right to be protected from serious harm. Another fundamental difficulty is that a decision to keep a suspect in detention is inevitably based on predictions about their future behaviour and these are notorious difficult to make. Hucklesby noted a tendency to over-impose remand in custody: less than half of those denied bail actually received a prison sentence, and almost a quarter were never convicted (Home Office, 2001). There appears to be a tendency to err on the side of protecting the public, at the expense of the interests of suspects.

In the US, suspects who are arrested and kept in custody normally appear before a magistrate within 48 hours (Smalleger, 1997). Following arrest most states require a magistrate's review in order to determine whether or not there is cause to detain the suspect. Release is subject to bail, which usually involves a monetary deposit, although there are alternatives such as conditional release and release on recognisance, which involves a defendant signing a promise not to flee from prosecution.

In the Netherlands every detained suspect is interviewed by an examining magistrate within three days of his/her arrest. This judge can impose remand in custody, which usually involves a suspect being transferred from a police cell to one in a remand prison. The suspect is entitled to have a defence lawyer present at their hearing. Examining magistrates need to make several assessments.

First they establish that the crime the suspect is prosecuted for is serious enough to allow remand. The general rule is that only for offences that carry at least four years imprisonment is remand in custody a possibility. The Dutch Criminal Code specifies maximum sentences for crimes, and four years can be given for most sexual crimes, most violent crimes, and the more serious class of property crimes. The sexual crime that is an exception is exhibitionism, so that those suspected of this offence cannot be remanded in custody (Corstens, 1999).

Second, the examining magistrate must be satisfied that the evidence as put forward is sufficient to warrant custody. The required level of proof is not beyond reasonable doubt, but it has to be considerably stronger than the reasonable suspicion required for arrest. The third assessment to be made is whether certain grounds apply to necessitate custody. These would include the strong possibility of the suspect re-offending, or of the suspect evading trial or disturbing the gathering of evidence. Finally, in cases of suspects without a fixed address in the Netherlands, the possibilities for remand in custody are somewhat widened.

In France, a suspect can be held at a police station for interrogation and questioning for 24 hours, which can be extended to 48 hours, and in exceptional cases to 96 hours (Vogler, 1996): the system of *garde à vue*. The suspect's rights relating to *garde à vue* have recently been improved, partly because of a number of European Union rulings against France. Only since 1993 do suspects have the right to:

- notify a relative by phone of the arrest;

- obtain legal advice, although with limitations – it is only allowed after 24 hours of detention, and the suspect does not have the right to have his/her lawyer present during interviews;

- call for a medical investigation straight away and not, as was the case before, after the initial 24 hours have expired. Relatives can request that a suspect be seen by a doctor as well;

- be told at once in a language the suspect understands about all relevant applicable rights and the legal limitations on the duration of *garde à vue*.

Garde à vue is initiated by a senior police officer and overseen by a prosecutor who has limited powers of extension as well. Remand in custody (*détention provisoire*) can only be imposed by an examining magistrate. Only those defendants charged with a grave offence carrying a penalty of at least two years' imprisonment or one year in case of an *offense flagrante* (a serious offence) can be remanded. Remand must be justified by reasons relating to the investigative process or for reasons relating to either the protection of society, the preservation of public order or for the sake of the defendant's own security. If the offence charged carries less than five years' imprisonment and the suspect has not previously served a prison sentence of at least one year, the remand period cannot exceed six months. In more serious cases, the custody can initially be for the duration of four months, but this period is renewable and the law does not state a maximum period of custody. Suspects can, at certain times, request the examining judge to lift custody, a decision that is open to appeal at a division of the Appeals Court called the *Chambre d'Accusation*.

From an English perspective, criticisms with regard to the position of the suspect in France are easily made. The fact that a defence lawyer is not entitled to attend police interviews is probably the main bone of contention. Despite significant changes to the system in the 1990s, defendants' access to legal advice remains limited. The system of pre-trial custody is not uncontroversial in France itself as well, and pre-trial arrangements seem to be ever-changing; but the position of the defence seems to be improved only with a certain level of reluctance. Vogler (1996) noted however that defendants do have four fundamental rights: the right to know the allegations against them; the undiluted right to silence; the right to counsel; the right to sufficient time to prepare a defence.

To what extent defendants will always be able to exercise these rights is a matter of debate. The consensus among French legal theorists seems to be that the immediate involvement of an independent judge is one important safeguard against police wrongdoing. The fact that all decisions affecting a suspect are reasoned, given in writing and can be appealed against is another. Third, careful regulations for the behaviour of police, prosecution and examining judge do also serve as indirect empowerment of suspects, who are certainly less well equipped to fight their corner directly than their counterparts in England and Wales.

The French situation, where a suspect is not entitled to have a defence lawyer present during initial police interviews, is an easy target for criticism. It is, however, not unique to France. In the Netherlands the suspect's rights are similarly limited with regard to the first police interview. The official reason is, ironically, that the presence of a defence lawyer would hinder the development of rapport between interviewer and suspect. The utility of this measure can be questioned, as it appears that most suspects in the hands of the Dutch police are happy to speak anyway. The issue periodically enters the political agenda, but change in the short term does not appear to be very likely (Corstens, 1999).

Despite occasional proposals to restrict the role or abolish the office altogether, the *juge d'instruction* remains a pivotal figure in French criminal justice (Hodgson, 2001). In Germany in contrast, the role of investigative or examining judge has been abolished. The examining judge used to gather evidence in serious trials in a process called *Voruntersuchung* (which translates literally as 'pre-investigation'). Legislation in 1974 abolished the examining judge because the post was considered unnecessary, costly and slow.

In the Netherlands the office of the investigative judge is alive and well. Investigative judges serve a dual role in criminal investigations. On the one hand they exercise their role as protector of the suspect's rights. Certain investigative actions are subject to an investigative judge's authorisation, including, in most circumstances, house searches. However, the law in this respect is hideously complex, with different legal frameworks coming into play depending on the objective of the search. Separate acts apply, depending on whether the police are looking for drugs, weapons, other goods or evidence, or whether the home or premises is entered in order to install technical equipment for the interception of communications.

It is telling that the investigative judge is, in certain circumstances, the actual supervisor of the investigation. It is curious that the person who is most capable of taking coercive measures against a suspect is also the one who is trusted with his/her protection against any overzealous application of these measures. Only in countries where the judiciary is generally trusted and held in high esteem is such an arrangement likely to work. Its importation into the UK has, in some circles, been contemplated, but never proposed with much force (Leigh and Zedner, 1992).

The figure of the investigative judge is, from a British perspective, a bit of an oddity. The concept of an independent judge being involved with the actual criminal investigation is unknown in the UK. The concept is at odds with the notion that independence of judges is their most important characteristic. With regard to that it is interesting to note that in France a change to the system is being contemplated at the time of writing. It has been proposed that two different offices be created: an examining magistrate to rule on issues of custody and a *juge d'instruction* to direct police investigations. It would in effect mean that the job of *juge d'instruction* would be divided into two in order to disencumber the role from its current and, some would say, conflicting duties (Hodgson, 2001).

Pre-trial custody in law and practice

Use of pre-trial custody is almost inevitably controversial. While no one disputes that those suspected of grave offences who are likely to re-offend should be held, pre-trial custody remains, by definition, the deprivation of liberty of the innocent, or at least the not yet proved guilty. In England and Wales the proportion of those held in custody and subsequently not found guilty was 23 per cent in 2000 (Hucklesby, 2002). Although, at the time, their remand might have been reasonable or necessary, the loss of liberty is particularly hard on these individuals (Ashworth, 1998; Uglow, 2002).

The issue of human rights violations is pertinent here. Article 5.1 of the European Convention for Human Rights guarantees the right to liberty and security and has implications for the use of pre-trial custody. It considers pre-trial custody lawful only when it is 'lawful arrest or detention of a person effected for the purpose of bringing him before the competent legal authority on reasonable suspicion of having committed an offence or when it is reasonably considered necessary to prevent his committing an offence or fleeing after having done so'. Article 5.5 of the European convention for Human Rights states that 'everyone who has been the victim of this Article shall have an enforceable right to compensation'. The extent to which, in practice, suspects are able to exercise this right is another matter, not least in England and Wales (Hucklesby, 2002).

In most Western states the rules with regard to pre-trial custody are quite specific. They usually prescribe the crimes for which remand may be considered, those who are authorised to impose it, and the kind of legal advice and legal remedies available to the suspect. While the philosophy underlying pre-trial custody might perhaps be similar across European jurisdictions, the actual practice is not. In some countries there seems to be more of a readiness to use this measure, while in others there appears to be more of a reluctance to do so. Table 4.1 lists the number of suspects in pre-trial custody per 100.000 inhabitants for 29 European jurisdictions.

The European average, based on the sample of countries given in Table 4.1, is about 38 people in pre-trial custody per 100,000 inhabitants. High-ranking are the Baltic states of Estonia, Latvia and Lithuania. Together they average close to 100 detained suspects per 100,000 inhabitants, and neighbouring Belarus also seems quite enthusiastic about incarcerating large numbers of suspects. These four countries, with Kyrgyzstan (which also has a relatively high pre-trial custody rate) are notably all former Soviet republics. In the former Soviet Union incapacitation, often combined with deportation, was a commonly used state strategy for dealing with criminals and dissidents. The current liberal use

Table 4.1 Pre-trial custody rates in 29 European jurisdictions

Country	Rate per 100,000 population
Austria	26.2
Belarus	114.4
Belgium	35.0
Bulgaria	18.9
Croatia	19.4
Cyprus	3.7
Czech Republic	85.4
Denmark	15.5
England/Wales	24.3
Estonia	115.1
Finland	5.7
Hungary	33.5
Italy	42.5
Kyrgyzstan	70.3
Latvia	88.9
Liechtenstein	51.6
Lithuania	80.6
Luxembourg	33.2
(FYR) Macedonia	7.4
Malta	18.4
Moldova	48.0
Netherlands	19.9
Northern Ireland	26.9
Portugal	37.0
Scotland	19.8
Slovakia	38.0
Slovenia	9.8
Sweden	11.7
Turkey	40.2

Source: Kangaspunta *et al.* (1998).

of pre-trial custody may well be a leftover from that period (McMahon, 1995).

Very low, on the other hand, ranks Finland, which is geographically very near the Baltic states. It has a pre-trial detention rate of only 5.7 per 100,000 inhabitants, about 20 times lower than Estonia, which is only a short ferry trip away and culturally said to be not dissimilar. The Finnish rules regarding pre-trial custody do not appear to be radically different from elsewhere in Europe. Under normal circumstances, remand is only applicable when there is probable cause that the suspect committed a crime that carries at least a one-year prison sentence. Additionally, it has to be judged probable that the suspect will flee to escape trial, seek to tamper with the evidence or influence witnesses or other parties, or continue his/her criminal activity. Only a court may remand a suspect in custody, and must do this within four days of the suspect's apprehension. The Coercive Means Act 1990 also states that a judicial chamber must rule on its renewal every two weeks (Joutsen, Lahti and Pölönen, 2001).

Finland's crime rate is relatively low. But the low number of people in pre-trial custody cannot be explained away by saying that there are simply not enough 'qualified' criminals available. Additionally, the Scandinavian countries of Denmark and Sweden have pre-trial custody rates that are at least twice as high as that of Finland, but also comparable rates of people imprisoned (Walmsley, 2002). It would thus seem that the criminal justice system in Finland is particularly successful in avoiding the incarceration of suspects. As the rules are not particularly restrictive, this seems to be a matter of practice rather than of legislation.

Pre-trial custody is an area, then, where its rules are not necessarily very predictive of the extent to which it will be used. I have used Finland as an example where the rules regarding remand in custody are perhaps relatively liberal: crimes for which one year of imprisonment can be imposed may be justifiable ground, in comparison to the Netherlands, where crimes punishable by four years imprisonment ought, in theory, to restrict the applicability of remand in custody. However, the *actual* use of detention in Finland is much lower than in other countries, including the Netherlands. In comparative criminal justice, rules only mean so much. What matters is their application.

Hucklesby has argued that police officers might use the threat of pre-trial custody to put pressure on defendants, or to 'give them a taste of prison' (Hucklesby, 2002). Such practices imply use of powers in a way not intended by law and suggest the possibility that laws are not simply followed but utilised to the advantage of those who apply them. When the police are looking to improve detection rates or the evidence in certain cases coercive powers may become tactical weapons. A similar argument applies to the reasons why police officers might decide to choose to prosecute evidentially weak cases. The reasons include acquisition of information; assertion of authority, and pressure to meet the expectations of victims (Sanders, 2002). Such practices, particularly in the difficult-to-penetrate pre-trial phase, are notoriously difficult to control or change.

We can see further illustration of such practices by looking at pre-trial custody in the People's Republic of China. The legal culture in China has traditionally been informed by the philosophy of Confucius. In this, the concept of social harmony takes precedent over justice for individuals. Alternative dispute-resolution by informal means has therefore been prevalent throughout history. China has thus been described as a country without law, because custom and natural law were seen to be more important than the letter of the law. Dispute-resolution was therefore strongly based on fact and not on legalistic styles of argumentation (Lu and Miethe, 2002).

In line with this tradition the Chinese communist government in the 20th century was slow to formulate a code of criminal procedure after assuming power: that took some 30 years, which probably meant that the longevity of informal measures of conflict resolution was extended. A negative result of this legislative vacuum was the development of the widespread use of detention. In the 1979 Criminal Procedure Law pre-trial custody was regulated to outlaw custody in ways and situations that were not spelt out. It failed, however, to stop extra-legal practices of detention from developing. The official phrase used for this practice was 'taking in for shelter and investigation' (Fairchild and Dammer, 2000), which was a measure originally intended to protect society's most vulnerable members. However, the way this measure was employed was as a catch-all ground for detention. Criticisms were levelled at the authorities because it was felt that this type of detention was used particularly to control and deter those whose political views and activities were not condoned by the authorities. It has been alleged that persons have been arrested and detained, sometimes for years, for their involvement in the famous Tiananmen Square demonstration in 1989 (e.g. see Amnesty International, 2002).

The 1996 revision of the Criminal Procedure Law aimed to rectify this situation. A number of improvements with regard to the position of suspects must be noted. It gives defence counsel better access to suspects at the pre-trial stage, although often in the presence of police officers and not at the first police interview. Another improvement is that defendants are given a minimum of ten days to prepare a defence. Other issues remain, such as the facts that the right to silence is not granted, and that many defendants are convicted and sentenced without ever having seen a defence lawyer (Lu and Miethe, 2002).

Diversion

Diversion is the process by which a prosecutor (or other state official) arranges for a case not to go to court but for it to be settled in a different manner (Miers, 2001). Offender–victim mediations have been in place in

Europe for about 20 years. The work of Norwegian theorist Christie (1976) has been influential throughout the continent, whereas the family group conference legislative framework has been quite successful in New Zealand and has also served as an example for other jurisdictions.

Christie's seminal article is called 'Conflicts as property' and it argued that a crime should be treated primarily as an issue between offender and victim. It put forward the suggestion that conflicts between people had been 'stolen' by the state and reconfigured as prosecutions against lawbreakers. He argued for the return of the conflict to the parties themselves, who should aim to seek a resolution via dialogue. Initiatives to bring this about were developed in Christie's native country of Norway.

The impetus for diversion in New Zealand had to do with an over-representation of the indigenous population, the Maori people, in the criminal justice system. It was felt that the way the system dealt with Maori youths, in particular, was not very successful. As a response the family group conference legislative framework was adopted in 1989. It is arguably a step toward the *indigenisation* of the New Zealand criminal justice system, as such conferences were the traditional way of solving conflicts within Maori culture. It has been reported to be very successful (Miers, 2001).

Since then such mediation schemes have been adopted all over the world. One of their advantages lies in the fact that they allow for a prominent role for the victim. Traditionally in many systems, there was hardly any role for victims in the criminal justice process apart from the provision of information upon which the authorities could act. In mediation conferences the views and wishes of victims can be properly taken into account.

Victim–offender mediation can occur at different stages in the criminal justice process. It may occur prior to any charge: the police may formally or informally suggest that a suspect make amends to the victim. When that succeeds, a charge may be avoided. Mediation may also operate before trial but after the suspect has been charged. The results of the mediation may help decide whether the trial should go ahead, and, if it does, the mediation results may be used during decision-making at trial. Mediation may also occur after completion of the trial, as part of a sentence or as a sentencing alternative. As this chapter is concerned with pre-trial justice, we will discuss mediation at that stage.

In many jurisdictions it is the police or prosecution who serve as gatekeepers to pre-trial mediation. In France the prosecutor refers cases to such schemes. The intended outcome of such an intervention is for the offender to take responsibility for his/her wrongdoing and in some way to compensate the victim materially. The result of the mediation is communicated back to the prosecutor who can, if it is successful, dismiss the case. Mediation schemes have to be formally accredited and are usually carried out by well-trained volunteers. About 55 per cent of mediations are deemed to be successful (Miers, 2001).

In Austria it also is a public prosecutor's job to decide whether an offender becomes involved in an offender–victim mediation scheme. The scheme cannot be invoked in case of offences for which more than five years of imprisonment can be imposed (or ten years if the offender is a juvenile). It must also have been established that no special measures are required to prevent re-offending. When the prosecutor does not invoke the scheme and the case goes to court, the court may invoke the scheme on its own accord. This does not happen very often but might occur further to a request from either the victim or the offender (Kichling and Loschnig-Gspandel, 2000). The prosecutor is, in effect, therefore the main but not sole keyholder to the scheme. The implementation of the scheme is in the hand of the *Aussergerichtlicher Tatausgleich* (ATA), which translates as 'Out of Court Conflict Resolution' (Miers, 2001). It is a private organisation funded by the Ministry of Justice. The actual case-work lies in the hands of mediators. The aim is to have the offender take responsibility for his/her actions and make amends. This often involves a face-to-face meeting with the victim, depending on the victim's willingness to participate. Where mediation took place in case of a juvenile offender an agreement was reached in 83 per cent of cases.

Our final European example concerns Germany. German prosecutors have an option of discontinuation when the offender has voluntarily made restitution to the victim or has reached some form of reconciliation. In minor cases that would mean an end to the case. In more serious cases mediation is still an option, but it is more likely to happen alongside a prosecution. The results of the mediation are taken into account by the court. Bannenberg (2000) has noted that pre-trial mediation is used only in a relatively small percentage of cases. It is also noteworthy that regional differences are large, which is probably to do with the substantial autonomy of the *Länder*, the states of federal Germany.

Umbreit and Greenwood (1998) identified 289 different victim–offender mediation schemes in the US. Most of those appear to involve juvenile offenders. Two thirds of the programmes in their survey were of the pre-trial diversionary kind, which is what we are concerned with here. Many of the agencies involved were either private community-orientated or church-based. The cases in which mediation took place were most often minor crimes with a clearly identifiable victim, such as theft and minor assaults. Experiences with these programmes seem to have been almost invariably positive, which is quite an achievement given the inevitable diversity of the schemes involved and those who administer them.

Miers' (2001) list of positive outcomes, based on Umbreit and Coates (1992) included the following:

- victim–offender mediation results in high levels of client satisfaction and perceptions of fairness, on the part of both victims and offenders;
- this effect is even more substantial for victims;
- mediation makes a significant contribution to the reduction of fear and anxiety among victims;
- mediation can be effective for first-time offenders as well as for repeat offenders;
- the majority of offenders indicated that they participated voluntarily;
- the vast majority of victims felt that their participation was voluntary, with less than one in ten indicating a feeling of coercion.

On the other side of the coin there is a concern that with the growth of mediation as a solution within criminal justice the elements of spontaneity and creativity might disappear. When properly incorporated into mainstream criminal justice it is feared that the subtlety as well as the success of such schemes may well be reduced.

The New Zealand family group conference

The Family Group Conference is firmly embedded in the pre-trial phase in New Zealand. It involves young offenders in the age range 14–17. Most offences committed by this group are minor, and are dealt with by the imposition of a police fine. Only offences that involve an arrest go to court, which means only 11 per cent of all offending youths (Morris and Maxwell, 1998). The wide intermediate range of offences is referred to a police body called the Youth Aid Section. This body sets up family group conferences, of which there are some 5,000 per year.

Family group conferences are made up of: the young person who has committed the offence; members of his/her family and those whom the family invites; the victim or his/her representative; a support person for the victim(s); a representative of the police; and the mediator or manager of the process. The manager of the process is a youth justice coordinator and is an employee of the Department of Social Welfare. The main goal of a conference is to formulate a plan about how best to deal with the offending. There are three components in this process. The first is to ensure that the offender actually did commit the offence: If the offender denies guilt at the conference, the case will normally go to court. The second involves the sharing of information to do with the offence, the offender, the victim, and other relevant circumstances. Once everybody has discussed the offending and options for making good the damage, the professionals and the victim leave the family and the young person to meet privately to discuss what plans they wish to make to repair the damage and prevent further offending. When the family is ready, the others return and the meeting is reconvened. A spokesperson outlines the plans to the conference. When there is agreement the conference ends.

The notion of family conferencing draws on the idea that the responsibility for juvenile offending lies beyond the individual. His/her immediate social circle is of vital importance in addressing behaviour and in generating ideas for making amends. While cynics say that this is one way for the state to resolve deviant behaviour without much of its involvement, others say that the natural locus for a non-adversarial fashion of addressing problem behaviour lies in the offender's support network and not in traditional courtrooms. The fact that the notion is borrowed from indigenous Maori traditions has no doubt added to its appeal among progressive law- and policy-makers in New Zealand. As in many other places, cultural sensitivity in criminal justice is of great importance.

Family conferencing has become popular across the world, most notably in Australia, but also in the UK, the US and Sweden. It is in place not only for criminal justice issues but also to deal with social welfare issues in general. These are regularly administered by social services.

Conclusion

Suspects need protection. Much of the traditional literature on pre-trial justice is indeed concerned with a suspect's protection against the power of the state. The main problem identified is that of the overzealous state official. This doctrine is traditionally strong in the US and the UK. Arrangements in these countries are often characterised by a certain level of rigidity in arrangements between law-enforcement bodies. Their relative independence and the separation of their powers are thought to be guarantees against the state coming down too hard on its citizens during criminal investigations. Furthermore, the role of the defence is judged to be vital in protecting suspects' rights.

These kinds of relationship between the criminal justice agencies are characterised by a higher level of interdependence on the European continent, where interaction and review serve as mechanisms for control. Police, prosecution and judiciary are constantly looking over each other's shoulders to ensure that everyone abides by the rules, although, as we have seen in the case of the Netherlands, that does not always guarantee that everyone always does. On the other hand, the miscarriages of justice that have plagued England and Wales in the recent past are perhaps testament to the fallibility of independence as a control in an adversarial structure, although most of these miscarriages took place before the CPS came into existence. Clearly, it is safe to say that neither system is perfect.

Another important aspect of pre-trial justice relates to the worldwide trend of relying on diversion, in particular for young offenders. It is often felt that the traditional adversarial courtroom does not offer the best environment for a constructive dialogue with the wrongdoer. It is therefore better to seek other solutions and venues to achieve that. While New Zealand and Norway could be said to have been frontrunners in this respect, such developments now occur on a global scale. The enhanced role of the victim in criminal justice procedures has certainly facilitated this process, as has the desire to accommodate indigenous ethnic features in criminal justice arrangements. This clearly is the case in New Zealand, while Christie's writings on crime as property were informed by his knowledge about indigenous justice in Tanzania. The acclaimed success of mediation and the fact that the Council of Europe is promoting the concept of restorative justice among its member states both confirm that mediation is here to stay.

Chapter 5

Systems of trial

Visiting a courthouse in a foreign country is an interesting experience. Although not usually an excursion advertised by tour operators, it is a good way of gaining knowledge about another country. Before entering, it is worthwhile to consider the building that serves as the courthouse. Its architecture can be more or less inviting or intimidating. The design may offer suggestions as to what extent security was a priority or whether public access was of primary importance. The presence and appearance of guards or caretakers might be of interest, in particular whether or not they carry arms.

Once inside the courtroom, it is interesting to observe the spatial organisation of the court. The positioning of judges and their attire can reveal information about their role and the esteem in which they are held. The presence or absence of a jury has invariably an impact on the way in which the courtroom is designed. Are spectators behind bullet-proof glass? Is it possible to look all participants in the eye? The level of formality, as well as the relative positions of the participants can provide hints to the actual goings on at trial, in particular about the relationships between significant persons such as judge, members of the jury, the prosecuting authority and defence counsel. Although not every courtroom necessarily looks the same within one justice system, there are interesting differences between countries in the basics of how the room is laid out.

In most English and Welsh Crown Courts, the higher courts of first instance, the defendant is physically far removed from the judge. The accused sits normally in a separate niche called the dock, whereas the defence lawyer takes a more central position. In most continental European courtrooms, in contrast, the defendant is seated very close to the judge, much closer than the defence counsel. The defence counsel is often literally right behind their client. In the Netherlands, no one is closer to the judges than the prosecutor. In the course of the chapter it will become clear that these spatial relationships reflect quite closely the actual relationships between the various actors.

Families of trial systems

Trial systems vary hugely around the world. Most people in the Netherlands know the jury system only from television programmes. Similarly, many people in the US will have difficulties in conceptualising the procedures in the more administrative Dutch courtroom. These differences are not superficial and deserve proper discussion. A significant portion of this chapter is therefore devoted to looking at inquisitorial versus adversarial modes of justice. Underlying these systems are deeply rooted differences with regard to how societies are organised. In particular, the role of the state in administering justice has important repercussions for the way trials are conducted.

In addition we need to understand how the trial itself is situated within the whole of the criminal justice process. It is important to realise that the differences between both modes of trial are not just different ways of performing the same function. Inquisitorial trials are more deeply embedded within the investigative process, whereas adversarial trials constitute more of an independent platform. As will become clear in this chapter, trials are, as it were, the closing ceremony of the inquisitorial process, whereas they represent the 'grande finale' in the adversarial process of justice. When comparing both modes of trial I shall focus on the higher courts, where the differences are most pronounced. In lower courts, particularly in case of cooperative defendants who do not contest their cases, procedures are quite administrative in any system. It is, however, in the higher courts where the adversarial element in adversarial trials truly blossoms.

I will also describe trials in the Islamic legal tradition. In *sharia* law the origins of trial procedures and of the system in which they are set is again rather different and based largely on writing in the Muslim holy book, the *Koran*. Finally, a description of so-called indigenous courts of justice is included by means of two examples, from Papua New Guinea and Alaska.

Inquisitorial trials in France

Although the French criminal justice system tends to receive a bad press, the following quotation is worth consideration:

The importance of the post-revolutionary French penal procedural codes as models for both European and global criminal systems cannot be overemphasised. Their influence is far more pervasive and extensive than that of the Anglo-American common law and both the intellectual coherence and the practical advantages of the great Napoleonic codification of 1808 have ensured its international popularity. (Vogler, 1996: 11)

As a result of the Napoleonic domination over much of mainland Europe, most European countries have criminal justice systems that originate from, and often still bear close resemblance to, the French blueprint. The French inquisitorial system of justice is the archetypical inquisitorial example. However, it should be borne in mind that although the systems in, for instance, Germany and Belgium are similar, they are by no means identical.

The principle underlying French trials is that all relevant facts will be placed before a court in order to judge the accused. This aim is achieved by conducting extensive pre-trial inquiries and by placing the onus of eliciting the evidence at trial on the judge rather than on the parties (Sheehan, 1975). Great emphasis is placed on these pre-trial inquiries. They are made in private: the evidence is examined publicly only at trial. The results of the pre-trial investigations are compiled into a case file, or *dossier*. The *dossier* is given to the presiding judge prior to the trial. If compiled properly, the evidence at trial will closely correspond to what is contained in the *dossier*.

In France as virtually anywhere, the type of offence determines, to a large extent, the eventual court of trial. The French penal code distinguishes between three different types of offence. The most serious are 'grave offences' (punishable by imprisonment from five years upwards). 'Serious offences' carry prison sentences from two months to five years. The least serious offences are minor offences and can attract penalties of up to two months' imprisonment. Grave offences are tried before a *cour d'assises* (assize court). It sits with three professional judges, a president and two assessors, and a jury of nine members of the public. It deals with about 2,700 cases a year (Vogler, 1996). The middle range of offences is usually tried in a *tribunal correctional* (correctional court). This court sits with a panel of three judges without a jury. Minor offences are tried before a single judge in a so-called *tribunal de police* (police court). The term 'police court' might be misleading: the police are not responsible for the prosecuting nor do they decide cases. The reasons for the name of this court are historical and it is worth mentioning that the term has been in use in England and Wales in the past as well.

Trials in the higher and lower courts in France have a different feel to one another. The atmosphere in the lower courts is characterised by informality. In these *tribunals de police* the case usually develops on the basis of a relatively unscripted dialogue between the presiding judge and the defendant. The president deals with the defendant's history and personal circumstances as presented in the *dossier* and asks, where it is needed, for clarification from the defendant. It is the judge who examines witnesses and the defendant. Both parties can have an input, but that is normally performed by means of suggesting questions for the judge to ask.

Instead of being examined in a strict question-and-answer format, the defendant is usually invited to give his version of events with regard to the allegations, and might be interrupted more or less often by questions from the president. Defendants are never under oath. When witnesses are called they are also dealt with in the same conversational manner. They are invited to relate their stories before specific questions are put. There is no distinct witness examination or cross-examination. In their closing statements, prosecutors can propose a sentence. Judgement may be given at once or reserved but is always made in open court.

In the *cour d'assises* the atmosphere is said to be more formal although procedures not dissimilar. The main difference between the two types of court is the presence in the *cour d'assises* of the nine-member jury. As I will deal with juries in more detail in the next chapter a few comments will suffice here. First, the jurors and judges decide together on both guilt and sentencing. An eight-to-four majority is needed for a guilty verdict, from a blind ballot. Sentencing decisions are arrived at by majority. Jurors do have the option of asking questions at trial, either by suggestion to the president or directly.

Despite the presence of a jury, the role of the president judge remains pivotal. As the president puts most of the questions to defendants and witnesses this judge is firmly in control of the happenings at trial. On top of that, the presiding judge is the only person who has the opportunity of reading the *dossier* prior to the trial. Neither assessor has the case-file at his/her disposal, and nor do the jurors. The system thus places a heavy burden on the presiding judges. It is their duty to take all steps to discover the truth. To that end they conduct the trial to elicit all relevant information and can call additional witnesses that neither party may have brought forward.

Closing speeches are given by both prosecution and defence, but these are followed by closing remarks from the president. The judge summarises the issues to be decided and instructs the jury on the burden of proof. In order to control the president's influence on the jury, the president cannot make statements in court that might reflect an opinion on the defendant's guilt. The law does not, however, forbid the assessors from doing that. In addition, the president is allowed to comment on, for instance, the credibility of witnesses in ways that would clearly give away their sentiments about the case. If this measure is aimed at protecting the jurors from the president's opinion of the defendant's guilt before deliberation, it is one that is certainly questionable as to its effectiveness.

Adversarial trials

Adversarial criminal justice originated in England and has been exported, as has the French system, across the world. In particular in many English-speaking nations, often former British colonies, the system enjoys an enduring popularity. An adversarial trial can be long-winded affair. To use the archetypical example of adversarial justice, in England and Wales the trial procedure in Crown Courts is as follows.

Initially, the indictment is read out, and the accused confirms his/her plea of not guilty. Subsequently, the jury is sworn in, after which the prosecution opens its case. It proceeds by calling witnesses, who are positioned in the witness box: the witnesses for the prosecution. Each witness is initially examined by the prosecuting barrister. Subsequently, each prosecution witness can be cross-examined by the defence lawyer. It is in these cross-examinations that much of the drama in adversarial courtrooms is to be found, as the questioning can be intense and confrontational. After cross-examination the prosecution has the chance of re-examining the witness. This procedure is followed for each prosecution witness, after which the prosecution closes its case. This phase often takes several days to complete.

Next it is the defence's turn to call witnesses to support its case. The defence witnesses are examined initially by the defence lawyer and cross-examined by the prosecution, after which a re-examination can be conducted by the defence counsel. Prior to their appearance in court, witnesses for both parties have been put under oath by an usher. During examinations in chief counsel (prosecution or defence) witnesses cannot be asked leading questions: the witness may only be guided. During cross-examination, leading questions are allowed and frequently used. Witnesses are expected to give 'evidence of fact' and not offer opinions (although expert witnesses constitute an exception to this rule). Additionally, they are not allowed to offer hearsay evidence: that means that they cannot testify as to statements made by others. It is a testament to the principle of immediacy that if the evidence of another person should be of relevance then that person should testify in person. However, there are exceptions to this rule as well.

When the examination of witnesses has been completed, the prosecution addresses the jury in its closing speech and the defence does the same. Subsequently, the judge sums up the facts of the case and directs the jury on points of law regarding the charges and with regard to the issue of proof. The summing up of the facts can also be quite lengthy, and should not in any way be leading. Perceived violations of this principle are frequently cited as reasons for appeal. The jury finally retires to reach a verdict in private.

There is a great deal of etiquette involved in participating in, or even attending, a Crown Court trial. Any attempt to interrupt proceedings may be considered contempt of court, and offences under the Contempt of Court Act 1981 carry prison sentences. The fact that judges and barristers wear traditional wigs adds to the sense of decorum and an atmosphere in which irreverence is out of place.

The atmosphere in US courtrooms is similar, but there are procedural differences. Examinations have been said to be more rigorous in American courtrooms. Another important difference is that judges in the US do not sum up the facts. Their role is somewhat more restricted and umpire-like, whereas judges in England and Wales can be, and regularly are, somewhat more dominant. Arguably, therefore, the US mode of trial is more truly adversarial.

Adversarial and inquisitorial justice in theory and practice

A number of differences between the system of England and Wales and that of France are readily apparent. I will elaborate on some of these because they help us to appreciate the core differences between the French inquisitorial tradition and the English adversarial way of conducting trials. Some key differences are the role of confessions and pleas, rules of evidence, and appeals and so-called reasoned verdicts.

In France, defendants do not plead. Because they are regarded more as the subjects of investigation such a declaration is not needed. In England and Wales, defendants are seen as parties in the conflict. Their plea implies their factual or tactical approach to the case, an aspect deemed unnecessary in the inquisitorial philosophy in which there usually are no separate procedures for suspects who do not challenge the facts or the charge. The inquisitorial court will always examine the evidence at trial regardless of the attitude of the accused. The onus on proving guilt lies with the prosecutor. This is most important in the pre-trial phase, in which the prosecution is heavily involved with the investigative process. As the judge is the primary fact-finder at trial, the role of the prosecutor is more limited at this stage. The prosecution's closing statement, in which he/she recommends a sentence, is nevertheless known to be influential.

Confessions made during the pre-trial phase are sometimes regarded with caution, especially when made during police investigation (when a defence lawyer might not always be present) and subsequently retracted. However, French courts have great freedom in weighing the value of a confession: it may be enough for a conviction, but it may also be discarded.

Rules of evidence in France, as well as in other inquisitorial systems, tend to be minimal. The courts are trusted with the experience and reasoning powers to judge any evidence on merit. That removes the need for protecting participants from evidence that might be irrelevant, improper or biased. Courts should be able to decide that for themselves and ignore such evidence if necessary. In principle all evidence should be presented at trial. This honours the principle of immediacy, which is upheld in France, but only in principle. Much of the evidence is merely mentioned, particularly if it is undisputed. Hearsay evidence is not admitted, but it is in some other European countries. Even evidence that resulted from improper investigative actions can be admitted. It is up to the courts to decide how to weigh it.

Because of the reliance on case files, inquisitorial trials tend to be shorter, especially in the case of confessing and cooperative defendants. Also, particularly when the cases are decided by judges instead of jurors, there is a lack of courtroom drama and examination skills, because there is not a jury to convince but seasoned professionals who know the prosecutors in their area often rather well. It makes courtroom interactions much more routine.

With the exception of cases decided by a jury in the assize court, appeals are open to both the defence and the prosecution. Appeals receive a full new hearing at the appellate court. An appeal by the defendant alone cannot lead to the imposition of a more severe penalty than was awarded at the first instance (Vogler, 1996).

Whereas juries are often strictly forbidden to explain their verdicts, judges in inquisitorial systems are often required by law to do so. These explanations often include the evidence they use as the basis for their verdict, and the reasons why competing items of evidence are rejected. Both prosecution and defence can scrutinise these reasons, and use them as a basis for appeals. Two doubts can be raised about the usefulness of offering these reasons. First, one cannot be certain that the reasons listed are the actual ones that swung the court's decision. Second, it is perhaps unlikely that court will phrase their reasons such as to provide the parties ammunition for appeals. Wagenaar *et al.* (1993) are rather sceptical about the actual practice of reasoned verdicts in the Netherlands. They argue that verdicts rarely contain more than standard formulations, such as 'given the evidence presented', and do not illuminate the court's decision-making at all.

There is great deal of legal-historical writing about the source of the differences between inquisitorial and adversarial systems (Damaska, 1986). The core difference between both systems can be understood in terms of the role that the state traditionally plays in different societies. In inquisitorial settings the role of the state is prominent. We therefore speak of an *active* state. Active states are associated with a strong state involvement in the provision of education, health care, and social welfare. The extent to which the state provides health care and education for all, or whether large sections of the population seek private education and health care, can be indicative of the position of the state. Strong and active states rely on higher levels of taxation as well.

Active states also tend to take responsibility for dispensing criminal justice. The traditional view is that it is up to the state to investigate both the crime and the accused so that justice can be done. The impartiality of the investigators and the court should guarantee that this process is carried out properly. The role of the defence is more limited: it is rather the prosecution with the investigative judge and the court who are supposed to ensure that the suspect's rights are respected. They do that by respecting them themselves and by keeping a close eye on police activities.

In adversarial systems the basic premise is that the state should not be relied on to the same extent. The role of the state in adversarial systems is limited and is therefore associated with societies in which the state is smaller and more passive. The passive state does not provide for the dispensation of justice but rather provides a platform for conflict resolution. At trial, both prosecution and defence are supposed to present the case to the best of their abilities, and an independent body, be it judge or jury, decides the result after having heard both sides of the argument.

The kind of welfare state established in many Western societies in the second half of the twentieth century has obscured this relation between the state and the mode of trial. In England and Wales the state at present certainly cannot pass for 'minimal' or passive. However, we have to bear in mind that modes of trial and the influence of the powers that be over courts, judges and juries has been shaped over centuries, whereas the phenomenon of the inclusive 'cradle to grave' welfare state is historically a relative novelty. The assumption that adversarial systems flourish as a response to a malevolent state, whereas inquisitorial justice fits a society in which the state is regarded as a strong and benevolent force, may still remain valid.

Although it is often left unsaid, inquisitorial systems are often associated by their opponents with the sinister operations of a state-run inquisition, persecuting its citizens and in which the 'truth' is found by means of torture and otherwise coerced confessions (Jörg *et al.*, 1995). It is certainly appropriate to say that adversarial systems have blossomed in response to a societal distrust in the state and its powers. This is especially true for the US, where the adversarial system became popular as a response to fears of an overbearing and oppressive state. When state officials cannot be trusted it makes sense to leave the administration of justice to 'the people', a jury of one's peers. Ordinary people are then trusted more easily than state officials with a vested interest in maintaining power. All the state needs to provide is a stage: a platform where an assessment of the suspect's guilt can take place in a rule-governed fashion. Those ideas form the basis of adversarial justice. In inquisitorial systems, on the other hand, the state is associated with objectivity and fatherly wisdom. When such sentiments are prevalent it makes sense to leave the dispensation of justice in its lap. Juries would be seen to be less important, and, as the state represents the investigating as well as the adjudicating body, there equally is no need to discount the information gathered prior to trial.

The difference between the role of the prosecution service in adversarial and inquisitorial systems is, in practice, often subtle but theoretically important: the prosecution in the adversarial system is geared more towards proving the defendant guilty. It is the defence whose task to advocate innocence. Therefore the role of defence counsel in adversarial systems is more prominent. In inquisitorial systems, however, the prosecution should aim to find the truth, and therefore takes on part of the function that, in adversarial systems, is left to the defence. Hodgson (2001) correspondingly found that in France the profession of defence lawyer is held in less esteem than it is in England and Wales. The right to have a defence lawyer is generally accepted, but their role is widely seen to be rather inconsequential to the case and its outcome.

Both systems have been accused of neglecting the defendant in proceedings, or of 'taking the conflict away from victim and offender' where it initially arose. In adversarial systems a contested case may be completed easily with hardly any contribution from the defendant. The battle is being fought between legally qualified actors, who argue over rules that often have little to do with the defendant or the charge. The defendant is, in a sense, removed from the actual conflict. This removal is also apparent in the spatial lay-out of the English Crown Court, in which the defendants are usually positioned further away from the judge than their representatives.

In inquisitorial systems the defendants, regardless of whether they protest their innocence or not, will normally contribute to proceedings. They are asked questions about the crime and their criminal record, and are free to speak for themselves. However, the defendant is more the topic of investigation than an actual party, and the *dossier* normally has answered all questions anyway. Thus, the fact that defendants in inquisitorial trials often sit in a more central position does not make them more powerful actors. Cynics would say that their close proximity is primarily to allow the judges to have a good look at the defendant, and not for defendants to have equal ability to scrutinise and influence proceedings in their trial.

Trials in the Islamic legal tradition

The third influential legal tradition is Islamic law. It is prevalent in the Middle East, and informs some or all of the legal system in countries such as Saudi Arabia and Iran. The principal source of Islamic law is the Muslim holy book, the *Koran*. The *sharia* is the body of rules of conduct revealed by God (Allah) to his prophet Muhammed whereby the people are directed to lead their life. According to the Muslim faith, the angel Gabriel called Muhammed to be a prophet. Muhammed preached about the need to replace old tribal customs, which drew heavily on blood revenge. Instead he preached for brotherhood among all people of the Muslim faith.

A number of features of Islamic law are worth noting. Its most important characteristic is its strong religious basis. While amplified by Islamic legal scholars, the source of the law is divine revelation. It has universal validity for Muslims even if not officially recognised by the state. Because of its divine status it is relatively inflexible, as room for interpretation is limited. Although other sources of law exist, such as the actions and words of Muhammed and the consensus of high-standing Islamic legal scholars, the strong basis in religion sets Islamic law apart from other legal traditions. While adversarial and inquisitorial justice systems are informed by Christian values, the connection between religion and law is nowhere near as strong as it is in the Islamic tradition (Fairchild and Dammer, 2001).

In some predominantly Islamic countries, Islamic law forms part of the legal system. In a minority of countries, it forms the basis for all law, often with only minor exceptions. In Saudi Arabia, for instance, Islamic law underlies the whole of the justice system, although Fairchild and Dammer note that 'certain concessions are made to modern exigencies of trade, banking (Islamic law does not allow the payment of interest), and industry' (Fairchild and Dammer, 2001: 61).

In substantive law a distinction is made between crimes against God and private wrongdoings against other people. Crimes against God are called *hudud* crimes. They include defamation, denunciation of Islam and

Box 5.1 Foreign influences on the Japanese criminal justice system

The early history of Japan is characterised by a great deal of isolationism. Only after Japan opened up to the West for trading in the middle of the nineteenth century was the door opened for influence in the criminal justice arena as well. The French Napoleonic Code was translated into Japanese and it proved influential.

A French scholar was asked to draft a penal code and a code of criminal procedure, which came into effect in 1880. The latter code of criminal procedure was heavily inquisitorial. The preliminary inquiry rather than the trial was trusted to provide the courts with the relevant facts. The code gave substantial discretion to the judge in questioning the accused and witnesses at trial, a jury was incorporated into the system only by the introduction of the Jury Act in 1928 (Nakayama, 1987).

Following Japan's surrender at the end of World War II a new code of criminal procedure was drafted by Japanese legal scholars, together with officials from the Allied forces. It came into force in 1949. The new system made a substantial shift towards a more adversarial fashion of proceeding. However, the jury system had never became popular following its earlier introduction and, further to its suspension during World War II, was not reintroduced. In the new code, the independence of the prosecution and the judiciary was given a stronger footing and the preliminary inquiry was abolished.

Western influences at various stages, and for different reasons, have left Japan with a criminal justice system that is truly mixed. Although there are adversarial elements, the absence of a jury and the central position taken by the prosecution are clear remnants of the older inquisitorial tradition. However, trials are more important than they tend to be in other inquisitorial countries, and they are of a slightly different form. Trials are not necessary full-time events, as they are in England and Wales or the USA. Rather, they may proceed over a longer period with only one or two sittings per week. True to the inquisitorial tradition, the evidence presented before trial tends to be influential (although defence counsel can object to it being used). Traditionally, much weight is given to confessions, and their value is not only evidential. Confessions are normally viewed as the start of the reconciliatory process, which for centuries, formed an important ingredient in the maintenance of social control. The Japanese example of the evolution of a criminal justice system is typical of those in many parts of the world: they evolve under influences of domestic traditions and foreign domination, and notably lack any master plan (Takayanagi, 1963; Castberg, 1990; Leishman, 1999).

also certain sexual offences such as sodomy and adultery. In case of crimes against God, it is for the state to initiate proceedings against a suspect. Penalties in case of *hudud* crimes tend to be fixed. Private wrongdoings are called *quesas* crimes. In such crimes a private party, such as the victim or their family, must initiate the case, and there is an emphasis on offender–victim negotiation. *Quesas* crimes may, however, also attract severe sentences as they can be serious crimes. Murder, for instance, is a *quesas* crime: not so much a crime against God, Islam, and the community of believers, but rather a crime against a private individual. In such cases, there may be scope for negotiation between the victim (or their family) and the offender. There certainly is a place in Islamic law for negotiation and restitution as a means for expressing forgiveness and charity. Many crimes against God, on the other hand, risk the death penalty or the amputation of limbs.

In procedural law, a number of elements are worth noting. Putting aside confessions, witness statements are all important. It could be said that in the absence of confessions Islamic law seeks the truth by statements made by reliable people. The burden of proof is on the accuser. Proof-taking occurs by calling reputable witnesses. In most Islamic courts evidence from a male witness counts heavier than from a female witness, and in some jurisdictions women hardly appear at all as witnesses.

Lying under oath is considered a serious wrongdoing, with severe legal and religious consequences. However, the oath works rather differently than it does in Western jurisdictions. Witnesses speak freely in court, and it is assumed that not everything that is being said is necessarily truthful. It is up to the judge to deduce who speaks the truth or not. The stakes become much higher when the evidence in a case is not decisive. One party may then challenge the other to take an oath in support of their assertions. The idea is that lying under oath is unthinkable, so that the party who is prepared to maintain their allegations under oath comes out as the winner. The rationale is simple: one may bend the truth in dealing with other people in everyday life but not under holy oath. The final decision about who should take the oath first rests with the *qadi*, the judge.

Saudi Arabia has adopted Islamic law since the beginnings of the modern state, in 1926. The territory of Saudi Arabia, which is mostly uninhabited desert, contains the holy cities of Mecca and Medina. The government has not disseminated a penal code or a code of criminal procedure, and few laws exist separately in published form, most being contained in religious writings.

According to official figures, the crime rate in Saudi Arabia is very low. While there are the problems of counting and compiling statistics (the

Arabic calendar year is shorter than that of the Western Gregorian calendar, for example), it seems that rates of murder, rape, and robbery are very low, even compared to other Arab countries. Souryal *et al.* (1994) claimed that Islamic law, with its strict punishments, has been instrumental in establishing a rather peaceful society.

To what extent these figures are reliable is open to debate. While in certain jurisdictions it is often relatively easy to obtain figures with regard to the criminal justice process, in Islamic criminal justice systems this often is not the case. One reason might be to do with the fact that in criminal justice systems on a more pragmatic footing, performance figures are vital for monitoring that performance. In the Islamic tradition, in which the doctrine is dogmatic rather than pragmatic, such information would be less necessary. Where policy-making is less at issue policy information is less likely to be readily available (see also Crystal, 2001, on criminal justice in the Middle Eastern region).

The status of the dossier in inquisitorial trials

It is worth a moment of reflection about what it means for a panel of judges to have access to the case-file before the defendant appears before them in court. Via its contents the court will usually know what the defendant said to the arresting police officers and what was found at a house search. The judges will be aware of whether defendants during interview sessions changed their story, and to what extent statements of possible accomplices or witnesses differ. Judges will have noted whether the investigative judge (after all, a colleague) felt that there was enough evidence for pre-trial custody, and what the suspect's attitude and level of cooperation has been throughout the pre-trial process.

The court will also have taken note of the defendant's criminal record. In adversarial systems it is often forbidden to mention or discuss any previous crimes the defendant may have committed. In most inquisitorial systems this is often done as a matter of course. It is evidence of the fact that the inquisitorial process comprises, to a larger extent, an investigation into the suspect's character, and not only into the individual crime. If these judges have done their homework they must feel that they know the case and the defendant rather well. It is fair to say that surprises do not very often occur: trials tend to confirm more or less the impression gained from studying the case-file.

In the Netherlands, the dossier is not just information. Information from the dossier can be used *in evidence*. This can go quite far: when a defendant denies his/her guilt at trial but did confess during police investigations, that earlier confession might be taken as evidence. Obviously a court needs to explain why it considers that confession more

---

Box 5.2 The unbearable shortness of Dutch trials

Trials in England and Wales tend to take days or even weeks. In contrast, trials in the Netherlands tend to take only minutes or hours. Straightforward trials of burglary, drunken driving or common assault take no more than half an hour from start to finish. More complicated cases may take several hours to one day, and only the most dramatic cases take more than a day in court to be completed. So-called 'mega-cases' are cases that take more than two days in court. In 1997 there were about 70 of them. For those familiar with trials in England and Wales this must sound almost farcical. How can justice be done in, for instance, a rape case with a defendant who denies his guilt, when his 'day in court' is not even a day, but rather a couple of hours?

A typical trial in the Netherlands runs as follows. At first, the presiding judge assesses the identity of the defendant, if present, and reminds the defendant of his/her right to silence. The prosecutor then rises to read the indictment. Subsequently, the presiding judge questions the defendant. However, since the judges will normally have read the case-file beforehand, usually little new information comes to light. After questioning by the judge, the prosecutor and defence lawyer may ask questions. Occasionally, but not usually, witnesses are called to appear at trial. Again, it is the judge who is the principal fact-finder, although both prosecution and defence can pose questions to witnesses, as can defendants themselves.

When the questioning is completed the prosecution presents its closing argument, which comprises a sentence recommendation. Following this *requisitoir* (in Dutch) it is the turn of the defence lawyer to make the final statement on behalf of the defendant, although defendants are entitled to speak for themselves. The defendant always has the last word.

Such a trial procedure is, as inquisitorial trials go, not out of the ordinary. What is striking however is their short duration. In order to understand the role of the trial within the context of the whole of the criminal justice process we have to think back to the pre-trial stage. We have seen that police investigation in France and the Netherlands is, to a large extent, governed by review by the prosecution service and the magistracy. Proper judges in serious cases have a great deal of involvement in ongoing police investigations. Whereas in England and Wales case-files are compiled to send to the prosecution, in the Netherlands and in countries such as France and Germany these case-files are sent to the courts.

Judges usually familiarise themselves with the contents of these dossiers. They contain summaries of witness and suspect statements, descriptions by police officers of investigative actions, the paperwork relating to coercive measures, and also the suspect's criminal record, which is usually discussed at trial (Nijboer 1995; Corstens, 1999). The facts are established during the investigation and they do not need to be repeated. The information needs only to be verified. This means that judges are not very often taken by surprise at trial, which helps to explain the routine and administrative nature of the trial process. In most cases, the trial is just a matter of wrapping things up. The battle over guilt or innocence does not start afresh in the trial itself.

important than the subsequent retraction, but in principle nothing stops a court from using self-incriminating statements made during the investigative stage as actual evidence on which they can base a guilty verdict.

Additionally, certain investigative actions take place at the pre-trial stage so that they need not be repeated at trial. Victims are often interviewed in the pre-trial stage by an investigative judge, usually in the presence of a defence lawyer. These interviews tend to be less confrontational and traumatic than a cross-examination in a courtroom might be. A court would normally rely on the accuracy of the record of such interviews, during which both parties have had a chance to examine witnesses. Although occasionally witnesses are called into the courtroom further to a request from the defence they would need to explain why they have left it until such a late stage to involve them. The appearance of vulnerable witnesses in particular is considered inappropriate at the trial stage.

Indigenous courts

Clegg and Whetton (1995) argued that a 'third world criminology' is lacking. Although there certainly is some writing in this area (e.g. Clinard and Abbott, 1973), on the whole the administration of criminal justice in developing countries is under-researched. As an example of trial systems outside of the Western world, I shall discuss how justice is dispensed in village courts in Papua New Guinea. It serves as a representative case for informal justice in other developing countries, such as Zambia and Kenya (Clegg and Whetton, 1995). Subsequently I shall examine how the trial function is given shape in the US state of Alaska.

The indigenisation of local justice in Papua New Guinea

Village courts were introduced in Papua New Guinea in 1974. These courts were established with the intention of handing the administration of justice back to the people and provide communities with a locally administered platform for conflict resolution. The country's last colonial power, Australia, had centralised criminal justice to a large extent, and the village courts were a way of reversing this trend. The move responded to the sentiment that traditional Papua New Guinean communities did not easily assimilate Australian law and legal culture, so that an indigenisation of trial procedures was seen to be a positive development. On the other hand, it has been mentioned that central government also wished to exert greater control on local justice. The way this was done was not by replacing the local systems of social control but by incorporating them into more formal structures, while preserving a certain level of autonomy. Supervisory district-court magistrates were influential in making recommendations for appointments and conducting regular visits to village courts, so that any autonomy would be mediated by a certain degree of oversight from more centralised bodies.

Magistrates at village courts deal with a range of criminal and civil matters in a semi-autonomous manner. These court officials are villagers selected by the local population. Village magistrates tend to be males, between 35 and 50 years old, and relatively influential in their community. Female magistrates have been rare. The wrongdoings dealt with are usually disturbances, fighting, abusive language and drunkenness, but also include absenteeism, theft, and adultery. The courts have developed an efficient, crisp interrogatory style, in which little deviation from the facts by parties or witnesses is allowed. Decisions are rendered without much delay and are usually unanimous.

This type of court does share characteristics with many courts around the world: the composition of the magistrates reminds one of England and Wales; the resulting conservatism is another feature that is widespread. On the other hand, its efficiency and effectiveness is not always paralleled in the Western world. It provides good example of 'developing' justice, in which the traditional means of achieving justice utilising trusted community members as arbitrators, combined with modern considerations involving the standardisation of procedures, produces something rather effective and suitable for the social fabric of the villages concerned (Paliwala, 1980; Fitzpatrick, 1982).

Courts in a cold climate: achieving justice for all in Alaska

The US state of Alaska is a remote place. Situated west of Canada, a land surface of over 571,000 square miles (over 6 times the size of the Great Britain) is home to only about 626,000 people. That makes the population density just over 1 person per square mile. To put that figure into context, in relatively densely populated countries this number is in the order of a few hundred. Of these people, 69.3 per cent are White; 3.5 per cent are Black or African American; 15.6 per cent are Native American (Indian) or native Alaskan, and 4.0 per cent are of Asian origin. 7.6 per cent indicated a different race or more than one race according to the 2000 Census. While much of the population is concentrated in the cities, such as Anchorage, there are countless remote villages and communities throughout the state. Many of those local communities consist, by and large, of native Alaskans (Alaska Justice Reform, 1996).

In a state where people are so few and far between there are challenges with regard to the provision of justice. Until the late 1980s many remote communities had become accustomed to a state of affairs that, in effect, meant a high level of self-governance. Policing functions were, to a large extent, administered by locals. There were usually also provisions in place to deal with minor wrongdoings. These indigenous arrangements were often extra-legal: not covered by any official law or statute.

A study of local governance, including 28 villages of between 70 and 700 residents that were 10–100 miles away from an urban centre, was carried out in 1995 (Alaska Justice Reform, 1996). The average native Alaskan population in these villages was approximately 82 per cent. Local government in these communities was often administered by a village council. The larger communities had a village police officer and a village public-safety officer. In spite of this, it was concluded that nearly all the communities surveyed were short of money to pay for local public-safety operations. Most villages had established local ordinances and rules to handle undesirable behaviour. In a few cases official tribal courts had been recognised by the state, but in most villages similar operations of an extra-legal nature were in place. Most inhabitants accept their jurisdiction either voluntarily or because of social pressure. It would appear that the law exclusively applies to local residents. Misbehaving guides, fishermen and hunters were normally handed over to official law-enforcement bodies instead.

In one community surveyed, sentences imposed comprised fines and a form of community service, which might involve helping the elderly or cleaning public facilities. The administration of justice was highly informal and predominantly informed by custom. In another community, the court used a handbook comprising a set of rules, and employed local, native security guards. The administration of justice was in the hands of village chiefs. Because of the fact that in this particular community it was common to walk in and out of one other's homes, no one seemed to think twice about entering homes to check on misconduct, such as the possession of alcohol, or to gather evidence. Such arrangements do not seem to be heavily informed by issues of privacy. Any form of judicial review of investigative methods seemed both non-existant and a non-issue. Apart from a range of lesser penalties, natives who repeatedly misbehaved could be asked to leave the village, temporarily, and in case of recidivism, permanently.

The study drew rather positive conclusion with regard to the operation of law and order in these villages:

> Most of the villages in this survey have seemingly well-understood community social control methods to handle problems beyond the scope of family responsibility. These methods sometimes do not reflect the western legal system and lack articulated recognition from the Alaska Department of Public Safety, the Alaska Court System, and most other governmental organisations. The village social controls tend, however, to be confined primarily to dealing with disruptive behaviour in the community. (Alaskan Justice Reform, 1996: 5)

It has been argued that such methods perform a useful ancillary role to the established criminal justice system. Communities who are able to resolve low-level disputes without the need for the established authorities to interfere probably help save resources. There is now increased contact between officials in formal and less formal modes of justice, which will no doubt help ensure an acceptable standard of justice that is not jeopardised by isolation.

There is also evidence that native Alaskans, in particular Yup'iks, are not always properly served by the formal criminal justice system, which they consider to be daunting and alien. This is because of differences in culture and language, but also on account of differing conceptions about what is involved in being held to account for wrongdoing (Morrow, 1993). Better education of the public, most particularly the harder-to-reach parts of the population, and an increased investment in translation and interpretation services are vital in securing some form of justice for all who live in Alaska (Shafer and Curtis, 1997).

We can note interesting similarities and differences between the Alaskan and Papua New Guinean examples of modes of justice. Both seem to be praised highly. Both seem to be operating by communal consent, and have a swiftness and directness that many Western criminal justice systems cannot achieve. Both have a rather informal feel, which will usually only enhance the quality of operations, as they are based in small communities. However, where civil liberties are at issue it is difficult to see how a firm but fair system of accountability could be incorporated.

An important difference lies in the genesis of each. The village courts in Papua New Guinea were reintroduced after colonial arrangements did not seem to fit the local population. Thus, they were instigated as a remedy. The Alaskan courts did not come into being as a response to any state-imposed bodies, but rather as a way of doing justice in the absence of formal criminal justice institutions.

A landmark case: the build-up to the Lockerbie Trial

Certain trials can be thought of a landmark event. Such trials include the O.J. Simpson trial in the US in 1995 and Adolf Eichmann's trial in Israel in 1961. O.J. Simpson, the former American football player and actor, was accused of killing two people, including his ex-partner, in the state of California; he was acquitted by a jury. The case highlighted issues of race within criminal justice, the value of forensic evidence, and also the role of the mass media in reporting on crimes and trials involving celebrities. Eichmann was abducted from Argentina by the Israeli secret service to be brought to trial for his involvement in the mass killing of Jews in Nazi concentration camps in World War II. That trial took place in 1961, and ended in a conviction. The Eichmann case raised issues regarding the nature of Nazi war crimes, and the legality of abducting war criminals from one country to bring them to justice in another. Both trials were not isolated events: they embodied the *Zeitgeist* of the period in which they were conducted.

The landmark trial I discuss here is the more recent Lockerbie trial, named after the Scottish town where a Pan Am Boeing 747 crashed down in 1988. I shall relate the events leading up to the trial . Much of this is based on articles in the British newspaper the *Guardian* (Brown, 2002) and the writings of the Scottish QC Black (1999, 2000; see also www.thelockerbietrial.com).

On 21 December 1988 Pan Am Flight 103 exploded over southern Scotland. It was on its way from London's Heathrow Airport to New York. All 259 passengers and crew died instantly, along with 11 people on the ground in the Scottish border town of Lockerbie. Following an investigation by the UK Air Accidents Investigation Branch it was concluded that the aircraft was brought down by means of an explosive device. The criminal investigation subsequently identified two suspects: both were of Libyan nationality and were thought to have planted the explosive device on board the aircraft.

From here on a battle ensued, which was as much diplomatic as it was judicial. The Libyan authorities were asked to hand over both suspects by the British, US and French governments. Libya refused to comply, and insisted that it would try both suspects under local laws. Subsequently, the United Nations imposed sanctions on Libya. These sanctions included a ban on arms sales and air travel to and from that country. Meanwhile, out of the public eye, diplomatic efforts continued in an attempt to bring both suspects to justice. In 1993, the defence lawyers for both suspects suggested that a trial be held at a neutral venue outside Scotland, because of the level of pre-trial publicity. This plan was not acceptable to either the US or Britain, who insisted that both men should be tried in either Scotland or the US. Meanwhile, while the deadlock continued, United Nations sanctions were tightened. They were extended to include a ban on imports of materials for Libya's oil industry, which was thought to be a body blow to the Libyan economy.

In 1994 the suggestion was made to hold the trial in the Netherlands. The first idea was for it to be conducted by international judges but under Scottish law (Black, 1999). This idea is not as far-fetched as it may have seemed. The International Criminal Tribunal for the Former Yugoslavia had just come into operation in the Netherlands, while the Netherlands also holds the seat for the International Court of Justice. The plan was nevertheless rejected by the British Foreign Secretary and the Lord Advocate, who maintained that the suspects should simply be handed over for trial in either Scotland or the US.

Three years later the plan of holding the trial in a third country but under Scots law was proposed by the Libyan authorities. While it was not what the UK and US authorities initially had in mind, it was finally accepted. This change of heart may well have been informed by the fact that global support for the sanctions against Libya was waning. This was particularly the case on the African continent and in the Muslim world. In 1998, therefore, a proposal was made by Britain and the US for the two Libyan suspects to be tried in the Netherlands under Scottish law, but with three Scottish judges instead of a jury. The plan followed months of discussions between Britain, the US and the Netherlands, initiated by the then British Foreign Secretary Robin Cook. This shifted the onus back onto Libya's leader Colonel Gaddafi to hand over both suspects. While an agreement was reached on the main issues, some final hurdles still needed to be overcome. A large sticking point was where the suspects, if convicted, would serve their no-doubt lengthy prison sentences.

Following intervention from Nelson Mandela, who flew to Tripoli to speak with Colonel Gaddafi with special UN permission in March 1999, an announcement was made that the Lockerbie suspects would be surrendered on, or before, 6 April. Both suspects indeed came to the Netherlands in April 1999. They were taken into Dutch custody after flying from Tripoli to an airbase near The Hague and formally charged with the bombing. The UN sanctions against Libya were suspended as agreed. The first pre-trial hearing took place on 7 December 1999, in

Camp Zeist, the Netherlands. Both defendants pleaded not guilty to all charges in February 2000. The trial could finally get underway, and was conducted by Lord Sutherland, Lord Coulsfield and Lord MacLean.

The above description illustrates a long build-up to a most unusual trial. In an army camp in the Netherlands, a trial was thus conducted against two Libyan defendants under Scots law, but not by jury. In the end one suspect was acquitted, while the other was convicted and sentenced to life imprisonment. This result has received plenty of criticism. Many people, including relatives of the victims, feel that the whole story has not been told. The convicted defendant lodged an appeal but it failed in 2002.

Despite its unique nature, the Lockerbie case shows a number of characteristics of international justice as it is administered in the world today. A defining characteristic of criminal justice in an international context is its entanglement with diplomacy. This is clearly exemplified by the Lockerbie pre-trial saga. While the actual trial was still a purely legal matter for judges and other legal professionals, to ensure that there was a trial in the first place did take a range of diplomatic efforts, not just from officials in the countries involved, but from many others as well. In the end, arguably the economic sanctions set by the United Nations may well have been vital in securing the necessary level of cooperation from the Libyan authorities. Without those sanctions the Lockerbie trial may never have happened in the first place.

The Lockerbie trial demonstrates amply that trials are not self-contained, isolated phenomena. To understand what happens at trial, it is important to have an understanding of what happens before a trial can actually take place. While the Lockerbie trial is an extreme example, it is important to remember that trials are embedded within larger criminal justice systems of which they are only one component. Additionally, trials of international crimes have to be contextualised in the stage of world politics and international relations.

Conclusion

There is no standard format for criminal trials. If we disregard appeals and the execution of sentences, a trial is where the prosecution of a defendant ends. In a minimal sense a trial is nothing more than a decision-making platform. It is where a decision is made about an alleged wrongdoing and then about what is to be done about the wrongdoer.

The nature of trials is, to a considerable extent, determined by the nature of the investigative phase that precedes it. The more extensive the investigation carried out under judicial supervision, the more is taken away from the trial as the all-decisive day in court. In adversarial systems, pre-trial information is usually discounted; it is only at trial that the evidence that really matters is produced. In inquisitorial systems the evidence gathered in the investigative phase is given much more weight.

Those who support the adversarial way of conducting trials often point out that it gives defence counsel the best chance to prepare and conduct a proper defence. The examination and cross-examination of witnesses in court, before a jury, is seen to be the fairest way for any defendant to be tried. It is also argued that suspects' rights are better protected by a partisan defence lawyer than by an investigative judge, who must balance these rights against the interests of the investigation. Opponents argue that adversarial trials are expensive and time-consuming affairs, and potentially traumatising for vulnerable witnesses. They argue that the involvement of the jury adds a 'hit and miss' element to the proceedings, because jury decisions are difficult to predict, and often not explained.

In this chapter I have sought to juxtapose both systems for analytical reasons. One could argue that this does not do justice to either system. In fact, there is hardly a country where the legal scholars accept their criminal justice system to be purely adversarial or inquisitorial. The Dutch system, although quite far to the inquisitorial end of the spectrum, has been called a mixture of both, as has the German system (Huber, 1996). Legal scholars do not seem to be keen to see their system pigeonholed as part of one category or the other. The Japanese criminal justice system might, perhaps, most justifiably be called a mixture, because of the influence of European and US legal scholars in different eras.

The differences shown relate to, as we have seen, history, foreign domination, and additionally differing philosophies about how justice can best be achieved. These philosophies in turn relate to how societies are organised and what role the state is given in them. Therefore, there is no easy way of judging which is better or worse. That would probably be a meaningless exercise. Crombag (2003) elaborated this point by arguing that adversarial and inquisitorial systems are incomparable because they seek to achieve different goals. Their *ultimate* goal is the same: to serve justice. However, in the methods of achieving, or at least approaching, that goal both systems settle for what Crombag called 'proximate goals', and here is where the difference can be found. Adversarial justice's proximate goal is fair play, whereas truth via inquest is that of inquisitorial justice, and *sharia* law's road to justice is related to religion. Each system, therefore, has a 'different commitment to the discovery of the truth' (Damaska, 1986: 583), and there are corresponding differences as to the perceived objective of the criminal justice process. Once more, we must conclude that comparing like with like is not without obstacles, so that understanding the various systems of trial is best achieved by appreciating their internal logic in their own contexts.

Chapter 6

Judicial decision-makers

Regardless of how criminal justice systems or criminal trials are organised, the ultimate decisions remain in the hands of people. We can identify two schools of thought as to who those decision-makers should be. The first argues for such decisions to be left to the wisest and most experienced people in society: they would be best placed to reach a balanced judgment on the offence and the offender. This is the *patriarch* doctrine. The other view is that such powers should be reserved for people who are as 'ordinary' as the person standing trial: people who are similar to the offender might be best suited to judge his/her behaviour. This represents the *peer* point of view. The idea of judges as arbitrators obviously corresponds to former idea, whereas juries are associated with the latter notion of the peer-review of wrongdoers.

In this chapter I shall examine jury selection and the appointment of judges and their roles and responsibilities in various inquisitorial and adversarial systems. I shall look at how these decision-makers are protected from undue influences and how they are empowered to carry out their tasks properly and effectively.

First of all, let us turn our attention to the appointment of judges and the role that the judiciary, parliament and the electorate play in making these appointments. Later I shall make a tour around Europe to see where and how the jury system is in operation. The role and powers of juries vary widely both in adversarial systems and in inquisitorial modes of justice. Where a criminal justice system incorporates the provision for jury trials to be held it is normally only the more serious offences that are tried in this way. Minor wrongdoings are usually left for a judge or a magistrate to deal with. To complicate matters, it is not necessarily all serious crimes that are eligible for jury trial. In many countries arrangements are in place to prevent the most complex or controversial crimes from being tried by jury. In some jurisdictions fraud cases are kept away from juries while in other jurisdictions terrorist crimes can be tried by judges only.

Safe pairs of hands: the judiciary

The rule of law dictates that judges be independent. This means that no individual or office should be able to tell a judge how to conduct a trial or decide on a case. The legitimacy of the judiciary is further enhanced by ensuring that its members are appointed in a manner that is seen to be fair and that results in a judiciary that is balanced in certain important characteristics.

The extent to which the judiciary constitutes a fair representation of the population as a whole is a perennial issue. In many countries in the Western world, judges tend to be White, middle-aged and upper- or middle-class men. Women, ethnic minorities as well as the lower strata in society tend to be under-represented. But in comparative criminal justice there seem to be exceptions to every rule. With regard to the gender balance in the judiciary many of these exceptions occur in eastern Europe.

In the Republic of Slovenia, formerly part of Yugoslavia, female judges outnumber men. Selih and Maver report a male–female ratio of 247:262. However, they also report that female judges work predominantly in the lower courts, whereas male judges predominantly populate the higher courts.

In the Czech Republic the situation is similar, as women make up 61 per cent of the judiciary. However, just as in Slovenia, the pattern is that the more senior the position the less likely the judge is to be female. The judiciary at the highest court in the land is overwhelmingly male (Osmancik). In Slovakia, formerly joined with the Czech Republic the distribution of male and female judges is almost equal (Hencovska) which is also the case in France in Western Europe.

Countries with a more traditional gender ratio include Germany, Canada and South Korea. In Germany, the proportion of women judges is about 20 per cent (Aronowitz) whereas in Canada, in 1991, 181 female judges made up only about 10 per cent of the judiciary (Cohen and Longtin). In South Korea there are well over a 1,000 judges and less than 50 are reported to be female (see *The World Factbook of Criminal Justice Systems*: www.ojp.usdoj.gov/bjs/pub/). Gender is only one issue to have on impact on the composition of the judiciary. Race is obviously another, and age is a third. A further area of potential controversy is judges' political affiliation and the corresponding lack of, or perceived lack of, impartiality.

Clearly, the appointment of judges can be rather a delicate matter. Judges are at the heart of the criminal justice process and the judiciary is responsible for the fair application of the law. That requires a high level of trust in the individual judges as well as in the judiciary as a whole. If you cannot trust a judge, whom can you trust?

Judges can be appointed in various ways. The way these appointments work might either enhance or reduce their responsiveness to certain groups or individuals in society. The four main methods are: direct election, election by the assembly (parliament), appointment by the head of state, and co-option by the judiciary.

Direct election occurs in many states in the US. (Most US prosecutors are also appointed using this method.) An advantage of this method is that it guarantees public support for the judge in office, at least at the time of the election. This method is also likely to increase the official's responsiveness to dominant values in the community. The downside is that impartiality might perhaps be compromised in light of particular public attitudes, when judges find themselves unduly influenced by mood swings in public opinion.

Election by the assembly is popular in some states in Latin America. While this method may also help to ensure that the judges appointed have the support of the people, political considerations may come into play through appointments because of political affiliation rather than competence (Hague *et al.*, 1998). In Venezuela, for instance, it is argued that the political parties have great control over the appointment of judges (Salas). Supreme Court judges are elected by Congress from a list forwarded by the president. Although a body called the Judicial Council has recently been given a role in the appointment of judges in order to depoliticise the process, in practice party politics is still regarded a dominant factor in judicial appointments.

Spain is another example of a country in which parliament is involved with judicial appointments. As in many other countries there are certain safeguards in place to protect the independence of the judiciary. Judges cannot be transferred from one position to another against their will. They also cannot be sacked unless via very thorough disciplinary procedures. A judicial body called the General Council of the Judiciary handles complaints against judges. There are about 1,500 complaints of various kinds each year, but very few actually result in disciplinary action (Canivell).

Appointments by the head of state also involve the danger of political partiality. This is most common for senior judges for the highest courts. These courts often have an important role in the development of a nation's laws. In most countries judges are appointed for life, and governments usually leave their trace in the composition of the judiciary in the highest courts. The US president who appoints Supreme Court judges is a good example. It is sometimes said that these appointments are some of the more lasting influences on public policy that any president can exert. The issue most notably relevant here at present relates to abortion, which was legalised in the US by a Supreme Court ruling (the famous *Roe vs. Wade* ruling of 22 January 1973). A particular configuration of Supreme Court judges may well make it more or less likely that this ruling will be overturned in the future.

Finally, option or co-option by the judiciary is a system in which judges themselves partly or completely decide who are to become their new colleagues. This way of appointing judges is probably preferable with regard to maintaining the judiciary's independence from politics, but might result in an inward-looking and out-of-touch judiciary. It is therefore the method of selection at the opposite end of the spectrum to appointing judges by direct election (Hague *et al.*, 1998).

The danger of appointments that derive directly from popular votes lies, as mentioned above, in the risk of producing a judiciary that is too focused on public opinion. A judiciary primarily appointed by other judges might become too resistant to change and out of touch with a changing society. It is perhaps unsurprising that judges are often therefore appointed via a hybrid system, in which, at various stages, the judiciary, parliament, the head of state, and/or the electorate have a say. It is also not uncommon for there to be different procedures for the appointment of senior high-court judges than other judges. In Sri Lanka, for instance, High Court judges are appointed by the president, whereas judges in first-instance courts are appointed by a council representing the judiciary (Karunaratne).

In authoritarian states, independence of the judiciary is often non-existent. Judges on the side of those in power are considered vital in order to enforce the law to the taste of the ruling party or individual. They are often called to convict defendants of such catch-all offences as 'offences against the people' or 'crimes against decency', which are common in many totalitarian states. In China, in the 1950s and 1960s, judges were selected for their party loyalty and were expected to uphold the party line in court. Hague *et al.* (1998) have argued that the willingness of judges to raise their heads above the parapet is often an early sign of liberalisation in such regimes, and tends to precede the final collapse of power.

Conversely when democracies are overthrown this often has severe consequences for the judiciary. Recent history shows some grim examples of this. They include Egyptian leader Nasser sacking 200 judges in one go in 1969. More recently, the now fugitive ex-president Fujimori in Peru was known to sack judges he regarded as performing 'unsatisfactorily'. In Uganda, in the 1970s President Idi Amin had his Chief Justice shot dead (Hague *et al.*, 1998).

Juries: an endangered species?

Juries are a remarkable entity. While criminal justice systems just about anywhere have seen an increase in professionalism, the ultimate decision-makers with regard to guilt or innocence are still often lay people. The oddities of the jury system are not lost on many, including Vidmar (2001a), who described jury service as follows:

> ... it brings together a small group of lay persons who are assembled on a temporary basis for the purpose of deciding whether an accused person is guilty of a criminal offence or which of two sides should prevail in a civil dispute. The jurors are conscripted and often initially reluctant to serve. They are untutored in the formal discipline of law and its logic. They hear and see confusing and contested evidence and are provided with instructions, most often only in oral form, about arcane legal concepts and sent into a room alone to decide a verdict without further help from the professional persons who developed the evidence and explained their duties. (Vidmar, 2001a: 1)

While the seemingly odd task the jury faces is widely appreciated, there is equal clarity about what is perceived to be its value. Juries ensure that community values have a place within the system. They can guard against a too rigid or unfair application of laws. Juries can serve as protection against the biases of police officers, prosecution officials and judges. Juries also have the power to ensure that harsh laws are not necessarily enforced. For these reasons, the institution of the jury is seen as the embodiment of fairness and propriety (Findlay and Duff, 1988).

Juries around the world are nevertheless a somewhat endangered species. In England and Wales, there are currently proposals, as there have been before, to reduce the number of cases that are eligible to be tried before a jury (see Auld, 2001). In other adversarial systems, such as those of the Republic of Ireland and Australia, a similar trend is apparent. Jury trials are, after all, costly, time-consuming and, some say, add an unnecessary element of chance to proceedings.

Ironically, in countries without a jury system there is sometimes a trend towards introducing or reintroducing it. Both Spain and Russia have introduced a jury system in the 1990s, while it is on the political agenda in other former Soviet states as well. But here there also are exceptions. Particularly in the Luxembourg and Netherlands there seems to be a widespread contentment with a jury-less criminal justice system. If this contentment is as widespread among the public, defendants and defence counsel as it is among the judiciary that would be indicative of the esteem in which the judiciary must be held.

'The lamp that shows freedom lives': the English jury

It is appropriate to start this discussion in England and Wales, where juries have been in existence for at least 800 years, although their independence became properly established after 1670. Before that, juries were commonly the victim of bullying or persecution if they did not return the verdict desired by those in power. Today, the jury is free to decide its verdict in any way it sees fit. In order to protect that freedom juries are not required to give reasons for their judgement. In fact, the Contempt of Court Act 1985 forbids them to do so. As jury decisions lack scrutiny, a jury is free to go against the law or the evidence without having to fear being held to account. Such a defiance of the law is called *jury nullification*. In order to honour the pivotal role of the jury, appeals against their decisions are difficult. Appellate proceedings are more often instigated because of the behaviour of the legal professionals in court than the fact that the jury may have been mistaken in its verdict (Lloyd-Bostock and Thomas, 2001).

Juries are, however, estimated to sit in no more than one or two per cent of all criminal trials in England and Wales. Most defendants plead guilty, and for them a jury trial is not an option. Additionally, most crimes are minor, which also starkly reduces the chance of a trial by jury. Only the most serious offences are automatically tried before a jury in a Crown Court. There is also a class of so-called *either-way* offences. These offences, representing the middle range in terms of severity, can be tried by either a judge or by jury. It is the defendants' right to opt for jury trial in case of an either-way offence. In case of a minor offence (called a *summary* offence) or when the defendant chooses to be tried by a judge in case of an either-way offence, the case goes to a Magistrates' Court. In this lower type of court the case is usually tried by a panel of three lay judges.

To qualify for jury service, a person must have been a resident in the UK for at least five years since the age of 13 and be between 18 and 70 years of age. Potential jurors are chosen from the electoral register. Excluded are those who have ever been sentenced to five years or more in prison. Those who have served a sentence within the previous ten years, and those who have been placed on probation in the previous five years, as well as those currently on bail, are disqualified as well.

Ineligible are people involved with the criminal justice process, such as police officers and court staff, along with the clergy and the mentally disordered. Others have the right to refuse to serve because of the demands of their profession. This includes Members of Parliament, medical professionals and those serving in the armed forces (Lloyd-Bostock and Thomas, 2001).

Prosecution and defence powers to exclude individual jurors before trial is limited. The reason is that that would fly in the face of random selection, which is the cornerstone of jury composition. Its advantage is the lack of intentional bias in the group of 12 people who form the jury. However, any random selection may by chance result in a jury that is imbalanced in terms of, for instance, race, gender or social status. The High Court has held that a racially balanced jury is not an automatic right, but the matter remains a sore point, especially in racially sensitive cases (Lloyd-Bostock and Thomas, 2001).

In England and Wales jurors are allowed to take notes. They can also ask questions, but they rarely do so. During deliberations they can send out questions, but this does not seem to occur regularly either. Verdicts should preferably be unanimous. However, when a jury cannot succeed in reaching a unanimous verdict, the judge can instruct that a 10–2 majority will suffice. According to government figures, this occurs in about 20 per cent of cases (Lloyd-Bostock and Thomas, 2001).

The relation between the judge and the jury is intricate. In principle the division of labour is very simple: matters of law are for the judge to deal with, whereas matters of fact are for the jury. In reality, the lines of demarcation are not that straight. One of the points at issue is the judge's summing up at the end of the trial. At this stage the judge will direct the jury on matters of law, but will also sum up the evidence. Here there is plenty of scope for the legal professional to influence the jury. A judge in England and Wales has considerable leeway in dispersing his or her views, much more so than US judges, who do not tend to sum up the facts. The fact that judges rule on the admissibility of evidence gives them a firm handle on the goings-on at trial. They do not decide on the facts, but they do have a grip on what evidence the jury hears in the first place.

Despite the fact that the vast majority of cases are dealt with without a jury there is no doubt that the institution is held in high esteem in England and Wales. Attempts to reduce opportunities for jury trials for reasons of expedience are usually opposed vehemently by the judiciary as well as by other commentators. The ideological love affair with the jury is exemplified by the term 'the lamp that shows freedom lives' coined by Lord Devlin. He argued that abolishing the jury would be the second act of any dictator, after dissolving parliament. The jury not only stands for fairness in criminal justice but seems to function as a symbol for propriety in politics and other areas of public life as well (see Findlay and Duff, 1988; Lloyd-Bostock and Thomas, 2001).

A secondary aim of jury service is to educate people about criminal justice via their participation. Most citizens are likely to be called for jury service at some point in their lives. The experience of a trial, and the subsequent deliberations and verdict, tend to make lasting impressions, for better or worse, about the justice that was done on that occasion. Jury service offers lay people the opportunity to be a part of the machinery that delivers justice. Its value therefore extends well beyond the interests of the defendant.

The American jury

There is arguably no country in the world in which the jury is of more importance than the USA. Because its jury system was imported from England, one might expect to find many similarities between both systems. However, specific features of US law and culture have influenced the shape of the jury system there. These include 'Americans' distrust of the judiciary, their passion for open procedures and unfettered public discourse about those procedures, their struggle to overcome racial and ethnic injustice, their commitment to adversarial adjudication, and the dual state-federal justice system' (King, 2001: 93).

In the US the right to a trial by jury is enshrined in the constitution. The Sixth Amendment promises a jury in all criminal prosecutions. However, the US Supreme Court has held that this right can be refused in the case of petty offences for which no more than six months of imprisonment can be imposed. Another departure from the basic premise that all trials should be jury trials relates to the possibility of defendants waiving their right to a jury trial. Federal legislation since 1930 allows for defendants to be tried by a judge in a so-called bench trial, provided defendants opt for that. In many states these bench trials occur rather frequently. The US state of Massachusetts is exceptional in that it allows for the possibility of a jury trial after a defendant has been found guilty in a bench trial. This is technically not an appeal, but a two-tier system. The initial trial by judge is optional (King, 2001).

Jury arrangements vary among states. All but four states, for example, require 12 jurors at trial (at least to begin with; *jury attrition*, which is a reduction in size of the jury because, for instance, of a juror falling ill, is sometimes possible). In some states note-taking is permitted, in others it is not. Normally, it is not for the judge to comment specifically on the evidence. Summing up does not occur in most states. Nevertheless, the role of the judge remains highly influential, as the judge rules on the admissibility of evidence, as is the case in England and Wales.

The differences between jury arrangements in England and Wales and those in the US are perhaps greatest when it comes to jury selection. The Sixth Amendment states that the jury should be impartial and drawn from a previously ascertained district. That, in effect, provides little guidance. A system for the random selection of jurors from electoral lists was adopted in 1970. Nevertheless, both parties have extensive powers to exclude potential jurors. Because of that, the actual composition of the jury often turns into a battleground, as if it were a trial before the actual trial itself. Many US lawyers believe that selection of the right 12 persons is paramount to victory or defeat at trial (Simon, 1977).

First there is the process of *voir dire*, by which both prosecution and defence can exclude a number of prospective jurors before trial without having to offer specific reasons why. The number of jurors that can be excluded can be up to 20 (Simon, 1977). Apart from that, both parties can *challenge for cause*, which means that jurors can be excluded for particular reasons, which need to be given and accepted by the court. The purpose of the whole exercise is to secure a composition of the jury that is satisfactory to both parties. The idea is that when both parties are satisfied, the jury is most likely to be a proper representation of the public, which will consider the evidence objectively and fairly.

An important secondary objective for jury selection is to get acquainted with the prospective jurors. The counsel for both sides may use it as their first chance to sell their case to the jury. The protracted American selection process ensures pre-trial interaction between parties and jurors of an intensity that does not occur in England and Wales. That will affect the relationship both parties have with the eventual jury, which might in turn have an effect on their conduct at trial.

While rapport with prospective jurors tends to serve as a strong informal predictor with regard to selection, many lawyers tend to use certain heuristic methods as to what type of juror would be beneficial to their case. Simon (1977) identified many rules of thumb that are commonplace among lawyers. A selection of them is listed below.

- A young juror is less likely to favour the defendant;
- A juror belonging to the same fraternal organisations, union or political party as the client or witness is more likely to return a verdict favourable to that party;
- A juror belonging to the same occupation or profession as the client will be more likely to give a favourable verdict;
- A woman juror is more likely to return a verdict unfavourable to a party of her own gender;

- A mixed jury, in terms of religion or ethnicity, will have a more difficult time agreeing on a verdict and is thus more likely to return a verdict more favourable to the defendant;

- An intelligent, courageous juror is more desired by parties who feel that they have a good case while a weak-minded jury is more desired by parties who feel that they have a doubtful case and are dependent on emotional, sympathetic appeals.

Groups who are believed to favour the defendant are:

- Women;

- Those who vote Democrat;

- People of middle and lower socio-economic status;

- Certain occupational groups; such as social scientists;

- Minority ethnic groups.

It can be debated to what extent such folk psychology has any real value. Valid or not, it can be argued that frequent use of exclusion without reason might put the ideal of juries as a cross-section of the population in jeopardy, particularly if certain social groups are more likely to be excluded than others.

King (2001) has argued that while jury trials are relatively rare and occur in only three to ten per cent of all felony cases, the notion of the jury is important to the nation's psyche. As is the case in England and Wales, it is felt by large sections of the population that jury trials are a fundamental human right and a prerequisite for justice.

What makes juries particularly significant in the US is the possibility for them to be involved, in most states, in decisions regarding the death penalty. Just as juries are left to themselves when reaching a judgement on guilt or innocence, the situation is essentially the same with regard to the ultimate issue of life or death.

The trial of a person charged with a capital crime (one for which the death penalty might be imposed) has two stages. The first stage is the traditional one, in which the evidence for guilt or innocence is considered. In the case of a guilty verdict, the second stage occurs, in which the same jury hears evidence concerning the appropriate sentence. The phase involving sentencing is also adversarial in nature. The prosecution will seek to prove that certain aggravating circumstances apply, whereas the defence will be looking to present evidence of mitigating factors. The jury needs to decide unanimously that aggravating circumstances apply before they can impose the death penalty.

In potential death penalty cases, the *voir dire* process centres, to a large extent, on the prospective jurors' attitude towards the death penalty. Prosecutors seeking the death penalty could, in the past, exclude prospective jurors who were opposed to it on principle. Nowadays however, only jurors who *cannot* in a particular instance apply the death penalty can be excluded for cause. Those who might sentence a defendant to death but might be reluctant to do so cannot be challenged for cause. The Supreme Court ruled that excluding anyone with a negative attitude towards the death penalty would violate the defendant's right to a fair trial and to an impartial jury under the Sixth Amendment. However, during peremptory challenges, the prosecuting party often still excludes many jurors whose attitude they find not to sufficiently favour the ultimate punishment (King, 2001).

Juries imposing the death penalty may well be a feature unique to the US. It arguably makes sense to leave the state's heaviest weapon against

---

Box 6.1 Juries around the British Isles

When looking around the British Isles outside the mainland of Britain, and for the moment we include in that Guernsey, Jersey, the Isle of Man as well as the Republic of Ireland and the province of Northern Ireland, we can observe quite striking local differences in jury arrangements.

As mentioned earlier, in England and Wales the jury consists invariably of 12 members, while in Scotland the number is 15. In the Republic of Ireland the jury consists of 12 members as well, but unlike in Scotland or England and Wales, the decision to render a guilty verdict must be unanimous or an 11–1 majority.

Notable in Ireland and Northern Ireland is the existence of procedures to try cases of a particularly sensitive nature without a jury. In Ireland there is the Special Criminal Court for this purpose, while in Northern Ireland so-called Diplock Trials can be held, in which a judge, not a jury, decides on guilt or innocence (Jackson *et al.*, 2001).

Meanwhile, on the Isle of Man a jury of 12 persons is required for charges of treason or murder. For other crimes, a jury of 7 members is sufficient. Their verdicts have to be unanimous. In the island of Jersey, off the west coast of France, any defendant in the Royal Court has the right to elect trial by jury. As is the case in England and Wales, unanimity is preferred, but 10–2 can suffice for the return of a guilty verdict. The situation on the neighbouring Isle of Guernsey is rather different again. Guernsey does not have a traditional jury system. Instead, it utilises 12 so-called *Jurats*, who are prominent citizens selected by an electoral college. There are over 100 of these Jurats, and 7 of them are required for a criminal trial. A simple majority will do for a guilty verdict (Vidmar, 2001b).

---

its citizens ultimately in the hands of the people. However, this does not mean that the practice of the death penalty and the way in which it is imposed is necessarily just, or fair. We will scrutinise this practice further in Chapter 7.

Juries in inquisitorial systems

The adversarial courtroom is the jury's natural habitat. The adversarial process, in which all evidence is orally presented at trial, fits the jury model well. The inquisitorial mode of trial, in which documentary evidence is more important, is less suited. Nevertheless, a fair deal of cross-fertilisation between adversarial and inquisitorial systems has occurred. Bench trials happen frequently in adversarial systems, and similarly in inquisitorial systems there often tends to be a place for the jury. However, the role of the jury across Europe is certainly more restricted, and it often involves judges and juries deciding verdicts in conjunction. We call such arrangements *mixed tribunals*. I shall briefly discuss jury arrangements in a number of European countries, after which I shall examine the state of affairs in Spain and Russia: both countries introduced the jury within their inquisitorial framework in the 1990s.

Regional courts in Austria hold trials by jury for serious crimes, which are defined as crimes that carry at least ten years of imprisonment. The possibility for jury trial also exists for cases that might lead to at least five years in prison. Juries deal also, as a matter of course, with crimes of a political nature, which is an arrangement enshrined in the Austrian constitution. Eight jurors decide on guilt, and in the case of a guilty verdict, sentencing is decided by judges and jury collectively (Vidmar 2001b).

The role of the jury is very limited in Belgium. Juries only feature in the highest court, called Assize Courts. In these Assize Courts, crimes are tried before a mixed tribunal, consisting of three judges and 12 jurors. The jury was abandoned during the Dutch rule, between 1815 and 1830, but following Belgium's independence it was reinstated, but only for trials involving crimes of a political nature. A majority of eight versus four is enough for a guilty verdict. However, when the majority is only seven versus five favouring guilt, the three judges may express their opinion as well and a unanimous vote from them could swing the verdict. The role of the jury has diminished over the last 50 years, and very few trials by jury are actually held nowadays. However, Article 98 of the constitution codifies the right to a trial by jury, and a change in the constitution is not very likely in the short term (Van den Wijngaert, 1993).

Trials by jury are also a rarity in Denmark. Only serious crimes threatening the defendant with four years of imprisonment or more can be tried before a panel of 3 judges and 12 jurors. However, economic crimes such as fraud and forgery cannot be tried before a jury. Judges and jury deliberate separately, and both have to find the defendant guilty by majorities of, respectively, 2–1, and 8–4. Juries also vote on sentencing, and may rule on legal issues, such as aggravating circumstances or insanity, as well. To ensure parity between judges and jury, one vote from a judge counts as four jury votes. As in Belgium, the constitution guarantees the existence of the jury system, but the constitution does not specify what crimes should be eligible for jury trial or what form the lay participation should take. Only around 60 to 100 cases per year are actually tried by jury. Greve commented that for some time there has been rather widespread discontent with the jury system (Greve, 1993).

Jury trials are held in the higher courts in France (Courts d'Assises), in a mixed tribunal setting. The panel consists of three judges and nine jurors, who deliberate together and come to a joint decision on guilt. As is the case in Austria, Belgium and Denmark, the jury is also involved with decisions on sentencing. The jury system in France is said to be in considerable demise (Pradel, 1993). Court d'Assises trials are regularly held without the involvement of the jury. That category includes political or otherwise sensitive crimes, such as terrorist offences.

In Germany lay judges can be members of higher and lower courts. They hold the same formal position as regular judges, which means that they decide on all matters with the same vote as their professional counterparts. However, their actual position is not entirely as influential. Professional judges also have the advantage of being able to inspect the case-file beforehand. Lay judges do not have access to the *dossier* prior to trial. There is no lay participation in cases heard in the first instance in the High Court: this is where cases of terrorism, treason and assaults against high representatives of the state are tried. As is the case in France and Denmark, cases with the most potential for political controversy are steered away from lay involvement. It is important to note that German lay members are not exactly jurors: their participation is not restricted to one trial. Rather, they serve for a period of time and sit on a number of cases (Kühne, 1993).

Lay participation occurs in mixed criminal courts in the first instance in Greece and sometimes, but not regularly, in appeal cases as well. Such mixed courts are presided over by one professional judge, who is accompanied by two other judges and four lay persons. As we have seen in other countries across the European continent, more complex cases do not tend to go before a jury, but the Greek constitution ensures the role of the jury in criminal and political trials. Jurors in Greece must be at least 30 years old and have completed elementary school. Juries decide on guilt and also have an input on sentencing. Professional judges decide on legal matters, such as the admissibility of evidence (Mylonopoulos, 1993).

In Italy Assize Courts deal with the most severe cases, and this is where lay participation is to be found. Such trials involve two professional judges and six lay persons. The involvement of jurors in proceedings is in demise, especially since in 1988 legislation was passed that reduced opportunities for jury trials considerably.

The Grand Duchy of Luxembourg totally abolished the jury in 1987. The reasons given did not relate to practicalities of jury trials but to the quality of justice administered by the jury system. Spielmann and Spielmann (1993) explained that there was no possibility of appeal against judgements of the Court d'Assises, which, it was argued, violated defendants' rights. Another reason was the fact that the jury did not give reasons for its decisions, which was also considered to be unfair to defendants.

In the Netherlands the jury system, introduced in the Napoleonic era, was abolished as early as 1813 and never to be seen again. Its reintroduction seems out of the question, as the jury does not seem to be desired by either the public or the legal profession (Swart, 1993).

In Norway, the jury consists of ten persons. They are drawn from a register of nominees, who tend to be respectable citizens with strong ties to the community. The first step of jury selection involves the selection of fourteen nominees from the register of nominees. These are always seven men and seven women, of which ten are ultimately chosen. For a guilty verdict a majority of seven versus three will do. No reasons are required, and it is forbidden to disclose the distribution of the votes. Interestingly, when the presiding judge is of the opinion that the evidence favours guilt, he/she can order a new trial, despite a jury acquittal. Courts in the first instance tend to be mixed tribunals, whereas appeals courts embody a jury as the sole decider of guilt or innocence.

In Portugal, lay participation occurs in jury courts, consisting of three judges and four jurors. They try only the most severe crimes, carrying a penalty of at least eight years' imprisonment, including crimes against the security of the state and crimes against peace or against humanity (De Figueiredo Dias and Antunas, 1993).

New jury systems

Although the Spanish constitution guarantees popular participation in criminal proceedings, it is the 1995 Spanish Jury Law that laid down specific arrangements for jury trials (Ruiz Vadillo, 1993). The decision to forward a case to jury trial lies with the investigative judge. This is an example of the European tradition of strong judicial involvement in the pre-trial phase. The trial itself is adversarial in nature. To secure an adversarial trial, in which all the evidence is orally presented, the judge does not have access to the case-file. Jury trials are an option only in cases of certain crimes, including those committed by public officials in the exercise of their duties, crimes against persons, liberty, security and arson.

Trials begin with an opening statement from the prosecution followed by the defence's plea, and continue in true continental style with an examination of the defendant by the judge. This is followed by the questioning of witnesses, including expert witnesses, which is performed by both prosecution and defence, although the judge can ask questions after these examinations as well. While the defendant has the right not to testify, and is informed of his/her right of avoiding self-incrimination, the vast majority of defendants do give a statement at trial. The trial ends with summations and, true to the European inquisitorial tradition, the defendant has the last word.

Juries in Spain do not simply render a verdict of guilty or not guilty; rather, they are asked to answer a set of questions not unlike those that judges are supposed to answer in many European inquisitorial systems. These questions relate to elements of the crimes charged, such as intent, aggravating or mitigating circumstances, and whether the jury regards the charges proven. The answers to these questions are subject to disclosure and may serve as grounds for appeal.

The difference between a simple guilty/not guilty verdict and the set of questions to be dealt with by the Spanish jurors is of importance. Such specifications take away some of the mystique and secrecy of jury decision-making. They may also serve as a safeguard against jury nullifications: it is very difficult for juries to go against the law when the questions they answer are of a legal nature. It is also clear that these reasoned opinions serve as ammunition for appeals.

The Spanish example shows an interesting mixture of inquisitorial and adversarial elements. The role of the jury, however, must seem odd, especially for those used to the jury in England and Wales and the US. Some of the virtues of jury decision-making are actually reversed in the Spanish structure: their verdicts are open to scrutiny, and appeals against jury decisions are possible and do happen. Thaman (2001) has argued that nowhere in mainland Europe does the requirement for juries to justify judgments go as far as in Spain.

The restrictive legal requirements surrounding jury decisions, however, did not prevent a high profile acquittal occurring in 1997. Mikel Otegi, a young Basque nationalist stood trial for murdering two Basque police officers, but was acquitted by a jury on the grounds of diminished capacity caused by intoxication and 'uncontrollable rage provoked by alleged previous police harassment'. The verdict shocked a nation that has suffered violence from Basque nationalist terrorism for decades. The suspicion was, on the hand, one of intimidation: jurors were suspected to have been afraid of revenge against them in the event of a guilty verdict. Basque nationalists on the other hand, could argue that the case showed the distrust in which the local community held the criminal justice system and the police in particular. Calls were made to suspend jury justice, at least in the Basque area (Thaman, 2001).

This is reminiscent of the situation in Northern Ireland, where the Troubles led to the introduction of so-called Diplock trials, in which a bench sits and rules instead of a jury. It reminds us of the fact that adherence to the ideal of jury justice in divided communities plagued by violence and distrust proves to be extremely difficult.

Advocates of the jury system perhaps will find it heartening that even in situations such as Spain, where its role is certainly more straight-jacketed than in England and Wales, the jury still finds ways of delivering verdicts that seemingly are at odds with much of the evidence presented and against the views of those in power.

As in Spain, the jury has made a reappearance in post-Soviet Russia. Trials by jury in Russia were common in the nineteenth century, but were abolished after the revolution of 1917. The right to trial by jury was reintroduced shortly after the collapse of the Soviet Union in 1993. Thaman explained that while juries have been introduced, this was not accompanied by an overhaul of the pre-trial phase. In a preliminary hearing the trial judge reviews the evidence contained in the case-file. On that basis a decision is made about whether or not a case should be committed for jury trial. Although the trial is adversarial in nature, no new evidence is presented at it: arguments have to be based on the contents of the dossier. The Russian mode of trial is distinctly continental European, although, unlike in France for instance, the examinations are usually performed by both parties. The defendant normally gives an unsworn statement, and has the last word. Thaman has noted that:

> For criminal justice systems that place emphasis on the presumption of innocence, the prosecution's burden of proof, and the defendant's right to remain silent, the interrogation of the defendant before any incriminating evidence has been presented to the fact finder is a lingering inquisitorial vestige. (Thaman, 2001: 335)

A further point of note is the fact that any mention of the defendant's criminal record is forbidden. In many inquisitorial systems that record is discussed as a matter of course. To achieve some measure of equality, defendants in Russia are not allowed to present evidence of good character either. Upon coming to a judgement, a Russian jury has to answer three rather legalistic questions. They relate to whether a crime has been committed, whether the defendant was the one who committed it and whether that makes him/her guilty of the charge. Jury nullification remains a possibility, as the jury may render a not guilty verdict, even if all necessary elements for a guilty verdict are present.

Finally, let us look at the jury in Brazil. Brazil has a jury system, which is guaranteed in the 1937 constitution. The right to jury trial extends to cases involving murder, infanticide, abortion and assisting suicide, and it involves seven jurors at trial. In the Brazilian scenario the jury does not deliberate. They simply vote, and a four against three majority will suffice for a verdict (Vidmar, 2001b).

The arguments for and against the jury are manifold. Below are some of the ones listed by Davies *et al.* (1998). They are by no means exhaustive or even mutually exclusive. The arguments favouring the jury are as follows:

- Juries represent a cross-section of the population, so that any accused party is tried by his/her peers;
- Juries enable the public's view of the criminal justice system to be reflected;
- Juries ensure that unpopular or 'unjust' laws cannot be enforced;
- Jury members are not 'case-hardened';
- The jury system is the cornerstone of the adversarial criminal justice process;
- Fact assessment is a common-sense matter and therefore best left to lay people;
- There is no acceptable alternative.

Common arguments against the jury can be listed as follows:

- Jurors are not representative of society as a whole;
- Juries are not able to handle complex issues, particularly in areas such as fraud;
- Juries are subject to prejudice and irrationality;
- Jurors tend to acquit the guilty;

- Juries tend to convict the innocent;

- Juries are too ready to believe the prosecution evidence;

- Juries are reluctant to believe the police.

The fact that the reasons for and against are not mutually exclusive is perhaps indicative of the fact that many commentators' opinions about the jury are partly emotional.

The type of person society decides to put its faith in with regard to dealing with alleged wrongdoers hinges on the answer to the question of whom to trust. Where magistrates and professional judges are assigned these responsibilities there will often be an underlying

---

Box 6.2   Systems without juries

What do Israel, Japan, Lithuania, Luxembourg, the Netherlands, the Philippines and Sweden have in common in their procedures? They do not have a jury in any shape or form. Whereas in some countries the right to a jury trial is equated with fairness and central to the concept of justice itself, other systems seem to manage perfectly well without a jury, and apparently without anyone really missing it.

As discussed elsewhere in this chapter, in Luxembourg the jury was abolished only in 1987. The reasons given were the facts that appeals against jury decisions were not possible and that the jury did not have to give reasons to support its decision. It was felt that it was in the interests of justice to have defendants tried before a panel of professional judges instead. Japan is a country where the jury has never really prospered. When introduced in 1928, its role was advisory only, and the advice did not concern the ultimate question of guilt, only matters of fact. The jury disappeared during World War II, never to be seen again in Japanese courtrooms. The Netherlands' acquaintance with the jury was even shorter. Only in the early 1800s was a jury system incorporated, but it was generally considered to be a mistake and abolished shortly after its instigation. Its non-existence is a non-issue in Dutch politics: no one seems to desire it.

Article 10 of the 1948 United Nations' fundamental Declaration of Human Rights, which fed into later human rights legislation, states that 'everyone is entitled in full equality to a fair and public hearing by an independent and impartial tribunal, in the determination of his rights and obligations and of any criminal charge against him'. The key words are 'fair', 'independent' and 'impartial'. The word 'jury' is, however, not mentioned. The right to trial by jury is by no means absolute, and the right to choose when the system has a jury option is even less so.

---

conviction that seasoned specialists are best equipped to fulfil that trust. Professionals may have the knowledge and the reasoning abilities to judge each case on merit. The fact that such people are respected pillars of the community adds to their suitability for such an instrumental role in achieving social control. In communities where learned and senior members are held in high regard, it is not unlikely that they are judges, magistrates or, in the case of Guernsey, Jurats. Guernsey and Norway are examples of an intermediate solution: the principle of random selection of jurors is upheld, but the pool from which the jurors are drawn is not the population as a whole but rather a subset of people judged competent to make life-altering decisions over offenders. The typical safeguard against wrongdoing on the part of these decision-makers is by means of a requirement to render reasoned judgements in writing. Via that mechanism these individuals are held accountable in a way that juries typically are not, although Spain is a notable exception in this regard.

Just as policing styles will differ depending on the communities that are being policed, so will community characteristics help understand what type of person is trusted with decisions on guilt and sentencing. Where there is distrust of official bodies, a jury a randomly selected group of ordinary people is likely to be seen as a good alternative. Where police, prosecution, or perhaps even judges cannot be relied on because of vested interests or perceived vested interests, the whole machinery of selecting and instructing a jury and presenting all the evidence in a way that is understandable to them is probably worthwhile.

Conclusion

This overview of judicial appointments and jury arrangements shows an impressive degree of diversity. In particular, the way in which different jurisdictions try to ensure a certain level of lay involvement in criminal trials is subject to immense variation. Sometimes lay participation occurs in mixed tribunals, in which both judges and jurors have to come to a verdict, sometimes together, sometimes separately. Sometimes juries alone decide on guilt, but quite often they play a role in the decision on sentencing as well. In certain countries they decide separately from the judge or judges, and elsewhere in conjunction with their professional counterparts. There are instances where jurors do more than decide on matters of fact only, but in Japan, during the short period in which juries existed there, the verdict of juries remained advisory only (Castberg, 1990).

Apart from emphasising this intriguing level of diversity, it is also worth considering a number of communalities. Lay participation seems to be in decline in many countries, including, if current government plans proceed, in England and Wales. There seems to be a tension between ensuring lay participation for the most serious crimes and efforts to steer lay participation away from the most complex cases where juror may have difficulties understanding the information presented to them. Jurors hardly anywhere in the world are involved with minor offences. That is why we call the jury an endangered species: highly valued, but rarely to be seen.

In countries where lay participation is rare their involvement is often in cases where, perhaps, the state should not be trusted because of its vested interests. Belgium for instance, reinstated the jury initially to deal with cases involving censorship and political crimes. Additionally, in Portugal jurors are involved only in the most serious cases and those involving crimes against peace, humanity and against the security of the state. On the other hand there are several examples where the jury cannot sit on, for instance, trials for terrorist offences, in which the state certainly is bound to have a vested interest.

In countries with a more inquisitorial system the demise of the jury is often explained in terms of the quality of justice delivered. It is often said that jurors might not understand complex trials. Another reason given concerns the fact that options for appeal against jury decisions are often limited. The fact that juries normally do not explain their decision is a third. In adversarial systems, in contrast, any restriction of the role of the jury tends to be inspired by pragmatic considerations. These often relate to expenditure, as jury trials are expensive.

Despite sentiments to that effect in England and Wales and the US lay participation is not a fundamental requirement for justice. More fundamental is the acceptance of decision-makers as independent and impartial. The state can only serve justice by providing those decision-makers when its dependability and impartiality is generally accepted. When that is not the case, lay decision-makers serve as an invaluable protection against the state.

Chapter 7

Punishment

It has been said that we can assess the quality of justice in a country by looking at the treatment reserved for offenders. Where offenders' human rights are respected and where there is an emphasis on compassion and rehabilitation we take that to be indicators of a high level of social cohesion and inclusiveness in society. Consider the following quotation:

> Africans believe that an offender is a member of the community and should be corrected in the community and not outside it. The community insists on the offender paying a fine coupled with a communion feast and sacrifices to propitiate the gods, depending on the gravity of the offence. Undeniably, in Africa south of the Sahara, public offences such as incest, patricide, matricide, or desecration of a holy shrine would demand a sacrifice to appease the gods in addition to a communion feast and other communal penalties. (Ebbe, 2000a: 287)

From a Western point of view, this practice of having a feast to appease the gods as part of a sentence is obviously outlandish. However, it tells us something about the sub-Saharan African orientation towards rule-breakers in their midst. In particular, the efforts not to cast out offenders are noteworthy. In Western societies there are more efforts to temporarily exile offenders from the community and send them to boot camps, prisons or other correctional centres.

Such differences in sentencing practices yield information about the perceived severity of offences. They additionally, tell us something about the position and perception of wrongdoers. Differences in sentencing practices are therefore likely to reveal meaningful information about other jurisdictions' visions of social inclusion and social control (Garland, 2001). Punishment is an area almost made for comparative research.

Sentencing and sentences are perpetual sources of controversy and debate. Perhaps the main reason for that is to do with the underlying goals of punishment. In order to understand this we need to look at why certain punishments are imposed and what society aims to achieve by their imposition. The literature distinguishes between *absolute* and *relative* theories of punishment. In absolute theories, the punishment constitutes an end in and of itself. Sentences are imposed because that is the proper thing to do in response to violations of law and social order. The aim of *retribution* falls into this category. In the philosophy of retribution, an offender should be punished because it is deserved and therefore just: it is their 'just deserts' (Walker, 1991).

• Relative theories justify punishment as a means to achieve a certain social goal. After all, punishment involves the infliction of suffering and should therefore be justified by assuming that something good will come of it. The first of such aims is *individual deterrence*. It aims to ensure that the offender punished will not offend again. Another is *incarceration*, the idea simply being that an offender will be unable to commit crimes as long as he/she is off the streets (discounting for the moment the fact that the committal of crimes in prison is far from impossible). A third utilitarian aim is *rehabilitation*: offenders may be punished to give the state the opportunity to 'better' these offenders by, for instance, improving their social or professional skills. The idea is obviously that the reformed offender is less likely to re-offend after their return to society. The fourth relative aim is *general deterrence*. By punishing one offender the system aims to dissuade others from committing the same offence.

In practice we often do not know the exact reason for a particular sentence. A judge might impose a certain sentence with a particular goal in mind, or with a mixture of objectives to be achieved. On the other hand the reality is that sentences are often imposed simply because of policies or tariffs that are in operation. In practice the philosophy that most systems operate is a hybrid one. It incorporates features of more than one of these objectives and, depending on the crime or the offender, one aim is prioritised over others. Typically, any punishment must be proportional to the crime and fit the offender, so that some of these goals have a reasonable chance of being achieved (Walker, 1991; De Keijser, 2000).

A complicating factor is that some of these sentencing goals are mutually exclusive. That means that achieving one aim will inevitably make it more difficult for other objectives to be met as well. Incarceration, for instance is achieved easily by putting an offender in prison. However, we know that the aim of rehabilitation is not achieved easily this way because the offender's subsequent integration into society is known to be difficult. In that way, sentencing poses a no-win situation to criminal justice systems: the completion of any sentence may constitute a success with regard to one objective but a failure in terms of another.

Comparative research may serve to assess how criminal justice systems deal with this sentencing conundrum. Criminal justice systems seek to strike a balance between retribution, deterrence and rehabilitation. Often in the case of young wrongdoers there is an emphasis on rehabilitation. In cases of more serious offences the element of deterrence is likely to be prioritised. We have seen that in *sharia* law, retribution is prevalent in responding to *hudud* crimes, which are crimes against Islam, whereas in case of *quesas* crimes there is an emphasis on rehabilitation. The fashion in which certain sentencing goals are given priority over others is indicative of the nature of state-operated social control.

Fairness and effectiveness

There are offences such as property offences for which, in Saudi Arabia, you might lose a hand. In England and Wales you might lose six months or a year of your life in prison for a similar offence. In other jurisdictions one might, perhaps, get away with a community service order. Different criminal justice systems certainly react differently to similar wrongdoings. The root of some of these differences lies in differences in the sentencing objectives discussed earlier. Another part of the explanation relates to differences in the perceived seriousness of offences and the perceived severity of certain types of punishment.

Key aspects of sentences are their fairness and effectiveness. Because sentences cause state-inflicted suffering, issues of fairness are pertinent. What actually constitutes fair punishment is not an easy matter to define. Sentences considered fair in one society are not in another. Additionally, perceptions of sentences have changed over time, along with changing attitudes on the value of human life, privacy and physical integrity. As far as England and Wales is concerned, the practices of corporal punishment, deportations and the death penalty have disappeared. As in most Western societies, the temporary or permanent confinement in prisons is the dominant serious form of punishment.

While the concept of fairness has a level of elasticity to it, certain minimal standards have been formulated in international law. Quite general but influential, nevertheless, is the Universal Declaration of Human Rights. It was published in 1950, and it lays out certain requirements for sentencing as it does for the ways in which defendants should be tried. Famous is the phrase contained in Article 5: 'No one shall be subjected to torture or to cruel, inhuman or degrading treatment or punishment.' However, what constitutes 'cruel, inhuman or degrading treatment' is a matter on which worldwide agreement is hard to find, although European case law has provided for certain specifications. Protocols from the Council of Europe outlaw the death penalty by any of its member states, because it is seen to be cruel. In this fashion international organisations play a significant role. The European Prison Rules, laid down by the Council of Europe (see the Council's official website, www.coe.int) are significant in this respect, as are several United Nations resolutions (accessible via the United Nations website, www.un.org). I will elaborate on these in the next chapter.

The second characteristic of sentences concerns their effectiveness. Usually, effectiveness is measured in terms of recidivism over a certain period after the completion of the sentence. We could however imagine alternative ways of establishing how effective a sentence has been. Victim satisfaction could be one of the criteria. A good sentence might be one that restores a victim's faith in the criminal justice system or in society at large. Another criterion could be of a procedural nature: perhaps the way in which the criminal justice system looked at all the evidence concerning the offence and the offender, and takes the view of all parties into account is of significance. These aspects, of evaluations of sentencing, usually receive less consideration than others.

There is a wealth of research on 'what works' in sentencing. All over the world ideas have been generated, varying from offender–victim mediation, boot camps, day fines, short sharp shock sentences, and so on. These ideas are often implemented in pilot schemes and evaluated after a certain period of operation. Under the assumption that what works in Quebec might just prove to be equally effective in say, Bavaria, there seems to be a certain hunger for information on effective ways of dealing with offenders. Unfortunately, it is usually far from easy simply to take an idea out of the context where it originated, implement it somewhere else and assume that it will work. Sentences are very much context-dependent.

To illustrate the importance of context, when I visited a prison in Mauritius I was told about the favourable local prison conditions. The evidence provided was that most inmates gained weight during their stay inside, and came out heavier than when they entered prison. The implication was clearly that prison took better care of those inside than they might have been able to manage themselves in the outside world. It reminds us that sentences have to be set against the conditions that those prisoners would find themselves in outside of prison. A strict prison regime in a welfare state may well feel harsher to inmates than basic prison conditions in a country that suffers from poverty.

In this chapter I shall discuss, to begin with, prisons. Second, the death penalty, perhaps the most contentious of modern forms of punishment will, be dealt with; and finally I shall look at studies of the effectiveness of sentencing and other forms of offender treatment in terms of recidivism.

Prisons and their comparative histories

Much of the earliest form of state-imposed social control was by means of ordering financial compensation. This practice, prevalent in the Middle Ages, involved offenders being ordered to pay a certain amount of money to the victim or his/her family. The motivation behind this was the need to prevent feuds. The amount of money to be paid depended on the status and position of both offender and victim. The rape of a high-status woman would require more compensation than the same offence against a victim of lower status. Similarly, a high-status offender would have to pay more toward the victim or his/her family than a wrongdoer of lower status. These levels of compensation would normally be set by rulers. Such financial penalties appeared to have been preferred over corporal punishment in the early Middle Ages and were clearly aimed at preventing future offences (Barrett and Harrison, 1999).

Despite its relatively late appearance on the sentencing scene, imprisonment is certainly popular in the world today. The advantages of imprisonment are obvious. Offenders are taken out of circulation, so that they will not commit crimes against the public while in prison. Victims will not have to worry about the offender for the duration of his/her stay in prison. Imprisonment additionally gives the state the chance of working with the offender. A major disadvantage is the cost of imprisonment. And as we will discuss later, there are serious doubts as to whether most offenders actually have been 'bettered' when they come out as compared to when they entered the prison system.

There is lively historical debate as to the birth of prisons (Hirsch, 1992). Penal historians have identified the processes to help us understand the popularity of imprisonment as a major form of punishment in the world today. Rothman (1990) analysed the rise of imprisonment in the US during the presidency of Andrew Jackson in the 1820s and 1830s. Rothman argued that at that time crime and social deprivation began to be viewed as social problems. Before then, crime was more likely to be regarded in terms of individual wickedness, liable to receive corporal, or in the most serious cases capital, punishment. Prisons or asylums were meant to take the offender out of society with its ample opportunity for crime and other temptations. In prison inmates would be subjected to order, perform labour and get accustomed to a strictly regimented lifestyle, with plenty of time to reflect on the error of their ways. During these Jacksonian years, imprisonment was no longer small-scale and haphazard but became part of a grand vision of social control, in which rehabilitation was the central focus (Rothman, 1990).

Foucault (1979), on the other hand, looked at the rise of the penitentiary in France before the French Revolution of 1789. In France, the king used to exercise corporal punishment in order to demonstrate and maintain his power over his citizens. Punishment was therefore highly public, so as to set an example. Following public disgust over its brutality and an increased sense of repression felt by the citizenry, punishment became further removed from the public eye. Punishment shifted from public places, such as markets, to the more private surroundings of prisons. Thus, Foucault argued, the birth of the prison in France had nothing to do with any Jacksonian sense of enlightenment. Arguably, the introduction of French prisons was not to punish less but to punish better.

Other commentators, such as Garland, have emphasised the strong relation between economic cycles and rates of imprisonment. During economic cycles, in which labour is abundantly available, convicted criminals are more likely to be imprisoned than when this is not the case (Garland, 1990). A further economic reason for the perpetuation of high levels of imprisonment relates to the fact that crime control has become a powerful industry, with huge employment rates, turnovers and lobby power (Christie, 1994). Simply for that reason alone, mass imprisonment is very likely to be with us for a long time to come.

Prisoner numbers

Worldwide there are over 8.5 million people imprisoned (Walmsley, 2002). Most of them are concentrated in a few countries with large populations and comparatively high prison rates. In particular, both the US and the Russian Federation score high, both in absolute and relative numbers of prisoners. The number of prisoners in a jurisdiction is normally expressed as the total number of people in prison divided by the total population in that jurisdiction. Its exact measure is usually the number of detainees per 100,000 of the population. It is called the prison ratio or prison rate.

It must be kept in mind that not everyone who is, in one way or another, kept by the state is in prison. People may be held in police cells, or in other jails or remand institutions. People may also be kept in secure hospitals or mental institutions. Alternatively people may be serving their sentence in a boot camp or Borstal, while people under house arrest are not technically imprisoned but still deprived of their liberty. The way in which the prison rate is calculated will depend on judgements about whether to include certain groups of people who are, in one way or another, physically constrained by the state.

Various researchers have established the prison rate for many countries and jurisdictions. Very elaborate is the one compiled by Walmsley (2002). Based on his data the worldwide top ten is as below, in Table 7.1:

Table 7.1 The ten countries with the highest prison rates

Rank	Country	Prison rate per 100,000 population
1.	United States	700
2.	Russia	665
3.	UK Cayman Islands	600
4.	Belarus	555
5.	US Virgin Islands	550
6.	Kazakhstan	520
7.	Turkmenistan	490
8.	Bahamas	480
9.	Belize	460
10.	Bermuda	445

Source: Walmsley, 2002.

In the first instance it might be difficult to make sense of these figures. The top three consists of countries as different from each other as is perhaps imaginable. Closer inspection reveals that apart from Russia three other former Soviet republics, Belarus, Kazakhstan and Turkmenistan, make an appearance in the top ten. That evidences the fact that in the former Soviet Union high prison rates used to be the norm. The Baltic states, also formerly part of the Soviet Union, still have rather high prison rates as well: 330 for Estonia, 355 for Latvia and 240 for Lithuania. Their shared Soviet legacy helps us make sense of these figures.

Throughout the world, we can identify regions where prison rates are relatively high or low. In Southern Africa prison rates tend to be high. South Africa's prison rate is 410; that of neighbouring Namibia 260. In Western Africa prison rates are much lower. Ghana's prison rate is 50, whereas that of Senegal is only slightly higher, with 55 prisoners per 100,000 of the population. That is lower than most European countries. Many of the world's lowest prison rates can be found in Asia. The exceptions are Singapore and the former Soviet states in central Asia, and Mongolia (with 265) and Thailand (with 220) are also comparatively high.

The Caribbean is another area with high prison rates. But, as many of the jurisdictions here are very small the actual number of prisoners is therefore quite small too. In Grenada, for instance there were 327 people incarcerated according to Walmsley, who based this particular figure on a UN survey. That translates into a prison rate of 330, as Grenada has a population of slightly less than 100,000 people. Similarly, the UK Cayman Islands' high position on the worldwide prison rate league table is based on only 220 prisoners. By contrast, the US' figure is based on 1.9 million people imprisoned, which is over 50 times the UK Cayman Islands' total population.

As far as the UK is concerned, England and Wales is listed as 125, Scotland 120, Northern Ireland 50, Guernsey 115, Jersey 150 and the Isle of Man 85. The table below lists the prison rates for the 15 countries currently in the European Union.

Table 7.2 Prison rates for the 15 European Union countries, in descending order

Country	Prison rate per 100,000 population
Portugal	130
United Kingdom	125
Spain	115
Germany	95
Luxembourg	90
Austria	85
Belgium	85
Netherlands	85
France	80
Ireland	80
Greece	80
Sweden	65
Denmark	60
Norway	60
Finland	55

Source: Walmsley (2002).

Comparing prison rates

Factors influencing prison rates are many. The extent of crime is the first one to mention, although comparative research has shown that the assumption that prison rates simply follow crime rates is erroneous. In the US for instance, crime rates have gone down consistently since 1990, but the prison population remains huge and continues to grow. In explaining prison rates, factors such as prison capacity, public opinion, legislation, attitudes among the judiciary, policing and prosecution policies and strategies, and developments in forensic science need to be taken into account, as do alternatives to prison and the availability of the death penalty.

An illustration of the fact that crime levels have little to do with prison rates is provided in a focused comparison by Downes (1988). He compared prison rates after World War II in the Netherlands to those in England and Wales. Both countries saw a steady increase in crime levels between World War II and the 1970s. In England and Wales, the prison rate rose along with it, but in the Netherlands a period of lowering of prisoner numbers, or *decarceration*, occurred. In 1950, the prison rate in the Netherlands was actually higher than that of England and Wales: 82 per 100,000 versus 64 per 100,000 inhabitants in England and Wales. By 1957 the rates of imprisonment had converged, and from then onwards the numbers of prisoners became more and more divergent. In real numbers England and Wales experienced a doubling of their prisoners by 1975. In contrast, the Netherlands had about half as many people incarcerated by 1975 as 25 years previously.

These opposing trends in prison rates cannot be attributed to levels of crime, as these were quite similar, albeit slightly lower in the Netherlands. Downes discussed a number of other reasons as possible explanations. The first factor was the differing limits of penal capacity. Unlike in England and Wales, one prisoner per cell has, for a long time, been standard practice in the Netherlands. That, in practice, means that a prison is literally full when each cell is occupied. The Dutch prison system can therefore not flexibly accommodate more prisoners than there are prison cells. To alleviate the burden on prisons, various policies were introduced to somehow try to match the number of available spaces with the number of prisoners sentenced to fill these cells. This applied equally to remand prison spaces as it did to prisons. As a result, in the 1980s prisoners sometimes had to wait to serve their sentences until a prison cell became available. Similarly, a large number of suspects to be detained in pre-trial custody were simply sent home because of a lack of available cells.

Second, Downes described a culture of tolerance in Dutch society and within the judiciary. This is evident in lower maximum penalties set by law for many offences, and a tendency among the judiciary to sentence more leniently. Long prison sentences were much less frequently imposed, and life sentences were, and still are, very rare indeed.

A third factor is the so-called politics of accommodation. Accommodation stands for a non-confrontational style of political life, which seeks consensus and compromise rather than confrontation and radical shifts. The politics of accommodation was, in the Netherlands, underpinned by a social stratification, that is called pillarisation. This is described by Downes as follows:

> Catholics, Calvinists, secular liberals and secular radicals each form their own constituency, to which their elites are responsive, and which therefore possess by proxy a stake in the system. The major price, so to speak, for such an arrangement is that the elites, both in and outside government and Parliament, are relatively insulated from criticism, unless in exceptional circumstances. (Downes 1988: 74)

The level of organisation was remarkable but has largely vanished today. There were separate schools, radio stations, clubs and social structures for members of each pillar. Nevertheless, this segregation never led to substantial social exclusion, as all pillars were represented in parliament and had a reasonable chance of getting into government. Because of a system of proportional representation in parliament, and without any of these pillars ever getting an outright majority, governments were, and are, invariably two- or three-party coalitions. While that may cause inertia in decision-making, it has also served as a further safeguard against radical or populist changes in penal policy.

Meanwhile the criminal justice system operated, and to an extent still does operate, its own version of accommodatory politics. Johnson and Heijder observed that:

> ... the setting of criminal justice policy operates largely detached from public monitoring ... a small professional elite, with a fringe of complementary groups, dominates practice in the field of criminal justice. Shared training, position, norms and values provide an effective boundary-maintaining system shielding the operations of criminal justice from public opinion. (Johnson and Heijder, 1983: 10)

Those shared norms and values certainly favoured decarceration in this period. Hulsman *et al.* (1978) argued that the low prison rate was in part a consequence of favourable economic developments, with corresponding high levels of employment, social security and health care, which all helped to produce a highly inclusive and cohesive society.

These arguments undoubtedly all carry weight. Prison rates are a result of various forces at work, including political discourse and attitudes and practices within the criminal justice system. To assume that prison rates are an inevitable response to, and therefore a straightforward function of, crime rates is simply incorrect.

A final remark must be made about the longevity of these states of affairs. While prison rates in the Netherlands in the 1970s were sensationally low, that simply is no longer the case. The Netherlands now takes a middle position in the European prison-rate league table, after an unprecedented increase in prison capacity and a resulting increase in the number of prisoners (see Pakes, 2000a).

In contrast, a European country in which prison rates have consistently gone down until, at least, 1999 is Finland. Twenty-five years ago Finland had one of the highest detention ratios in Western Europe; but today it has one of the lowest, with 55 per 100,000 (Walmsley, 2002). We saw in Chapter 4 that pre-trial custody rates were low in Finland as well, and, most importantly, consistently decreasing. That decrease is attributed to the political desire to achieve it. Attitudes among policy makers and sentencers seem to be the key factor in securing lowering rates of incarceration (Törnudd, 1993; Joutsen et al., 2001).

The effectiveness of imprisonment as a device for rehabilitation depends on the circumstances inside the prisons. The Finnish prison system is also, in that regard, a positive exception to the rule in most countries. Prisoners do not tend to wear uniforms, and the uniforms worn by prison workers are distinctly non-militaristic. Prison officers are also usually unarmed. Where possible, barbed wires have been replaced by camera surveillance. The aim is for the deprivation of liberty to be the actual punishment, and for the reduction of any further harm, stemming from incarceration, as much as possible. There is an emphasis on rehabilitative work, most prominently in dealing with problems of addiction. Most prisoners in Finnish prisons do paid work, and about half pursue some kind of education. Education certificates are phrased so as to hide the fact that they were obtained in prison. About 5 per cent of prisoners even seek education at university level. Apart from these provisions, the system also offers care and leisure activities in the form of sports, crafts, discussion groups as well as religious ceremonies (Criminal Sanctions Agency, 2003).

This state of affairs stands in stark contrast to the life inside in many American prisons. Here the emphasis has shifted away from rehabilitation. The focus instead has become the managing of groups of people seen to represent a risk. Mass incarceration is often justified by pointing to its role in protecting the public, a situation in which working with the individual offender has come to play second fiddle. Feeley and Simon have called this the New Penology, a discourse in which prison populations are viewed as unruly groups to be controlled, rather than as individuals to be rehabilitated (Feeley and Simon, 1992).

Box 7.1 The use of imprisonment in Nigeria

Below, in table 7.3, are official data from the Nigerian Police Force Annual Reports. They are from 1987, and reported in Ebbe (2000b). One can see that across the board the number of prosecutions is about half the number of arrests. Three additional matters are worthy of discussion. Firstly, it can be noted that relatively few people are prosecuted for fraud. Ebbe notes the possibility that politicians and corporate executives sometimes successfully attempt to prevent certain prosecutions from occurring. The crime of fraud might be particularly susceptible to this form of corruption.

Table 7.3 Numbers of arrests, prosecutions, discharges and imprisonments for seven offence types in Nigeria. Percentages of the number of arrests, per offence, in brackets

Crime	Arrested	Prosecuted	Discharged	Imprisoned
Assault	33,019	20,341 (61.6)	9,874 (48.5)	1,316 (6.5)
Stealing/Theft	31,281	14,077 (45.0)	2,163 (15.4)	4,722 (33.5)
Rape	1,116	471 (42.2)	113 (24.0)	358 (76.0)
Armed Robbery	1,012	579 (57.2)	66 (11.4)	125 (21.6)
Murder	716	441 (61.6)	38 (8.6)	147 (33.3)
Manslaughter	618	339 (54.9)	102 (30.1)	237 (69.9)
Fraud	169	60 (35.5)	22 (36.7)	38 (63.3)

Source: Ebbe (2000b).

The second issue to arise from table 7.3 relates to the administration of assault cases. Of the over 33,000 cases where there was an arrest, only 1,316 individuals actually received a prison sentence, and almost half of all prosecutions do not end in a guilty verdict but in a discharge. This imprisonment rate is very low. This is an instance in which the perceived severity of the crime of assault helps explain the sentences imposed. Fighting has traditionally been a relatively accepted form of conflict resolution between friends. Despite the fact that these behaviours were criminalised under British colonial rule, which lasted until 1960, the practice refused to die out. Most of the time such cases do not lead to a prison sentence, as they tend to be reserved for more serious (or perceived as such) cases of assault.

Finally, the reader may observe relatively low incarceration rates for the crimes of murder and armed robbery. That is because 256 murderers (63 per cent of those convicted) received the death penalty for murder. Additionally, 388 armed robbers (75 per cent of those convicted) were sentenced to death (Ebbe, 2000b).

These data show that sentences can be considered sensibly only if you also take into account the sentencing alternatives available to courts. A low rate of incarceration for assault requires an explanation wholly opposite to that for armed robbery. While the former are sent home, the latter are sent to the hangman.

The death penalty

Before discussing the practice of the death penalty one must make a number of distinctions. It is not necessarily clear, for example, what it means for a jurisdiction to 'have' the death penalty. First, it is a fact that not everyone who is sentenced to death will actually be executed. Prisoners on death row may be pardoned or their cases may be re-opened. Their sentences might be changed into custodial ones after appeals or review processes. In the US state of Texas, for example, only about 15 per cent of all death sentences given were actually carried out between 1977 and 1993. In many US states this percentage is lower still (Bedau, 1996). Throughout the US, many prisoners on death row are subjected to the uncertainty of not knowing if, let alone when, their execution might take place.

Another issue relates to the statutory status of the death penalty. Many countries do have the penalty in their law books, but reserve it only for special circumstances, such as for particular crimes in times of war. These countries are usually still called *abolitionist*. Other countries have the death penalty as a sentence available to courts but have a policy in place to prevent its imposition. Such countries are called *abolitionist in practice*. Then, there are states in which the death penalty may be imposed, but where it is decided that, temporarily, no executions will take place. Such a state of affairs is called a *moratorium*. Finally, there are *retentionist* countries. In these countries there is a real chance of convicts dying for their crimes (Hood, 1996). However, in the case of certain Caribbean countries the picture is more complex still. While the local laws do contain the death penalty, it is their highest appeal court, the Privy Council in London, that has the ability to block its usage. This state of affairs is discussed in Box 7.2.

Arguably, the strongest indicator of a commitment to abolition principles is when states have explicitly dismissed the death penalty in their constitutions. Constitutions tend to be very robust pieces of legislation, which are difficult to change. When a country's constitution explicitly outlaws the death penalty, that serves as a safeguard against its reintroduction at any point in the future.

Abolitionist and retentionist countries

Following are lists of countries in the four categories: abolitionist for all crimes, abolitionist for ordinary crimes only, abolitionist in practice; and retentionist. The lists (sourced from Amnesty International, updated 23 November 2000) include a few territories whose laws on the death penalty differ significantly from those of other countries within the same group. First to follow is the list of countries whose laws do not provide for the death penalty for any crime.

Andorra, Angola, Australia, Austria, Azerbaijan, Belgium, Bulgaria, Cambodia, Canada, Cape Verde, Colombia, Costa Rica, Côte D'Ivoire, Croatia, Czech Republic, Denmark, Djibouti, Dominican Republic, East Timor, Ecuador, Estonia, Finland, France, Georgia, Germany, Greece, Guinea-Bissau, Haiti, Honduras, Hungary, Iceland, Ireland, Italy, Kiribati, Liechtenstein, Lithuania, Luxembourg, Macedonia (Former Yugoslav Republic), Malta, Marshall Islands, Mauritius, Micronesia (Federated States), Moldova, Monaco, Mozambique, Namibia, Nepal, Netherlands, New Zealand, Nicaragua, Norway, Palau, Panama, Paraguay, Poland, Portugal, Romania, San Marino, São Tomé and Principe, Seychelles, Slovak Republic, Slovenia, Solomon Islands, South Africa, Spain, Sweden, Switzerland, Turkmenistan, Tuvalu, Ukraine, UK, Uruguay, Vanuatu, Vatican City State, and Venezuela.

The following list comprises countries whose laws provide for the death penalty only for exceptional crimes, such as crimes under military law or crimes committed in exceptional circumstances.

Albania, Argentina, Bolivia, Bosnia-Herzegovina, Brazil, Cook Islands, Cyprus, El Salvador, Fiji, Israel, Latvia, Mexico, and Peru.

The countries listed next retain the death penalty for ordinary crimes such as murder, but can be considered abolitionist in practice because they have not executed anyone during the past 10 years and are believed to have a policy, or established practice, of not carrying out executions. The list also includes countries that have made an international commitment not to use the death penalty.

Bhutan, Brunei Darussalam, Burkina Faso, Central African Republic, Congo (Republic), Gambia, Grenada, Madagascar, Maldives, Mali, Nauru, Niger, Papua New Guinea, Samoa, Senegal, Sri Lanka, Surinam, Togo, Tonga, and Turkey.

The final list consists of countries that retain the death penalty for ordinary crimes.

Afghanistan, Algeria, Antigua and Barbuda, Armenia, Bahamas, Bahrain, Bangladesh, Barbados, Belarus, Belize, Benin, Botswana, Burundi, Cameroon, Chad, Chile, China, Comoros, Congo

(Democratic Republic), Cuba, Dominica, Egypt, Equatorial Guinea, Eritrea, Ethiopia, Gabon, Ghana, Guatemala, Guinea, Guyana, India, Indonesia, Iran, Iraq, Jamaica, Japan, Jordan, Kazakhstan, Kenya, Kuwait, Kyrgyzstan, Laos, Lebanon, Lesotho, Liberia, Libya, Malawi, Malaysia, Mauritania, Mongolia, Morocco, Myanmar (Burma), Nigeria, North Korea, Oman, Pakistan, Palestinian Authority, Philippines, Qatar, Russian Federation, Rwanda, Saint Christopher and Nevis, Saint Lucia, Saint Vincent and Grenadines, Saudi Arabia, Sierra Leone, Singapore, Somalia, South Korea, Sudan, Swaziland, Syria, Taiwan, Tajikistan, Tanzania, Thailand, Trinidad and Tobago, Tunisia, Uganda, United Arab Emirates, US, Uzbekistan, Vietnam, Yemen, Yugoslavia (Federal Republic), Zambia, and Zimbabwe.

Amnesty International recorded about 1,600 official executions in 1998. This number was about twice as high in 1981 (Amnesty International, 2001). There is, if one takes a historical perspective, a slow but definite decline in its use, so that conceivably the world might be getting nearer to its total abolition. In 1899 only three countries had abandoned the death penalty. These were Costa Rica, San Marino and Venezuela. The US state of Michigan has been quoted as the first jurisdiction to formally abolish the death penalty, which it did as early as 1847 (Bedau, 1996). By 1948 the number of abolitionist countries had risen to eight, and to nineteen by 1978. In 1998, there were 67 countries without the death penalty.

The death penalty in the US

The Western country where the death penalty is most widely accepted and used is the USA. The death sentence can be imposed for certain federal crimes, and most, but not all, states have the death penalty on their books as well. The extent to which the death penalty is imposed in these states varies widely.

The death penalty has had a checkered history in the second half of the twentieth century. It was not in use during a period in which the Supreme Court had ruled against it, on the grounds that it considered the protracted death-penalty procedure cruel and unusual punishment. This process, which tends to take years, inevitably induces great uncertainty for convicts regarding the 'if and when' of their execution. This moratorium lasted from the late 1960s until 1977. Since then, the number of executions has been steadily on the rise.

In the previous chapter I explained how juries in the US decide on capital punishment. In this chapter I shall consider the actual practice.

Box 7.2 Executions in Trinidad and Tobago

There is a global trend towards the abolition of the death penalty. However, there are a number of trend-breakers. One of these is the Caribbean country of Trinidad and Tobago. A dramatic increase in violent crime relating to drugs plagued the country in the late 1990s. This prompted public opinion to favour strongly the reintroduction of capital punishment, in the hope that it would deter criminals of international notoriety from using the country as a safe haven. In 1999 those in favour of capital punishment got their way.

Dole Chadee (more colloquially known as the notorious Cocaine Chadee), Joey Ramiah, Ramkalawan Singh, Joel Ramsingh, Russell Sankerali, Bhadwandeen Singh, Clive Thomas, Robin Gopaul and Stephen Eversley were hanged on 4, 5 and 7 June 1999 (Amnesty International, 1999). Dole Chadee was seen as the ringleader of a gang that dealt in large quantities of drugs, and was widely thought to be responsible for a sudden rise in violent crime on Trinidad.

These executions were the first in Trinidad and Tobago for five years. The actual implementation of the death sentences hinged on a legal development that took place far away from the Caribbean. Trinidad and Tobago's highest court of law is the UK's Privy Council. The islands are not alone in this, as the Privy Council serves as the highest court of appeal for several British or former British colonies and territories, varying from the Cayman Isles to Jersey. The case of the five went on appeal to the Privy Council. A chamber of five Law Lords upheld their verdicts as well as the sentences, as it felt that Trinidad and Tobago should be able to exercise its constitutional right to sentence offenders to capital punishment. The Privy Council had, however, ruled against the death penalty in the past because of its cruelty, which is the accepted position across Europe.

Public opinion in Trinidad and Tobago seems to be strongly in favour of the death penalty. The British newspaper *The Independent* reported that 80 per cent of the population has been consistently in support of the capital punishment. Public opinion also seems to be that the influence of the Privy Council over such matters is an out-of-date colonial leftover (*The Independent*, 5 June 1999). That view, and the recent Privy Council ruling, is very bad news indeed for the 100 or so prisoners on death row (at the time of writing) in Trinidad and Tobago.

Table 7.4 shows the total number of US executions since 1977. The second column shows the number of people on death row waiting to be executed; the third column whether child offenders can be eligible for the death penalty and how many have been executed. The final column indicates the number of people sentenced to death but subsequently exonerated.

Table 7.4 The practice of the death penalty in the US

State	Executions 1977–99	Death row at 1/1/2000	Child offenders executed[1]	Exonerated 1973–99
Alabama	19	185	12	2
Arizona	19	121	3	4
Arkansas	21	40	1	
California	7	561	n/a	3
Colorado	0	5	n/a	
Connecticut	0	7	n/a	
Delaware	10	18	0	
Florida	44	389	4	19
Georgia	22	134	3	6
Idaho	1	21	0	
Illinois	12	160	n/a	13
Indiana	7	43	0	2
Kansas	0	3	n/a	
Kentucky	2	39	2	
Louisiana	25	87	3	3
Maryland	3	17	n/a	1
Mississippi	4	63	5	
Missouri	41	83	2	2
Montana	2	6	n/a	
Nebraska	3	9	n/a	
Nevada	8	89	2	
New Hampshire	0	0	0	
New Jersey	0	0	n/a	
New Mexico	0	0	n/a	4
New York	0	0	n/a	
North Carolina	15	224	1	3
Ohio	1	199	n/a	2
Oklahoma	19	149	1	7
Oregon	2	27	n/a	
Pennsylvania	3	232	3	2
South Carolina	24	67	4	3
South Dakota	0	3	0	0
Tennessee	0	101	n/a	
Texas	199	462	26	7
Utah	6	11	0	
Virginia	73	31	2	2
Washington	3	17	n/a	1
Wyoming	1	0	0	
US Government	0	21	n/a	
US Military	0	7	n/a	
TOTALS	598	3,659[2]	74	86[3]

There are substantial differences among the various US states with regard to the death penalty, as there are with regard to many other aspects of criminal justice. First or all, we must remember that certain states do not have the punishment on the books at all. Abolitionist states are in a minority, as there are currently only twelve (and the District of Columbia). They are Alaska, Hawaii, Iowa, Maine, Massachusetts, Michigan, Minnesota, North Dakota, Rhode Island, Vermont, West Virginia, and Wisconsin. Apart from Hawaii, they are all northern states. In some of these states efforts have been made to reintroduce the death penalty, but they have not been successful so far.

The way in which executions take place also varies between states. Many authorise death by lethal injection, whereas electrocution by means of the so-called electric chair is used in others. Montana, New Hampshire and Washington allow for the possibility of hanging. Idaho and Utah retain the possibility of using a firing squad to carry out executions but also use lethal injections (Bedau, 1996).

The minimum age of persons eligible for capital punishment is subject to similar variation. In 2000, 15 states had legislation in place to prevent juveniles from being eligible for the death penalty. Where specified, the threshold is often 18 years of age, as is the case in, for instance, the states of California, Ohio and Tennessee. Sixteen states have a lower minimum age. These include Georgia and Texas, where the age is 17 years, Mississippi and Oklahoma, where it is 16 years of age, while Arkansas is reported to have a statutory 14 years of age as the minimum age eligible for capital punishment (Bedau, 1996).

The final column of Table 7.4 yields disturbing results. In total, 87 people during this period were sentenced to death who, it later transpired, did not commit the crime they were accused of. That is a worrying number of miscarriages of justice, with potentially fatal consequences. Apart from these miscarriages of justice, a further persistent point of critique is an alleged bias in its application. It has long

---

Notes to table 7.4:

[1] Child offenders are defined as those under the age of 18 at time of crime (n/a = death penalty not applicable for this age group).

[2] The number of individuals under sentence of death is actually 3,652, as the total of 3,659 includes seven prisoners sentenced to death in more than one state.

[3] The total number of people sentenced to death and later exonerated is 87 (one man was sentenced to death in Massachusetts in 1971 under earlier death penalty laws, and released in 1982).

Sources: Criminal Justice Project of the NAACP Legal Defense and Educational Fund, New York; Death Penalty Information Center, Washington, D.C.; Amnesty International, International Secretariat, London, UK.

been held that Black defendants are more likely to receive the death penalty than White defendants. More specifically, and more worryingly, there is evidence that Black defendants convicted of a crime against a White victim are statistically most likely to be sentenced to death. Almost 43 per cent of prisoners on death row are Black. Of all those executed between 1977 and 1999 over 35 per cent were black. This means that Black/African American prisoners are overrepresented in both these statistics, as the proportion of African Americans in the general population is only about twelve per cent (Amnesty International, 1999). Additionally, it has been shown that Whites are the victims in over 82 per cent of death-penalty crimes. Overall, however, only 50 per cent of all murder victims are White. These aggregate data seem to validate the view that Black offenders get sentenced to death particularly for crimes against Whites. Amnesty International reports many a case where it is argued that racial issues have played a crucial role in death-penalty decisions (Amnesty International, 1999).

The data on miscarriages, as well as the data on race, provide strong ammunition for the anti-death penalty lobby (see also Bedau and Ratelet, 1987). Further evidence against it is derived from empirical studies, which demonstrate a lack of a general deterrent effect. Crime figures from abolitionist countries fail to show that abolition has harmful effects with regard to crime rates. In Canada, for example, the homicide rate per 100,000 population fell from a peak of 3.09 in 1975, the year before the abolition of the death penalty for murder, to 2.41 in 1980, and since then it has remained relatively stable. In 1993, 17 years after abolition, the homicide rate was 2.19 per 100,000 population, 27 per cent lower than in 1975 (Hood, 1996).

Reviewing the evidence on the relation between changes in the use of the death penalty and crime rates, a study prepared for the UN in 1988, and updated in 1996, stated that: 'the fact that all the evidence continues to point in the same direction is persuasive *a priori* evidence that countries need not fear sudden and serious changes in the curve of crime if they reduce their reliance upon the death penalty' (Hood, 1996: 187).

Yet, despite the arguments that the deth penalty has failed to prove to be effective from a general deterrent perspective, in some societies the individual deterrent element ('we at least make sure that this person will not re-offend') and/or the retributive element ('when someone commits a certain type of crime, they lose their right to live') might be arguments still powerful enough to retain it.

How the death penalty (just about) disappeared from Europe

In Europe the death penalty is becoming a thing of the past. Many Western European countries stopped carrying out executions shortly after World War II. Striking the death penalty off the books became more of a matter of urgency after 1985, when the 6th Protocol to the European Convention of Human Rights was drafted. To understand the significance of that protocol, we need to examine the body that issued it, the intergovernmental organisation called the Council of Europe. The Council of Europe should not be confused with the European Union, as the two organisations are quite distinct. The 15 European Union states, however, are all members of the Council of Europe. (We will discuss the European Union in the next chapter.)

The Council of Europe (see www.coe.int) was created shortly after World War II, in the aftermath of Winston Churchill's speech in which he advocated a United States of Europe. Today, any European state can become a member of the Council of Europe provided it accepts the principle of the rule of law and guarantees human rights and fundamental freedoms to everyone under its jurisdiction. In total, 45 European states are currently members, with Belarus as a notable exception. Armenia, Bosnia-Herzegovina, and Serbia and Montenegro have recently joined. The Committee of Ministers is the Council of Europe's main decision-making body. It comprises the foreign affairs ministers of all the member states, or their permanent diplomatic representatives. Its headquarters is in the *Palais de l'Europe* in Strasbourg, France. The Council of Europe established its mission as promoting the ideals of a democratic society and protecting the rights and freedoms of individuals from arbitrary interference by a state and/or its officials.

The European Convention on Human Rights is an agreement between a number of countries with the status of international law. The original members of the Convention, of which the UK was one, wrote and signed this Convention to guarantee a number of fundamental human rights. The Convention was ratified in 1951 and it sought to set standards for the behaviour of states and the parameters of individuals' rights. Countries who sign and ratify such a document make a pledge to abide by it. Since 1951 the Convention has been added to by means of protocols.

Since 1 March 1985, the 6th Protocol to the European Convention of Human Rights and Fundamental Freedoms established the abolition of the death penalty by legal obligation under international law. With the exception of Turkey, all of the member-states of the Council of Europe have now signed this Protocol. Russia is the only country that is yet to ratify it. The 6th Protocol is nine articles long, but Article 1 is the one that matters most. It reads: 'The death penalty shall be abolished. No one shall be condemned to such penalty or executed.' In Article 2 the possibility for the death penalty in times of war is acknowledged:

A State may make provision in its law for the death penalty in respect of acts committed in time of war or of imminent threat of war; such penalty shall be applied only in the instances laid down in the law and in accordance with its provisions. The State shall communicate to the Secretary General of the Council of Europe the relevant provisions of that law.

In 2002, however, a further protocol on the death penalty was drafted. This 13th Protocol effectively seeks to ban Article 2 from the 6th Protocol. Although this protocol has yet to come into force, it shows the pan-European intention of outlawing the death penalty under any circumstances.

What works?

The phrase 'nothing works' has been a cliché in criminal justice for quite some time. It has characterised practitioners', policy makers' and academic sentiments about the supposed situation in which whatever you did with or to offenders, it never seemed to lead to a substantial reduction in re-offending rates (Martinson, 1974). While there are doubts whether the initial research actually justified the emergence of the 'nothing works' maxim (McGuire and Priestley 1995) accumulated research since 1985 has disproved this 'nothing works' school of thought.

McGuire and Priestley's results of comparative research are certainly worth reporting here. While they conclude that a 'nothing works' position can no longer be maintained, there certainly are treatments that simply do not achieve lower rates of re-offending. 'Treatment' in this context is a broad term. It does not, strictly, refer to psychological or social-work interventions, but to anything that is purposefully done with the aim of changing offenders' future behaviour.

Any treatment can be said to be effective if there is evidence that a group of convicted criminals re-offend less than one would expect after having received that treatment. That usually means that this group is compared with a control group of comparable individuals who did not receive the same treatment.

McGuire and Priestley concluded that psychotherapy does not seem to be very effective. While doubtless very helpful in certain contexts, there is little evidence that psychotherapy helps to reduce re-offending. A meta-analysis showed a net destructive effect of imprisonment: incarceration seems to increase the rate of re-offending rather than decrease it, overall. It appears that specific deterrence, making sure that an offender is punished to stop this particular offender from re-offending, is an aim not generally served by imprisonment (McGuire and

Priestley, 1995). A similar argument applies to general deterrence. McGuire and Priestley noted that:

> In general, while the possibility that a small number of individuals are deterred by imprisonment cannot be ruled out, this proposition cannot be tested directly, as other factors may have contributed to their desistance from crime. There is certainly little evidence that the deterrent effect of impact of the prison is substantial or even satisfactory. (McGuire and Priestley, 1995: 11)

This finding may be counterintuitive. The common-sense idea that prison is an unpleasant consequence of the commission of crime seems to make its deterrent effect inevitable. However, the following factors disturb this link between criminal behaviour and the consequence of imprisonment.

For punishment to be effective, it needs to meet the following criteria. In the first place, punishment should be inevitable: when the undesirable behaviour is displayed, it should always receive punishment. It also should be immediate, and not, as happens in criminal justice, be administered months after the fact. Punishment should also be sufficiently severe. Additionally, deterrence of unwanted behaviour works best when there are clear alternatives available to the offender. That may often not be the case, and prison is likely to further reduce an offender's chances in life after it has been served. Finally, punishment should be comprehensible to the offender. While no doubt most offenders will grasp that a sentence is given for a crime committed, they are likely to feel singled out ('many others do what I did and get away with it'). Alternatively, they may feel that their crime has been singled out ('I've committed dozens of burglaries, and was just unlucky with the one that I got caught for'). In short, criminal justice systems cannot succeed in meeting these conditions. Official punishment is therefore, in these terms, not very likely to succeed in reducing recidivism.

To move on to the good news, it is argued that some interventions do work, at least to some extent. Lipsey (1992, 1995) reported a 10-per-cent reduction in re-offending for juvenile delinquents based on a meta-analysis of some 400 studies into the treatment of juvenile offenders. When looking at re-offending over a six-month period, the average re-offending rate for delinquents not receiving any treatment was 50 per cent: one in two delinquents had re-offended within six months. This figure came down to 45 per cent because of treatment, which is a net gain of 10 per cent across the board.

While 10 per cent may not sound that impressive, it certainly is statistically significant, and would decrease crime by an amount that most Western governments would immediately sign up for. Meanwhile, it was found that alongside this reduction in offending these juveniles also improved in other measures, such as academic performance and interpersonal adjustment. It must, however, be borne in mind that not every type of treatment works equally well and not every offender is equally susceptible to treatment. With regard to type and modality of treatment, it is difficult to do justice to Lipsey's review of 400 studies in just a few sentences. However, he found that finding employment for an offender to be very successful indeed. Also, behavioural and skill-oriented programmes come out favourably. Less successful is counselling. Whether it is family counselling, group counselling or individual counselling, the results tend to be only marginally successful.

The field has moved away from the pessimism embodied in the 'nothing works' phrase. Certain treatments actually do seem to work, to an extent. The next step is the formulation of guidelines to which treatment programmes should adhere, in order to enhance their chances of being successful. For this, I quote Lipsey (1995):

The best general practical advice for treatment sponsors that can be derived from the results of this meta-analysis is as follows:

- Focus treatment around behavioural, training or skills issues appropriate to the clientele using concrete, structured approaches as much as possible. Assemble treatment in appropriate multi-modal packages, possibly including psychologically oriented elements in the package.

- Monitor, supervise and implement the treatment well. Have a treatment plan and maintain fidelity to that plan in the service delivery so that the intended treatment is actually delivered to each intended client.

- Provide a sufficient amount of service, preferably 100 or more total contact hours, delivered at two or more contacts per week over a period of 26 weeks or more. (Lipsey, 1995: 77–78)

This advice reflects the new trend in the academic study of dealing with offenders. It has moved away from sentencing as a means of effectively doing this. It also talks less about what should be done, and more about how programmes should be formulated and implemented. It is phrased in terms of approaches, implementation and service, which shows that the question is no longer whether prisons, the death penalty or fines work, but how should programmes be devised so as to enhance their chances of making a real difference on recidivism rates.

Conclusion

We often learn about sentencing abroad by means of media reports on persons sentenced by foreign courts. It is, however, near impossible to base sweeping statements on the level of 'punitivity' in any country on such isolated instances of sentencing. In almost every criminal justice system there is discretion available for those who do the sentencing. It is therefore certainly possible that particular individuals are being sentenced much more severely, or more leniently, than might generally be expected. It is therefore important to bear in mind that any isolated verdict is not necessarily a reflection of general practice.

In the Netherlands, it has occasionally happened that murder sentences have been punished rather minimally: when medical doctors were found to slightly overstep the guidelines laid down for legally committing euthanasia, they ran the risk of being charged with murder. If such cases led to a conviction, they would not usually lead to imprisonment. However, any assumption on the basis of this that the Dutch do not take murder very seriously is far from the truth. One nominal sentence for what technically constitutes murder does not necessarily imply a careless attitude towards human life.

Sentencing must, therefore, be viewed in the wider societal context, in which public discourse, fear of crime, perceived seriousness of offences, and agreed severity of punishment combine to give shape to sentencing practices. These practices do vary significantly across countries, not only in actual practice but also with regard to the philosophies that underlie these practices. I have discussed these orientations in terms of the fairness and the effectiveness of sentences.

The first orientation is the one that most of this chapter has focused on: that of fairness. Human rights legislation gives us a handle on discussing these matters. One can see that, historically, the death penalty is slowly but surely, though not quite everywhere, in decline, most particularly because of its perceived cruelty. But, as we have seen, definitions of cruelty have changed over time. The point remains that cruelty is, to an extent, a culturally defined concept.

The second issue is that of effectiveness of sentences. Although it is fair to say that criminal justice has moved beyond the 'nothing works' catchphrase, this is another area where clear answers are not easy to obtain. The trend seems to be that it is impossible in terms of specific types of offences to predict their effectiveness (usually measured in terms of re-offending rates), but that general guidelines can be put in operation that might ensure that any intervention will have a reasonable chance of being effective.

It is worth repeating that international agreements, such as those set out by the Council of Europe, set standards in criminal justice. Some of these pertain to sentencing, as we saw with regards to the death penalty in Europe. States sign up to such agreements make a pledge to abide by them. In this way, democratic governments are accountable not only to the electorate but also to international bodies. Such agreements help strengthen the position of citizens across countries and are instrumental in setting minimal standards of what treatment citizens deserve to receive from the state.

From a comparative perspective it is perhaps unfortunate that as far as sentencing is concerned, it is focused more on what we should condemn, rather than on what can be learned from other criminal justice systems. In many a country minimal standards of justice are not adhered to. In others, lip service is paid to human-rights legislation, but behind-closed-doors violations of these rights may frequently occur. Amnesty International is a non-governmental organisation that plays an important watchdog role in monitoring and publicising such violations.

I conclude this chapter on the methodological note that the technique of meta-analysis discussed in Chapter 2 is probably at its most effective in the 'what works' arena. The work of Lipsey, which is drawn from empirical studies from all over the world, has yielded convincing results about which types of programmes reduce re-offending and what kind of treatments fail to achieve individual deterrence. That helps us appreciate that comparing findings across countries and cultures are certainly feasible and their results are there to be utilised worldwide.

Chapter 8

International and transnational criminal justice

Before considering the arrangements in place to combat transnational and international crimes, it is important to distinguish between them. *Transnational* crimes are offences the inception and effects of which involve more than one country. Money laundering, drug trafficking, many forms of organised crime and many internet crimes are often transnational in nature. Simply put, transnational crimes occur across countries. In contrast, *international* crimes are by their very nature crimes of a global calibre. International crimes we define as crimes against the peace and security of mankind. Such crimes include genocide, wars of aggression and grave acts of terrorism. When we speak of crimes against humanity as a blanket term we refer to this category.

I shall begin this chapter by looking at transnational offending. When discussing this type of crime it is important to understand the causes and effects of globalisation. Also, the role played by illegal markets in the causation of transnational crimes must be appreciated. As I shall be concerned with two particular forms of transnational offending in the next chapter, I shall here discuss the more general issues. As both terrorism and cyber-crime are particularly topical today they will be discussed in Chapter 9, which deals with new trends in comparative research.

Later in this chapter I shall look at the development of the concept of human rights. In particular, the Universal Declaration of Human Rights and the European Convention for Human Rights will be examined. Both documents inform criminal justice systems around the globe. Subsequently I shall look at past and present war-crimes tribunals and the workings of the European Union as well as the United Nations. Both of the latter are international organisations concerned with protecting human rights, fighting international and transnational crimes, and upholding the rule of law.

Transnational offending and policing

The difficulties faced by law-enforcement bodies when a suspect flees across a national border can be immense. Officers on either side of the border might speak different languages, and might be embedded in rather different organisational and hierarchical structures. Who is to say that when making an arrest is the priority of the chasing officers this will be also be the case for their colleagues across the border? It is even conceivable that the crime for which the suspect is being chased is only a minor misdemeanour in the neighbouring country, or perhaps not even a crime at all. In short, in the absence of any pre-emptive agreements, police officers either side of a border may have much negotiating to do before any action can take place. It therefore useful to have agreements that deal with local acute situations, and it pays off to coordinate and harmonise efforts at a higher level.

Traditional transnational police cooperation was involved with individual suspects crossing borders, and focused on transferring offenders back to the jurisdictions of their crimes. The challenges posed by modern transnational crime are of a different nature altogether. Many contemporary transnational crime problems are associated with the process of globalisation. Factors that have led to an increase in the forms and incidence of transnational offending include the increased mobility of people and the reduction in the cost of international travel, the move towards a free market, and the increased technological sophistication and access to the World Wide Web. Cyber-crime, as we will see in the next chapter, is particularly facilitated by the latter development.

The process of globalisation has acted as a criminal market accelerator (Norman and Spalek, 2002). As Williams has stated, 'what is new is not transnational crime as such but its scale and diversity: the range of activities pursued by criminal organisations has been broadened significantly while the enterprises engaged in such activities have become more diverse' (Williams, 1998: 58).

Connected to the process of globalisation is the development of increasing *criminogenic asymmetries*. The main global asymmetry is between the wealthy, consumerist and highly regulated North (particularly Western Europe and North America) and the poorer and less regulated South. Passas (1998) has argued that such asymmetries are criminogenic for three reasons. In the first place, they generate or enhance the demand for illegal goods and services. Second, they generate incentives for particular actors to engage in illegal transactions; and third, these asymmetries reduce the ability for authorities to control such activities.

Passas has used the example of the dumping of toxic waste. The legislation regarding toxic waste tends to be underdeveloped in many developing countries. That provides for a solution to evade the cost of disposing of toxic waste in the more industrialised countries. It brings about the practice of companies in richer countries paying money to third parties to dispose of toxic waste in poorer countries. It evades regulation and saves a good deal of corporate money (Passas, 1998). Transnational criminal activity thrives on such differences in regulations among countries and regions and differences in the rigour with which they are enforced.

Such asymmetries constitute fertile grounds for illegal markets, one of which involves the trafficking of people. The trafficking or smuggling of people has been a problem for decades. As early as 1949 there was a United Nations Convention addressing it (UN Convention for the Suppression of the Traffic in Person and the Exploitation of the Prostitution of Others 1949). It primarily regarded trafficking as a means for producing forced prostitution. However, human trafficking with the aim of forced labour was not specifically addressed in the 1949 convention, although it is covered by optional protocols to the Convention against Transnational Crime 2000. It is difficult to obtain data on the extent of the problem. Estimates for the United Kingdom vary from 140 to 1,400 cases per annum (Kelly and Regan, 2000) but these may already be dated. The worldwide incidence may well involve millions of people (Aronowitz, 2001).

The aforementioned asymmetries help explain the growth of this human trafficking. In particular, the wide disparity in income explains why there is a draw towards the Western market. Other, possibly more specific, factors that enhance that draw include political and religious persecution and political unrest, while the weakening of border controls (in particular, the collapse of the former 'Iron Curtain' between Western and Eastern Europe) is certainly an important factor as well.

These asymmetries make transnational crime a structural factor in today's world. The fight against it takes place at various levels. At the intergovernmental level, conventions and treaties are in operation, but the everyday practice of law enforcement is still to a large extent to do with border control. In order to analyse these cooperative developments, Benyon et al. (1994) suggested the following thematic structuring of cooperative activities.

The highest or *macro* level of cooperation relates to the harmonisation of national legislation and regulations. Agreements at this level require conventions and treaties signed by governments, as they involve issues of state sovereignty (see also 1994; Den Boer and Walker, 1993). One such area involves agreements that grant police forces operational powers across borders. Such powers would obviously solve many of the problems identified above.

The intermediate, or *meso*, level is concerned with operational structures, practices and procedures. The issues identified at this level are common databases, and mutual access to intelligence information. Much of it relates to speaking the same tongue, quite literally so in terms of languages, but it also concerns information systems' ability to communicate with one another and the identification of common terminologies for offence types and judicial procedures. Given that there are 80 separate police forces across Europe, with different origins, structures and legislative frameworks, the meso level of cooperation contains much scope for potential mishap.

The *micro* level relates to the investigation of specific offences. This is the traditional level of police cooperation, which is invoked when a particular offender, after the commission of a crime in one jurisdiction, travels to another.

One of the oldest organised bodies in international police cooperation is Interpol. Its mission is to facilitate the investigation of transnational and international crimes between member countries by the mutual exchange of information between police agencies. Its headquarters is in Lyon, in France. Interpol is best known for its International Notices of Wanted Offenders. Information on wanted offenders is spread via Interpol to police forces across the globe. An important information system is the so-called Automated Search Facility. This database contains information on crimes and criminals, including stolen vehicles, counterfeit currencies, fingerprints and stolen passports. It consists of hundreds of thousands of pieces of data (Interpol, 2000).

Although Interpol is a global affair, it is said to be predominantly European in practice, with European countries the most frequent providers and consumers of information (Benyon *et al.*, 1994). It has been argued, however, that Interpol's role in enhancing transnational policing is limited. That is because Interpol's remit has traditionally been interpreted in a restrictive fashion. Article 3 of its constitution forbids Interpol from undertaking activities of a political, military, religious or racial character (Benyon *et al.*, 1993), which has limited its involvement in, for example, activities against Nazi war criminals and terrorist activity in the past. However, a resolution adopted in 1984 changed the interpretation of Article 3, so that terrorist activity is now seen to fall under Interpol's remit. Another constraint on Interpol's impact has been the fact that it deals particularly with ongoing investigations and rather less with policy-making on a transnational level. It is therefore less likely to serve as an impetus for change on levels of policy or legislation. Interpol may well remain largely a 'clearing house' for enquiries (Benyon *et al.*, 1993).

European policing: Europol

Europol is a European law-enforcement organisation that aims to improve the effectiveness and cooperation of authorities in the European Union member states in preventing and combating terrorism, unlawful drug trafficking and other forms of serious and organised transnational crime. It was established in 1992, but took up its full activities only in 1999. Its headquarters is in The Hague in the Netherlands. The current mandate of Europol includes the prevention and combat of the following criminal activities where there are factual indications that an organised criminal structure is involved and two or more member states are affected (Europol, 2000):

- illicit drug trafficking;
- crimes involving clandestine immigration networks;
- illicit vehicle trafficking;
- trafficking in human beings including child pornography;
- forgery of money and means of payment;
- illicit trafficking in radioactive and nuclear substances;
- terrorism;
- illegal money-laundering activities in connection with these forms of crime.

In comparative terms, Europol is a more ambitious project than Interpol. Whereas Interpol aims primarily to facilitate the exchange of information, Europol aims to harmonise and enhance the policing of transnational crimes in the European Union. As there is substantial diversity in terms of European police organisations coupled with telling differences in judicial review over criminal investigations, such efforts have proven, and continue to prove, a challenge. At the Tampere Summit Conference in October 1999, the European Council called for a number of measures, including the setting up of joint investigation teams.

As mentioned earlier, not all investigative cooperation takes place at the level of policing. There are, similarly, judicial provisions in place that deal with the extradition of suspects, for instance, and many countries have arrangements in place for foreign nationals convicted in their country to serve sentences in their country of origin.

Relatively little known is the International Association of Prosecutors (see www.iap.nl.com). It was established in 1995 and aims to promote the effective, fair, impartial and efficient prosecution of criminal offences. Additionally, it aims to assist prosecutors internationally in the fight

---

Box 8.1   Europol's Operation Bravo

Operation 'Bravo' is described as a good example of transnational investigative efforts (Europol, 1999). Several months of close cooperation by Dutch, German, Belgian, Spanish, Danish, Swedish, French and Finnish law-enforcement authorities and Europol uncovered a large-scale drug trafficking organisation, which had been operating in various member states for several years. The organisation was also active outside the European Union, particularly in the Russian Federation. The result of this joint effort by the various member states' law-enforcement services concerned culminated during the night of 12 December 1999, when 12 persons were arrested simultaneously in different parts of southern Finland. At the same time, the investigation led to substantial drug seizures, totaling 179kg of hashish, 21kg of amphetamines, and 7kg of marijuana. The main part of the seizure was found on a Finnish licensed truck, in which the drugs had been smuggled into Finland. Soon afterwards, five additional arrests took place. This seizure of 207kg of drugs is the largest in history in Finland.

The alleged leader of the organisation was from Kotka, in Finland. He was previously convicted of an aggravated narcotics offence and was released on parole at the end of 1998. The organisation concerned was suspected to be one of the largest importers of drugs into Finland and maintained contacts and conducted activities in several countries. It was suspected that this organisation smuggled similar amounts of drugs into Finland on other occasions.

The Finnish Police and Customs worked together on this case for several months with the objective of identifying the organisation and apprehending its members. However, a crucial factor in the success was the close international cooperation. The role of Europol as a coordinator of operational work, exchange of information and analysis of information was significant. The Europol Liaison Officers' contribution was vital in facilitating and overcoming various practical problems (Europol, 1999).

Europol exemplifies the relationship between an increased contact between criminal justice systems and the level of policing. It is useful to appreciate the immense potential difficulties in arranging such international investigative teams. In some countries there would be a senior public prosecutor involved, in others perhaps an investigative judge, while and in other systems the police themselves would control such operations. A practical understanding of foreign systems is vital for the smooth running of this kind of collaborative effort.

---

against organised or other serious forms of crime by promoting international cooperation in gathering and providing evidence, in tracking, seizing and forfeiting the proceeds of serious crime, and in the prosecution of fugitive criminals. There are members from over 90 countries, and its headquarters is also in the Netherlands. The International Association of Prosecutors is another illustration of the rapidly expanding scene of international criminal justice.

The nature of international law

Legislation to combat transnational crime is often international in nature. In fact, criminal justice everywhere is more and more determined by international law. International law is the system of rules that states and other bodies regard as binding in their mutual relations. However, there is no such thing as a global constitution, nor is there a universally accepted international criminal code. The nature of international law is more diffuse than that. That is why it is called *soft law*, as opposed to the hard law of codes and constitutions. International law is used, on the one hand, to regulate how states should treat each other, and on the other hand is concerned with how states should treat its citizens. It derives from treaties, custom, accepted principles and the views of legal authorities (Hague *et al.*, 1998).

International law impinges on criminal justice in four ways. First, international law defines states and statehood, and sovereign states remain responsible for much of the way in which criminal justice is organised. Second, international law may form part of national law: the Human Rights Act 1998 in England and Wales is a good example. The provisions in this Act were already legally binding as international law before the Act came into effect, but its incorporation into domestic law has enhanced their enforcement. Third, international law can apply directly against individuals: this is so in the case of the International Criminal Tribunals for the Former Yugoslavia and Rwanda, as we shall see later. Finally, international agreements can act to mould the parameters of actions by national legislators. Such agreements can set out the objectives that national governments should put into effect.

There are also four sources of international law. The first comprises international conventions and treaties; the second is international customs which have been ripened into international law; the third consists of generally accepted principles of law; and fourth there are judicial decisions and judicial teachings and writings.

The first source is the most important. International conventions and treaties are often drafted by diplomats and other government officials, who come together for a short period of time to produce an agreed document. When the final draft is written the delegates may sign it, and this signature carries a certain degree of weight. However, a diplomatic signature does not mean that the diplomat's country has accepted the statute, treaty or convention. For that, ratification is required: the formal agreement of the state's government to the statute. This will usually require for the treaty to be formally agreed to by a parliament or other representative body, which can take considerable time. It is a fact that not every state whose diplomats sign a treaty will eventually ratify it.

Additionally, the fact that an agreement exists does not necessarily make it part of international law. For that it is important that it is widely ratified. That is an indication of the level of global consensus, which is important with regard to whether the content of the agreement is binding. The right not to be subjected to the death penalty, for instance, is laid down in the United Nations Optional Protocol for the Abolition of the Death Penalty. However, it is signed by fewer than 40 countries (Robinson, 1999). As there are over 180 countries that could have decided to sign up, that number of signatories not enough for it to be considered widespread. Thus, convicts on death row cannot claim that international law prevents the death penalty from being imposed. Any principled ban on the death penalty is not part of international law, and countries where the death penalty occurs are therefore not violating principles of international law. We have, however, seen that the situation in Europe is different: the protocols to the European Convention of Human Rights do outlaw the death penalty, but only in Europe.

There are treaties that condemn certain actions or practices and treaties by means of which the signatory nations promise each other to make certain efforts. These include the combatting of terrorism, cyber-crime and human trafficking. It gives signatories the obligation to pass national legislation on such matters and carry out other measures to fight such crimes effectively. Finally, UN conferences can lead to other specific results, such as the production of documents such as the Universal Declaration of Human Rights, or the creation of bodies such as the International Criminal Court (discussed later).

The organisation of the United Nations

In international law, the United Nations (UN) is the most important legislative body. The United Nations was established on 24 October 1945 by 51 countries committed to preserving peace through international cooperation and collective security. Today, almost every nation in the world belongs to the UN: membership totals 189 countries in 2003, and the list includes Afghanistan, Libya and Iraq. Recent additions are Tonga, Tuvalu and the Republic of Yugoslavia.

When states become members of the United Nations, they agree to accept the obligations of the UN Charter. This is an international treaty, which sets out basic principles of international relations and the workings of the United Nations. According to the Charter, the United Nations has four purposes: to maintain international peace and security, to develop friendly relations among nations, to cooperate in solving international problems while promoting respect for human rights, and to be a centre for harmonising the actions of nations.

The United Nations has six main organs. Five of them – the General Assembly, the Security Council, the Economic and Social Council, the Trusteeship Council and the Secretariat – are based at UN headquarters in New York. The sixth, the International Court of Justice, is located in The Hague, the Netherlands. For our present purposes it is the General Assembly and the Security Council that are the most important of these.

All UN member states are represented in the General Assembly. It is a kind of parliament of nations and meets to consider the world's most pressing problems. Each member state has one vote. Decisions on important matters, such as international peace and security, admitting new members, and budgetary issues are decided by two-thirds majority. Other matters are decided by simple majority. Special efforts are made to reach decisions through consensus rather than by taking a formal vote.

The UN Charter gives the Security Council primary responsibility for maintaining international peace and security, and it may convene at any time, whenever peace is threatened. Under the Charter all member states are obliged to carry out the Council's decisions. There are 15 Security Council members. Five of these, China, France, the Russian Federation, the UK and the USA, are permanent members. The other ten are elected by the General Assembly for two-year terms. Decisions of the Council require nine 'yes' votes. Except in votes on procedural questions, a decision cannot be taken if there is a 'no' vote, or veto, by a permanent member. This gives the five permanent members strong control over peace and security matters around the world, yet they do not always agree as was shown in the build-up to the war with Iraq in 2003.

Normally, when the Security Council considers a threat to international peace, it first explores ways to settle the dispute peacefully. It may suggest principles for a settlement or undertake mediation. In the event of fighting the Council tries to secure a ceasefire. It may send a peacekeeping mission to help the parties maintain the truce and to keep opposing forces apart. The Council can take measures to enforce its decisions, including economic sanctions or an arms embargo. On rare occasions, the Council has authorised member states to use 'all necessary means', including collective military action, to see that its decisions are carried out.

The Council's subsidiary bodies meet regularly and report back to it. The Commission on Human Rights, for example, monitors the observance of human rights throughout the world. Other bodies focus on such issues as social development, the status of women, crime prevention, drugs and environmental protection. Five regional commissions promote economic development and the strengthening of economic relations in their respective regions. The Secretariat carries out the substantive and administrative work of the United Nations, as directed by the General Assembly, the Security Council and the other organs. At its head is the Secretary-General, who provides overall administrative guidance.

The International Monetary Fund, the World Bank group and 12 other independent organisations known as *specialised agencies* are linked to the UN through cooperative agreements. These agencies, among them the World Health Organisation and the International Civil Aviation Organisation, are autonomous bodies created by intergovernmental agreements. These bodies report to the General Assembly or the Economic and Social Council, and have their own governing bodies, budgets and secretariats.

Universal human rights

While human rights can be traced back to the Medieval English Magna Carta, the United Nations Charter of Human Rights, formulated soon after World War II, certainly was a turning point. It led to the setting up of a commission to draft the Universal Declaration of Human Rights. This Declaration was adopted on 10 December 1948, and it was the first time that human rights were given statutory status. It was three years after the end of World War II, and in the voting the newly emerging world order was already apparent. The Soviet Union, for instance, did not vote in favour of adopting the Declaration; South Africa abstained as well. The Universal Declaration must, with hindsight, primarily be viewed as a declaration of good intentions: there was no enforcement machinery along with it. Nevertheless, it was an influential document, perhaps not least because no state has ever been prepared to boast about a breach of it, which is of course not to say that breaching never occurred in the decades that followed (Robinson, 1999).

The rights of freedom and equality are guaranteed in Article 1. This, however, does not mean that the state can never legitimately take away its citizens' freedom. It can do so, for instance, when an independent court finds a person guilty of an offence in a way consistent with national legislation and international standards.

Box 8.2 The Universal Declaration of Human Rights

The preamble to the Declaration asserts that if man is not to be compelled to have recourse, as a last resort, to rebellion against tyranny and oppression, that the rule of law should protect his human rights. To this end, the articles of the Universal Declaration include rights to:

- Article 1 – Freedom and equality in dignity and rights;
- Article 2 – The entitlements of the Declaration without discrimination;
- Article 3 – Life, liberty and security of the person;
- Article 4 – Freedom from slavery or servitude;
- Article 5 – Freedom from torture or cruel, inhuman or degrading treatment or punishment;
- Article 6 – Recognition everywhere as a person before the law;
- Article 7 – Equality before the law without discrimination;
- Article 8 – An effective remedy for acts violating fundamental rights;
- Article 9 – Freedom from arbitrary arrest, detention or exile;
- Article 10 – Fair and public hearing by an independent and impartial tribunal;
- Article 11 – Presumption of innocence;
- Article 12 – Privacy of family, home and correspondence;
- Article 13 – Freedom of movement;
- Article 14 – Asylum from persecution;
- Article 15 – A nationality;
- Article 16 – Marriage and family;
- Article 17 – Property ownership;
- Article 18 – Freedom of thought, conscience and religion;
- Article 19 – Freedom of opinion and expression;
- Article 20 – Freedom of peaceful assembly and association;
- Article 21 – Participation in the government of one's country, to have equal access to public service in one's country and to vote in periodic and genuine elections under universal suffrage and secret ballot;
- Article 22 – Social security and economic, social and cultural rights;
- Article 23 – Work, just remuneration and equal pay for equal work; the right to form and to join trade unions for the protection of his interests;
- Article 24 – Rest and leisure;
- Article 25 – An adequate standard of living and the protection of children;
- Article 26 – Education;
- Article 27 – Participation in the cultural life of the community.

An account of the development of the Declaration is in the United Nation's 'Blue Book' (United Nations, 1995: 23–7).

Article 3 specifies the right to life. However, we have seen that that does not make the death penalty necessarily illegal. Even this most fundamental right is a qualified one: it can be watered down, since there are circumstances under which the state may lawfully take the life of a citizen. Article 4 reads: 'no one shall be held in slavery or servitude; slavery and the slave trade shall be prohibited in all their forms'. This right is absolute: slavery is never permitted, and any state that engages in it is in violation of international law.

Box 8.2 lists the rights guaranteed in the European Convention of Human Rights. Although in content it is not dissimilar to the Universal Declaration of Human Rights, there are important differences. The most important difference is in practice: it is better observed (Merrills and Robertson, 2001). One reason for this is that the group of nations that subscribed to it is smaller in number and perhaps more homogeneous, as they are the member states of the Council of Europe. The more important reason is that this Convention (with its additional protocols) comes with a court of law to enforce it. The European Court of Human Rights in Strasbourg, France, is the venue where citizens in Europe can seek justice if they feel that that human

---

Box 8.3 Excerpts from the European Convention for Human Rights

Convention for the Protection of Human Rights and Fundamental Freedoms, as amended by Protocol No. 11, guarantees:

- Article 1 – Obligation to respect human rights
- Article 2 – Right to life
- Article 3 – Prohibition of torture
- Article 4 – Prohibition of slavery and forced labour
- Article 5 – Right to liberty and security
- Article 6 – Right to a fair trial
- Article 7 – No punishment without law
- Article 8 – Right to respect for private and family life
- Article 9 – Freedom of thought, conscience and religion
- Article 10 – Freedom of expression
- Article 11 – Freedom of assembly and association
- Article 12 – Right to marry
- Article 13 – Right to an effective remedy
- Article 14 – Prohibition of discrimination
- Article 15 – Derogation in time of emergency

(see conventions.coe.int for this, and all other, Council of Europe conventions).

---

rights are violated by any member state within the Council of Europe.

Article 2 (the right to life) is the first article to specify a particular human right in the European Convention. Article 3 specifies the right to not be subject to torture or to cruel, inhuman or degrading treatment or punishment. Torture is defined as the intentional infliction of severe pain or suffering, whether physical or mental, by or with the consent of a public official, although it specifically excludes suffering attendant on the imposition of lawful punishments (Robinson 1999). The fact that the torture must be carried out under the auspices of the state is important. Human rights particularly seek to protect citizens from the state and not from the wrongdoing of private citizens.

Article 6 secures the right to a fair and public trial by an independent and impartial tribunal for any criminal charge. It also enshrines the principle that the courts shall presume that anyone charged with a criminal offence is innocent until proven guilty. Minimum rights are specified in relation to being informed of the charge, time to prepare a defence, the right to legal representation, the right to call witnesses and to have the services of an interpreter.

Other rights include the right to marry and to be regarded as a family, the right to free movement, the right to freedom of opinion and expression and the right to privacy. This right to privacy requires explanation. Article 8 prohibits arbitrary interference with privacy, home or correspondence by state officials. Nevertheless, this right to privacy can also not be said to be absolute. After all, there might be legitimate reasons why the state would want to intercept citizens' mail, tap their telephones or enter their homes. Such reasons might involve a suspicion that a person has committed offences or might be planning a coup or a terrorist attack.

The current position, reinforced by the European Court of Human Rights, is that countries can invade the privacy of their citizens for law-enforcement purposes only if certain conditions are met. States must ensure that there is a procedure of prior authorisation (typically by a judge) in place, which law-enforcement officers must follow. Such a procedure is designed to safeguard against arbitrary or overzealous interference of state officials in the lives of citizens (Wright, 2002b).

The right to be protected from media intrusion is not part of international law. Just as international law is less concerned with the behaviour of individuals, it is also not aimed at protecting the public from other bodies, such as the press.

The European Court of Human Rights is the venue where European citizens can seek redress in cases of human-rights violations. Its internet website is accessible on www.ichr.coe.int. The European Court's main function is to decide whether any measure or decision by a member state could constitute a violation of that state's obligations under the convention. The Court's workload has grown exponentially: between 1959 and 1969 there were only ten judgements given; in 1997 alone, the number was 150 (Merrills, 2001). The number of applications is far higher still.

Apart from citizens, states and non-governmental organisations may all seek access to the European Court. They can do this only when all routes to seek redress under the national legislation have been exhausted. That process will usually take years, so that the road to Strasbourg can be very long and exasperating. Citizens who win their cases often get compensation. Apart from exerting an effect in individual cases, national laws have been known to be amended after the European Court has ruled that the application of that law violated a suspect's human rights.

The adjudication of the European Court of Human Rights in relation to *T and V v UK* (1999) shows that the Court will apply very strict principles of fairness where they believe there has been a violation. In this case, the applicants were convicted of the murder of a 2-year-old child when they were only themselves 11 years old. The defence counsel argued that putting them on trial in an adult court constituted both inhuman and degrading treatment (Article 3) and a contravention of Article 6, which guarantees a fair trial because of the very nature of the proceedings. The European Court of Human Rights accepted the latter claim (Wright, 2002b).

The European Court of Human Rights has also consistently upheld the right to silence as an important factor in the presumption of innocence under Article 6. In *Funke v France* (1993), the Court held that the state infringed the right to silence when it sought to compel the individual to produce bank statements. Similarly in *Saunders v UK* (1996) the validity of the requirements of Section 2 of the Criminal Justice Act 1987, relating to the requirement to provide information and documents to the Serious Fraud Office has also come into question. A more recent Scottish case has held that requiring details of a driver of a vehicle also contravenes the right to silence (Wright, 2002b).

In the Belgian case of *Piersack* the court that tried the defendant was presided over by a judge who had been a prosecutor in the past. His office had dealt with Piersack's prosecution, and that made his presence on the bench inappropriate. The European Court concluded that this constituted a violation of Article 6, the right to a fair trial. In particular, it violated the principle of a defendant's right for his/her case to be dealt with by an independent and impartial tribunal.

The European Convention casts its shadows on prospective legislation. Lawmakers across Europe make efforts to ensure that any new legislation will not contravene the Convention. Having said that, the Convention does provide for 'opt out' clauses in situations where national security is at issue. However, it also restricts the applications of such clauses to ensure that any such measures do not remain in force indefinitely.

The European Court consists of as many judges as the Council of Europe has member states. This does not mean that every member state is represented by one judge. There can be several judges from one country, and each judge is supposed to sit independently and not represent his/her country. The Court consists of four chambers and the judicial process is public and adversarial. Judgments are made by majority vote. Dissenting opinions can be added to the reasoned verdict. All final judgements of the Court are binding on the member states involved.

War-crimes tribunals

In the 1990s a pressing need for so-called war-crimes tribunals was identified. Atrocities of a scale not seen on the European continent since World War II took place in the territories of the former Yugoslavia, and within the United Nations it was felt that the prosecution of those responsible should be part of the peace process. At the same time, the world was shocked by the eruption of violence and mass murder in the African state of Rwanda. A very similar tribunal was set up to deal with those responsible for these acts. Both the International Criminal Tribunal for the Former Yugoslavia (ICTY) and the International Criminal Tribunal for Rwanda (ICTR) are *ad hoc*: they are instigated for specific purposes and with narrowly defined jurisdictions. They are also meant to be temporary. Apart from discussing both present day tribunals we will also look their predecessors. These are the post-World War II tribunals in Nuremberg and Tokyo.

The Nuremberg Tribunal

After the end of the World War II the allied powers France, the Soviet Union, the United Kingdom and the United States convened in London to decide on how to bring high-ranking Nazi war criminals to justice. On 8 August 1945 they signed the so-called London Agreement, which laid out the Statute of the Nuremberg International Tribunal and a set of guiding principles for the trial that was to be conducted. The allied powers nominated four judges, one from each country, and similarly four prosecutors. These prosecutors prepared cases and conducted the prosecutions at trial. Defendants could be charged with one or more counts of three crimes, defined as follows: *Crimes against Peace*: planning, preparation, initiation or waging of a war of aggression, or a war in violation of international treaties, agreements or assurances, or participation in a common plan or conspiracy for the accomplishment of any of the foregoing; *War Crimes*: violations of the laws or customs of war, which included murder, ill-treatment or deportation to slave labour or for any other purpose of civilian population of or in occupied territory, murder or ill-treatment of prisoners of war or persons on the seas, killing of hostages, plunder of public or private property, wanton destruction of cities, towns or villages, or devastation not justified by military necessity; and *Crimes against Humanity*: murder, extermination, enslavement, deportation, and other inhumane acts committed against any civilian population, before or during the war; or persecutions on political, racial or religious grounds.

In Nuremberg, the city of the Nazi party's headquarters, there were 22 defendants. They included Rudolf Hess (seen by many as Hitler's right-hand man), Hermann Goering, commander in chief of the Nazi Air Force, and Albert Speer, the minister of armaments and war production. They all were tried together in one mega-trial. Each defendant pleaded not guilty. Nevertheless, most were found guilty, and 11 defendants received the death penalty. Eight others were given prison sentences. (Yale University runs a research project on the Nuremburg Trial. See www.yale.edu\lawweb\avalon\imt for a wealth of documentation.)

The Tokyo Tribunal

Almost simultaneously with the London conference, but at a different venue, the so-called Tokyo Charter was drafted. This occurred in Potsdam, near Berlin, in July 1945. The Tokyo Charter set out the constitution, jurisdiction and functions of the International Military Tribunal for the Far East, or, in short, the Tokyo Tribunal. Unlike the Nuremberg Statute this document was not the result of combined efforts by the Allied powers, but drafted exclusively by US officials. They decided that the bench should be composed of nine judges, and during the trial two judges were added. They did not come exclusively from victors' countries, but included representation from the Philippines and the Netherlands. The one prosecutor was American.

In the Tokyo trial there were 28 defendants, including the prime minister, the minister of foreign affairs, as well as several diplomats and high-ranking military figures. All pleaded not guilty. Nevertheless, all were found guilty on majority verdicts (either 9–2 or 8–3). Seven defendants were sentenced to death. Others received prison sentences, ranging from seven years to life.

Evaluating both tribunals

Both tribunals were landmark events in the history of international law. Nevertheless, they have been subjected to severe criticisms, both at the time and by later generations. First, there is the legal issue of introducing legislation and applying it retrogressively. After-the-fact legislation is generally considered shaky, although the actions of the Japanese and German aggressors were widely considered criminal at the time anyway. The fact that what they did was not illegal in their native countries at the time was, probably appropriately, not given much weight.

Second there was the distinct feeling that the tribunals were primarily about the winners of the war judging the conduct of those who were on the losing side. Various characteristics of both tribunals suggest this. The prosecutors and judges in Nuremberg were exclusively of victor countries. This was not the case in Tokyo, but here the statute was drafted exclusively by the Americans. The suspicion that the US was particularly keen to try Japanese officials to seek revenge for the Japanese surprise attack on Pearl Harbour in Hawaii may well have merit. As no individual from the Allied nations was ever investigated, let alone prosecuted, it appeared as if only nationals of the countries that lost the war could have committed war crimes. This selectivity is nowadays regarded as a shortcoming.

Further deficiencies related to the defence counsel in both trials. Because the US was influential in both tribunals, the proceedings on the whole had a rather adversarial feel. Native trials in both Germany and Japan were, at the time, and to a large extent today, more inquisitorial. The proceedings therefore must have felt alien both to defendants and their counsels. As Tokyo Judge Röling observed, 'the majority of the judges were accustomed to an Anglo-Saxon trial and gradually many Anglo-Saxon features crept into the proceedings by majority decision of the court. Thus it became a kind of trial Japanese lawyers were not accustomed to' (Röling and Cassese, 1993: 36).

When this aspect became apparent it was agreed that each defendant be assigned a US defence counsellor, better equipped to operate effectively at trial. On the other hand, it must also be said that there were distinct inquisitorial elements in both trials. Defendants were permitted to give unsworn statements at the end of the trial. That is a typically inquisitorial feature. Additionally, the rules of evidence were as relaxed as they often are in inquisitorial systems. Evidence merely had to be probative to be admitted and hearsay evidence was allowed, and very frequently used. There also was no jury.

Perhaps most significant was the fact that there was no appeals procedure. Defendants simply did not have that right. Those convicted in Nuremberg could request only that the Control Council of Germany (the temporary Allied forces' administration in Germany) to reduce or change their sentences. All requests were rejected, and ten of the eleven defendants who received death sentences were hanged two weeks later. (The 11th had committed suicide in prison while awaiting execution.)

ICTY and ICTR

After 50 years of relative silence in the area of prosecuting crimes against humanity both present-day *ad hoc* war-crimes tribunals emerged. Both the International Criminal Tribunal for the former Yugoslavia (ICTY) and the International Criminal Tribunal for Rwanda (ICTR) started operating in the 1990s. It was the first time that such bodies existed under the umbrella of the United Nations.

The ICTY was established in 1993 by the UN's Security Council. Its specific assignment is to prosecute and sentence persons responsible for the violations of international humanitarian law in the Former Yugoslavia since 1991. The part of its statute that constitutes the Criminal Code consists of four clusters of crimes. These are Grave Breaches of the Geneva Convention 1949 (Article 2 of the Statute), Violations of the laws and customs of war (Article 3), Genocide (Article 4), and Crimes against Humanity (Article 5). Genocide is defined as:

Any of the following acts committed with intent to destroy, in whole or in part, a national, ethnical, racial or religious group, as such:

- killing members of the group;
- causing serious bodily or mental harm to members of the group;
- deliberately inflicting on the group conditions of life calculated to bring about its physical destruction in whole or in part;
- imposing measures intended to prevent births within the group;
- forcibly transferring children of the group to another group.

The following acts shall be punishable:

- genocide;
- conspiracy to commit genocide;
- direct and public incitement to commit genocide;
- attempt to commit genocide; and
- complicity in genocide.

Genocide is defined more elaborately in the ICTY Statute than it was in the Nuremberg Statute. It specifies that incitement to commit genocide as well as attempts to effect it classify as war crimes. Another novelty within the Statute is the status of the offence of rape. When rape takes place as a part of a systematic and widespread campaign it might constitute a crime against humanity, or even genocide following a recent ruling at the Rwanda Tribunal. The Statute also specifies that both individual and command responsibility might make one guilty of such offences. Finally, acts as well as failures to act in order to stop atrocities from occurring may constitute war crimes and may accordingly fall under both tribunals' jurisdiction. It is also worthy of note that *crimes against humanity*, often used as a catch-all term for war crimes and other crimes of a global calibre, are specifically defined in ICTY's Statute (Akvahan, 1993; International Criminal Tribunal for the former Yugoslavia, 1993).

The sister court of the Yugoslav Tribunal, the Rwanda Tribunal (ICTR), came into operation in 1995. The Security Council Resolution that led to the establishment of the tribunal was, ironically, voted against by the state of Rwanda itself. The state had three objections. First, it wanted the tribunal to be able to impose the death penalty. Second, it wanted to give the tribunal jurisdiction over crimes going back to 1990, instead of to 1994. Finally, Rwanda proposed that the tribunal be based in Rwanda and that local judges conduct the trials. None of Rwanda's proposals were implemented. the tribunal cannot impose capital punishment, the jurisdiction was not put back to 1990, the tribunal is based in Tanzania, and the judges are not Rwandan (Robinson, 1999). The tribunal consists of two trial chambers in Arusha, Tanzania, and an appeals chamber at ICTY in The Hague, shared by both tribunals. ICTR's first completed trial was that of Jean-Paul Akayesu, former major of a town called Taba. On 2 September 1998 he was found guilty of genocide and crimes against humanity. The verdict was historic in the sense that it was the first conviction by a UN tribunal for genocide.

Both tribunals' legislators were keen to ensure that they would improve on the Nuremberg and Tokyo tribunals. A few differences between those earlier tribunals and the ICTY, in particular, are worth discussing. First, in the Nuremberg and Tokyo trials there were certain restrictions placed on the conduct of the defence. Any potential wrongdoing by the Allied forces was not to be discussed as it was ruled not relevant to the charges being brought. The ICTY, in contrast, is not intended to be, and clearly does not want to be seen to be, a victor's tribunal, and neither does the ICTR.

The judges at the ICTY and ICTR more accurately represent the world community then the benches in Nuremberg or Tokyo. In both present-day tribunals judges are appointed after a vote by the UN's General

Assembly. In order to be nominated, judges have to be eligible for the highest judicial offices in their home countries, and of high moral character, integrity and impartiality. Judges are appointed for four years, with the possibility of re-election. Not more than one judge per country can be appointed.

Finally, the judges in Nuremberg relied, to a relatively large extent, on paperwork, because sizeable dossiers containing documentary evidence were available to them. This measure to enhance the trials' expedience helped to ensure that the Nuremberg trial took no more than 11 months to complete. The Tokyo trial lasted approximately two and a half years. Because, at the Yugoslav Tribunal, the principles of immediacy and orality are much more strictly adhered to, some trials there involving a single defendant have lasted almost as long as the Nuremberg trial as a whole.

A consequence of the prime importance of what happens in the courtroom is that many vulnerable witnesses have to testify in court when, in the more inquisitorial trial systems, they would often not need to. The Yugoslav Tribunal has the full modern range of technological options available to accommodate the needs of vulnerable witnesses, such as video links, masking devices for appearance as well as voice distortion, while, on occasion, a satellite link with a witness in the former Yugoslavia has been used.

ICTY in action

By August 2002 the ICTY had sentenced 12 people in a final (i.e. post-appeal) sentence. The first was Erdemovic, who was sentenced to five years imprisonment, and who has completed his sentence in Norway. Contested trials have resulted in convictions among others for Tadic, Alexovski, and three of the four defendants who were tried together in the so-called *Celebici* case. Of these four, only Delalic has been found not guilty on all counts. He regained his freedom after having spent two and a half years in pre-trial detention.

The tribunal has encountered scepticism about whether it would ever be able to try the so-called 'big fish' of the Bosnian conflict. While indictments against former heads of state Milosevic and Karadzic (as early as 1995) were served, many believed that they would never be arrested and brought to justice. The fact that Slobodan Milosevic is currently being held accountable for his actions is nothing less than a historic breakthrough.

A principal objective of the tribunal is to help create the conditions that might lead to a lasting peace. It is difficult to say to what extent the tribunal affects developments in the former Yugoslavia. Sometimes, it is argued that justice should play second fiddle as a too rigorous attempt to bring people to justice might spark civil unrest. After World War II one of the compromises arranged in this light was for the prosecutor in Tokyo to 'overlook' the role of the Japanese emperor. It was feared that his indictment and arrest would demoralise the Japanese people and destabilise the nation and the region. A similar argument would, however, have applied to Milosevic. While certainly not overlooked by the prosecutor who served an indictment against him, the sentiments were that his capture would be rather unlikely. The pessimists, in this case, have been proven wrong.

Tochilovski has explained that the style of trial proceedings is predominantly adversarial. He has argued that this decision was informed not so much by theoretical assumptions underlying modes of trial, but by practical concerns. The advisors most forthcoming in the preparatory stage were said to be from an adversarial background, most notably from the USA, so that an adversarial system of trial proceedings emerged as the natural choice (Tochilovski, 1998).

An obvious departure from the adversarial tradition is the absence of juries anywhere in the proceedings. A panel of three judges decides on guilt as well as on sentencing. A majority finding of 2–1 is sufficient for a guilty verdict, a state of affairs that has not escaped criticism (Pruitt, 1997). Another difference is that the prosecutor at the ICTY has extensive rights of appeal against acquittals. Defendants have, unlike in Nuremberg or Tokyo, absolute rights to appeal against any conviction (O'Brien, 1993).

It is worth investigating further the role of the judges at trial. After all, they are the actual decision-makers on guilt or innocence as well as on sentencing; in addition, the rules of procedure allow them considerable latitude to decide how to conduct a trial. The panel of judges might decide to be largely reactive. They can decide to let prosecution and defence do their witness examinations and rule only on objections and other issues, such as the admission of items of evidence. On the other hand, judges might adopt a more active position. Judges can ask factual questions, and it is up to them to decide to what extent they wish to exercise that right. In addition, the court has the right to call witnesses itself. Again, it is a matter of choice or preference to what extent judges regard this as the proper interpretation of their role.

Since judges work at the tribunal for a limited period of time after having been on the bench in their home countries for, probably, many years, it is not unreasonable to assume that judges might 'bring their domestic legal culture with them' when they sit at this international court. One might expect judges accustomed to an adversarial manner of trial proceedings to be more reactive, and judges from an inquisitorial tradition to conduct their trials in a more active and domineering fashion.

There is evidence for judges conducting their trials differently depending on their background (Pakes, 2000b). When comparing the behaviour of American presiding judge MacDonald with French presiding judge Jorda in the cases of Tadic and Blaskic respectively, clear differences can be found. The French judge asked a greater number of factual questions and interrupted examinations more often. The bench in the case with the French presiding judge also called a number of witnesses itself. The bench over which the American judge presided did not.

As always when discussing inquisitorial-versus-adversarial modes of justice, the question of which is more appropriate emerges. It could be argued that in case of war-crimes tribunals the answer to that question is perhaps relatively straightforward. Indeed, a good case can be made for a relatively inquisitorial mode of trial procedure. After all, the tribunal is more than a platform for conflict resolution. One of its aims is the discovery of the complete truth of what happened. The ICTY itself is quite clear on this:

> Ensuring that history listens is a most important function of the Tribunal. Through our proceedings we strive to establish as judicial fact the full details of the madness that transpired in the former Yugoslavia. In the years and decades to come, no one will be able to deny the depths to which their brother and sister human beings sank. And by recording the capacity for evil in all of us, it is hoped to recognise warning signs in the future and to act with sufficient speed and determination to prevent such bloodshed (International Criminal Tribunal for the former Yugoslavia, 1998: paragraph 294).

It is hard to overestimate the importance of this aim. It would therefore be fitting if the way in which the tribunal does its business bears it in mind. We have seen that finding the truth is a characteristic associated with inquisitorial justice in which the judge actively pursues the presentation of evidence. An active judge, whose duty will encompass an obligation towards the finding of the truth, is more appropriate in this regard than judges who regard it as their role to witness the battle between prosecution and defence unfold. Ticholovski (1998) has phrased this as the choice between trials as either battle or as scrutiny, with a preference for the latter.

The International Criminal Court

Both the ICTY and ICTR have increased the profile of international justice tremendously. The next step, currently being undertaken, is the establishment of a permanent International Criminal Court (ICC). In 1998 the decision was made to establish such a court at the Rome Conference. The reasons for its establishment have been given as follows:

The principal aim is to achieve justice for all. An international criminal tribunal has been described as the missing link in criminal justice. Its establishment will help to achieve justice for victims of genocide and crimes against humanity where in the past this was not achieved. Effective deterrence is another primary objective. It is hoped that those who would incite genocide, embark on a campaign of ethnic cleansing, murder or rape, or use children for barbarous medical experiments, should no longer find willing helpers. To what extent warlords and warmongers will indeed be deterred by the abstract threat of being tried before a tribunal in a foreign country remains to be seen.

Third, the International Criminal Court should enhance the prospects of a lasting peace. Although there is a question of to what extent peace and justice may be achieved simultaneously, both the existing *ad hoc* tribunals and the ICC are clear in their intention to help to secure peace by bringing those responsible for war crimes to justice. Finally, this court should not suffer from the deficiencies of *ad hoc* tribunals, which by definition, are established only after the fact. As investigations are best carried out when the events are still fresh, the ICC would have an obvious advantage.

The following quotation of UN's secretary general Kofi Annan illustrates the optimism and good will that underlies the establishment of a permanent war-crimes tribunal:

In the prospect of an international criminal court lies the promise of universal justice. That is the simple and soaring hope of this vision. We are close to its realisation. We will do our part to see it through till the end. We ask you ... to do yours in our struggle to ensure that no ruler, no State, no junta and no army anywhere can abuse human rights with impunity. Only then will the innocents of distant wars and conflicts know that they, too, may sleep under the cover of justice; that they, too, have rights, and that those who violate those rights will be punished. (Kofi Annan, www.un.org/law/icc/index.html)

The International Criminal Court Statute clearly defined what it deems a crime against humanity. It states that *crime against humanity* means any of the following acts when committed as part of a widespread or systematic attack directed against any civilian population, with knowledge of the attack:

(a) Murder;

(b) Extermination;

(c) Enslavement;

(d) Deportation or forcible transfer of population;

(e) Imprisonment or other severe deprivation of physical liberty in violation of fundamental rules of international law;

(f) Torture;

(g) Rape, sexual slavery, enforced prostitution, forced pregnancy, enforced sterilisation, or any other form of sexual violence of comparable gravity;

(h) Persecution against any identifiable group or collectivity on political, racial, national, ethnic, cultural, religious, gender or other grounds that are universally recognised as impermissible under international law, in connection with any act referred to in this paragraph or any crime within the jurisdiction of the court;

(i) Enforced disappearance of persons;

(j) The crime of apartheid;

(k) Other inhumane acts of a similar character intentionally causing great suffering, or serious injury to body or to mental or physical health.

This definition encompasses more acts than ICTY's definition of crimes against humanity. In particular, the addition of apartheid is new. The Statute defines it as 'inhumane acts of a character similar to those referred to in paragraph 1, committed in the context of an institutionalised regime of systematic oppression and domination by one racial group over any other racial group or groups and committed with the intention of maintaining that regime'.

The use of the term 'enforced disappearance' reminds us of the practice during Argentina's dictatorship where political opponents and dissidents 'disappeared'. In the UN's terminology the phrase means the arrest, detention or abduction of persons by, or with the authorisation, support or acquiescence of, a state or a political organisation, followed by a refusal to acknowledge that deprivation of freedom or to give information on the fate or whereabouts of those persons, with the intention of removing them from the protection of the law for a prolonged period of time.

Nothing but good intentions underlies the foundation of the International Criminal Court. However, the practicalities of establishing a

Statute have proved to be extremely difficult. A main bone of contention relates to the role and powers of the prosecutor. Many countries felt that the prosecutor should enjoy complete independence, in particular from the UN and its Security Council. Others, most notably the US, felt that these powers should be constrained. The underlying reason is the idea that when a prosecutor has unlimited freedom in deciding where and when to investigate, this might hamper the maintenance of peace in those regions. It also involves the risk of frivolous or political prosecutions.

To counter such issues the suggestion was made that the UN Security Council have the final say with regard to giving the go-ahead for prosecutions. However, the fact that certain countries in the Security Council have the right to veto decisions might, in effect, mean that these countries are able to prevent prosecutions taking place. It has been argued that the USs' preference for this arrangement is a means to ensure that US nationals are unlikely ever to appear as defendants at the ICC.

The concession that has been made is that the Security Council's agreement is required when prosecutions are intended to be brought against individuals in non-UN member states. The Security Council may also request prosecutions be halted for a one-year period. Nevertheless, the US is one of the countries that will not ratify the Statute. Another non-signatory is Israel. It is debatable to what extent a tribunal that lacks the support of the US can have an impact on the reinforcement of human rights on a global scale. After all, the tribunal will not have a police force, and will rely on states for funding, information, and the apprehension of suspects. When the US is unwilling to be involved, the court's ability to act could be severely curtailed.

The International Court of Justice

The final court of justice I shall discuss is the International Court of Justice. This court has, for a long time, been the principal judicial organ of the United Nations. Its seat is at the Peace Palace in The Hague, the Netherlands. It began work in 1946, when it replaced the Permanent Court of International Justice that had been in operation at the same venue since 1922. Its main role is to settle in accordance with international law, the legal disputes submitted to it by member states. (See www.icj-cij.org, which is the source for many of the details below.)

The court is composed of 15 judges, who are elected to nine-year terms of office by the United Nations General Assembly and Security Council, sitting independently of each other. It may not include more than one

Box 8.4 The European Union

The crux of the European Union is that member states have given up some of their sovereignty and handed that over to the Union. The idea is that the states share the same goals so that a common pursuit of them would suit all member states. The Union's principal objectives are to:

- *Establish European citizenship.* It aims to protect fundamental human rights and civil liberties.
- *Ensure freedom, security and justice.* That involves police and judicial cooperation, such as via Interpol and Europol.
- *Promote economic and social progress.* The introduction of the Euro is a good example of this as are policies to benefit the poorer regions within the Union.
- *Assert Europe's role in the world.* This is performed by formulating joint policies on economy and trade, as well as on combating terrorism and on issues of justice and home affairs.

The Union was initiated in 1950. Six countries (Belgium, Germany, France, Italy, Luxembourg and the Netherlands) took part from the very beginning. Today, after four further waves of entry (1973: Denmark, Ireland and the United Kingdom; 1981: Greece; 1986: Spain and Portugal; 1995: Austria, Finland and Sweden) the EU has 15 member states and is preparing for enlargement through the admission of a number of eastern and southern European countries.

The legal process underlying European legislation is complex. Ideally, legislation is passed by broad consent, but the more the Union grows the more difficult consensus will be to achieve on any issue of substance. Unanimous votes are necessary in certain vital areas, whereas it is specified that in other areas a qualified majority will do. This works by giving the more influential countries more votes than others in the *Council of the European Union*. Where a qualified majority (62 out of 87 votes) is required, votes are distributed as follows: France, Germany, Italy and the United Kingdom have ten votes each; Spain has eight; Belgium, Greece, the Netherlands and Portugal, five; Austria and Sweden, four; Denmark, Finland and Ireland, three; and Luxembourg, two.

The European Union consists of a number of institutions. There are five main bodies. The *European Parliament* consists of Members of the European Parliament (MEPs), who are directly elected by Europe's citizens. It has 626 seats, with the larger countries having more seats than smaller countries. The United Kingdom has 87 seats. Only Germany has more, with 99 seats. Luxembourg, on the other hand, has only 6. The *Council of the European Union* is the Union's main decision-making body. It is made up of ministers from the 15 member states, with responsibility for the policy area under discussion at a given meeting: foreign affairs, agriculture, industry, transport and so on.

The *European Commission* drafts legislation, is a driving force behind their implementation, ensuring it comes into force in the member states. (There are other EU bodies with which we are not concerned here because they do not operate in the field of criminal justice. These include the European Court of Auditors and the European Central Bank.)

The management of these issues in the context of a dramatic enlargement in the years to come will be a big challenge for the Union. The desire to achieve consensus on the main issues runs the risk of becoming a factor that will increase sluggishness and inertia in decision-making, while not adding to its transparency.

A number of European treaties are of importance to the criminal justice area. The Maastricht Treaty 1992 regulates three areas of cooperation among European Union member states. The first pillar relates to economic cooperation; the second pillar to a common foreign and security policy; and the third cooperation with regard to justice and home affairs. One of the achievements on the justice and home affairs front was the establishment of *Europol* (see Fijnaut, 1993). The Amsterdam Treaty in 1997 further enhanced the level of cooperation, as did the 1999 Tampere Treaty.

judge of any nationality. Elections are held every three years for one-third of the seats. The members of the court do not represent their governments but sit as independent magistrates.

The judges must possess the qualifications required in their respective countries for appointment to the highest judicial offices, or be jurists of recognised competence in international law. As is the case for the International Criminal Court the composition of the court has to reflect representatively the main cultures and the principal legal systems of the world. In 2003, the 15 judges were from Brazil, China, France, Egypt, Germany, Japan, Jordan, Madagascar, the Netherlands, the Russian Federation, Sierra Leone, Slovakia, the UK, the US, and Venezuela.

Only states may apply to, and their representatives appear before, the court. The cases that the court tends to be involved with include disputes between countries over land and maritime boundaries. As the court is more of a civil-type court rather than one to do with criminal justice, this discussion will suffice here.

Conclusion

In this chapter I have discussed several transnational and international bodies involved with criminal justice on a global or European plat-form. Of the bodies discussed, four – Europol, ICTY, ICTR and the

International Criminal Court – have been established since the 1990s. Europol is certainly growing in importance since the Tampere conference in 1999, while the International Criminal Court is the newest entity yet. International criminal justice is certainly going through a rapid process of institutionalisation. In these fast-paced developments, two trends are worth highlighting. First, there are the increased levels of international cooperation in fighting transnational crime, especially organised crime. The enhanced role of Europol is a good example. The more that European countries engage in joint operations, the more important becomes communication and harmonisation. While micro-level cooperation has a long history, the increasing harmonisation at macro level is one of the most intriguing developments in international criminal justice.

Second, the 1990s saw unprecedented efforts and achievements in indicting, arresting and bringing to justice those responsible for war crimes and violations of international humanitarian law. Despite the fact that it is progressing fast, the process of establishing an international criminal court of justice is fraught with difficulty. While both the current *ad hoc* war crimes tribunals have their limitations, the instigation of the International Criminal Court proves not to be without controversy either. Fundamental disputes are still lingering over the independence of the prosecutor at this court.

Some commentators fear that the ICC may well become a lame duck if the prosecutor cannot investigate and prosecute without the consent of the UN's Security Council (on which the permanent members states have the right to veto). The safest attitude to adopt is one of 'wait and see'. The ICC is in existence, but not yet in operation. Although no one doubts that justice is served by bringing war criminals to justice, the exact process by which this is to be achieved, and to what extent this will help secure peace in the regions concerned, remains unanswered at present.

Chapter 9

New directions in comparative criminal justice

Comparative criminal justice has been fuelled by the need for coordinated responses to common threats. New directions in comparative research relate particularly to such issues. Highest on this agenda, since 11 September 2001, is the threat of terrorism. The second issue I shall discuss in this chapter is the threat that is posed by cyber-crime.

The threat of terrorism

It has been said that nothing would be the same after the events of 11 September 2001. Such a broad statement is as difficult to prove as it is to disprove but there is no doubt that the terrorist attack on New York and Washington has had profound effects on many an area of public life (Halliday, 2002). In this chapter we will look at terrorism and the measures states have taken against it. It is an area where international cooperation and harmonisation is vital and in which international organisations, such as the United Nations and the European Union, play a pivotal role.

Terrorism is nothing new, and neither is its high position on the political agenda (Laqueur, 1999). However, the obvious truth is that only since 11 September the debate about combating it has been as vigorous as it is today.

The US Federal Bureau of Investigation (FBI) has defined terrorism as 'the unlawful use of force or violence against persons or property to intimidate or coerce a government, the civilian population, or any segment thereof, in furtherance of political objectives' (Federal Bureau of Investigation, 1999).

In 1999 the FBI identified 29 active terrorist groups. The list includes various groups in the Middle East, including Al Qaeda, the most infamous terrorist organisation in operation at present. Al Qaeda's self proclaimed leader is Osama bin Laden, who established Al Qaeda by bringing together Arabs who fought in Afghanistan against the Soviet invasion in 1980. Al Qaeda helped finance, recruit, transport, and train Islamic extremists for the Afghan resistance. Its current goal is to re-establish the Muslim authority in areas throughout the world. Al Qaeda has been alleged to work with allied Islamic extremist groups to overthrow regimes it deems non-Islamic and remove Westerners from Muslim countries, notably from Saudi Arabia, considered the Muslim holy land. Al Qaeda is generally assumed to be behind the 11 September terrorist attack, and a host of other attacks, both before and after 11 September.

The US State Department keeps a record of terrorist attacks worldwide since 1980. Until 2001, the hayday of terrorism in terms of numbers of attack was the middle to late 1980s, when over 600 terrorist attacks took place annually between 1985 and 1988. In 1999 this number was reduced to 392. When looking at the 1990s, the number of casualties was by far highest in Asia, followed by the Middle East and Europe. The United States saw relatively few casualties between 1994 and 1999. The State Department report lists a death toll of 7 in this five-year period, whereas the number for Asia is several thousands, and the total number of people killed in Europe is, altogether, over a thousand.

After 11 September measures against terrorism were swiftly taken. The UN's Security Council passed a resolution as quickly as 12 September 2001, in which it condemned the attacks (United Nations, 2001). On 28 September UN Resolution 1373 specified that states should prevent and suppress the financing of terrorist acts; take the necessary steps to prevent the commission of terrorist acts, including by provision of early warning to other states by exchange of information, and deny safe haven to those who finance, plan, support, or commit terrorist acts.

The European Commission also held an emergency meeting on 12 September. It formulated a plan of action very similar to that of the UN. It specifically states that member states will share with Europol systematically, and without delay, all useful data regarding terrorism. A specialist anti-terrorist team has been set up within Europol, which cooperates closely with its US counterparts.

In Britain the Anti-Terrorism, Crime & Security Act 2001 was passed. The Act has several goals. It is aimed at tackling terrorist finance but is also aimed at streamlining immigration procedures. The new legislation furthermore contains provisions against inciting religious hatred or violence. New offences to do with weapons of mass destruction were introduced as well. The Act also aims to tighten security legislation with regard to airports and nuclear sites. New powers of detention provided for by the Act have been criticised from a human-rights perspective. The government argued that the provisions of the Act were compatible with the European Convention on Human Rights, but it finds it necessary to derogate from Article 5(1) of the Convention in respect of the detention powers in the Act. Article 5 relates to the right to liberty and restricts the situations in which any state can impose detention on a citizen. The Government's argument is that the existence of an emergency situation necessitates such measures, and that the measures are not intended to persist indefinitely.

Canada, similarly, sought to change its Criminal Code, so that terrorist activity in various guises can be effectively prosecuted. In Canada, terrorist activity is defined in the Criminal Code as an action that can take place either within or outside of Canada, and which is an offence under one of the UN anti-terrorism conventions and protocols; or an act that is committed or threatened for political, religious or ideological purposes and threatens the public or national security by killing, seriously harming or endangering a person, causing substantial property damage that is likely to seriously harm people or interfere with or disrupt an essential service, facility or system. (The definition is carefully circumscribed to make it clear that disrupting an essential service is not a terrorist activity if it occurs during a lawful protest or a work strike and is not intended to cause serious harm to persons.)

Knowingly collecting or providing funds, either directly or indirectly, in order to carry out terrorist crimes will carry a 10-year prison sentence. Knowingly participating in, contributing to, or facilitating the activities of a terrorist group will carry a maximum sentence of 10–14 years in prison. This participation or contribution itself does not have to constitute a criminal offence, and would include knowingly recruiting into the group new individuals for the purpose of enhancing the ability of the terrorist group to aid, abet or commit indictable offences. The maximum sentence for the offence of participating or contributing would be 10 years' imprisonment. The maximum sentence for facilitating would be 14 years' imprisonment. To instruct anyone to carry out a terrorist act or an activity on behalf of a terrorist group (a so called *leadership offence*) carries a maximum life sentence, whereas knowingly harbouring or concealing a terrorist carries a 10-year prison sentence (Canadian Ministry of Justice, 2002).

A set of investigative powers was also introduced in Canada. The Anti-Terrorist Act 2001 gives the police the power of preventative arrest. Police may use preventative arrest provisions to bring a suspected terrorist before a judge where there are reasonable grounds to believe that a terrorist action might be carried out, and reasonable grounds to suspect that arrest is necessary to prevent it. The threat must be specific, and must involve a specific individual. Judicial review of such arrests should occur within 24 hours. The Act will be subject to evaluation by a parliamentary committee after three years (Canadian Ministry of Justice, 2002).

Initiatives of this kind have been implemented throughout the world. They often have been passed in the context of concerns for civil liberties. Powers of arrest and detention have usually been enhanced. This has been the case in the US, the UK and Canada. An argument put forward in both the UK and Canada is that these enhanced powers of detention are needed at present, but not indefinitely, and that the use of such powers should be carefully reviewed. To what extent the aftermath of 11 September will become permanent in terms of the form of such pieces of legislation is an open question.

Cyber-crime

Consider the case in Box 9.1, reported by the press agency Reuters. This case helps us to illustrate several points about the nature of cyber-crime. The suspect is accused of fraud using the internet. Fraud is nothing new, but there is no doubt that the internet has tremendously enhanced the possibilities for it. The second characteristic is its transnational nature. The suspect is Canadian, but is prosecuted in the USA. Other suspects are currently abroad, which is where much of the money may have gone as well. The investigation required international police cooperation, and the victims come from no fewer than 60 countries. The scam shows the complex nature of cyber-crime and the challenges it provides to transnational policing.

The internet, without doubt, is one of the most exciting and profoundly changing developments of our time. Thanks to it we can do our banking 24 hours a day, book flights, buy books and send emails from any hooked up computer. Many of us have daily access to the internet. While it enhances and changes much of our daily business, it has also provided an opportunity for the abuse of its potential. That is what we colloquially call cyber-crime. The term 'cyber-crime' is broad but usually indicates the use of computer technology during the commission of some form of crime or display of harmful behaviour.

Wall (2001a) has described three ways in which the internet has impacted on criminal and/or harmful activity. First, it has facilitated the exchange of information regarding existing crimes. Information on the internet about how to produce bombs is a good example: it is not that the information is novel, but the fact that the internet makes it much more widely accessible that is the important new development. Second,

---

Box 9.1   Man pleads guilty to £41 million online fraud

A Canadian man has pleaded guilty to participating in an online scheme that cheated some 13,000 investors out of nearly $60m (£41m) in what officials said was one of the largest Internet investment fraud cases in the nation. The US Attorney's office for the Eastern District of California and the FBI said Cary Waage, 26, pleaded guilty on Monday to one count of mail fraud and one count of conspiracy to commit money laundering relating to the Internet-based Tri-West Investment Club. According to officials, the club solicited incremental investments of $1,000 on the Web by promising a 120 per cent annualised return from promissory notes issued by key prime banks. But some 13,000 investors from 60 countries instead lost millions of dollars as Waage and others running Tri-West used the money to snap up property in Mexico and Costa Rica as well as a yacht, helicopter and fancy cars, officials said.

Waage also admitted that millions of dollars were funnelled to dozens of bogus shell corporations created in Costa Rica to hide the illicit profits.

Waage, who could not be reached for comment, faces up to 25 years in prison and fines of up to twice the value of victims' losses, officials said. The scam unravelled in September 2001 when Costa Rican authorities in cooperation with the FBI and US Attorney's Office seized and froze numerous Tri-West assets. Officials have also brought fraud charges against Waage's father Alyn, the scheme's alleged leader, and James Webb, who allegedly designed Tri-West's Web site. Both men are in Costa Rica fighting extradition to the United States. Alyn Waage's sister Lynn Johnston and his wife Michelle also face criminal charges for allegedly participating in the scam. They are currently fugitives, officials said.

(Source: Reuters, 30 April 2002).

---

the internet has created a transnational environment for the commission of crimes in a way previously not possible. Online fraud can serve as an example here: the use of the internet and the increase in electronic banking have opened the doors for the commission of a type of fraud that is entirely new. Third, the internet has allowed for new forms of criminal conduct to emerge: gaining unauthorised access to classified information via a computer link is an example.

The nature and extent of cyber-crime

Wall (2001a) has listed four types of cyber-crime. The first is cyber-trespass. It is the unauthorised access to computer systems where rights of ownership or title have already been established (Wall, 2001a). This is commonly known as 'hacking' and those who do it are termed 'hackers' (Taylor, 1999). Young (1995) distinguished between four types of hackers, depending on their differing motivations. The *utopians* regard their trespassing as a service to society: they relish the intellectual challenge of gaining access to sensitive material and want to demonstrate the vulnerability of internet security. *Cyberpunks* are anti-establishment, and intend to cause harm when trespassing. Young further distinguished between *cyber-spies* and *cyber-terrorists*, whose motives and methods may well be quite similar. It would appear that the image of the hacker has shifted away from the idealistic bright young mind, who finds a challenge in taking on the electronic establishment, to that of a reckless or terrorist offender, who is abusing the electronic highway to do maximum damage.

The second type of cyber-crime Wall described is cyber-deception and theft. This includes credit-card fraud and the raiding of electronic banks and bank accounts. A related form is cyber-piracy, which is the appropriation of new forms of intellectual property. It often concerns unlicensed software or music.

Third, there is cyber-pornography and obscenity, which concerns the publication and/or trading of sexual explicit material on the internet. This form poses particular law-enforcement problems, as the rules on pornography vary widely among countries.

Finally, there is a range of behaviours that Wall (2001a) has classified under the header of 'cyber-violence'. It is the violent impact of the activities concerned on an individual or social or political group. Violence, in this context, does not typically involve physical violence. However, threats of violence and incitement can easily be communicated via email and the internet. A particular instance of cyber-violence is cyber-stalking (Ellison, 2001).

There are problems with establishing the extent of cyber-crime. First, there is a lack of official statistics. There are reports that estimate the annual level of commercial damage done by cyber-criminals (e.g. Parker, 1998). However, such estimates do not always report counting method-ologies or offer a definition of cyber-crime. It is therefore difficult to put such figures in context. Consequently, not a great deal is known about the offenders. Cyber criminals may well be not very typical of the general offending population.

Additionally, we do not know too much about the victims either. One reason for this is that victims can be unwilling to report, as is no doubt the case with commercial victims who do not wish to expose their vulnerability. Corporations are known to favour civil remedies to retrieve damages rather than necessarily involve the criminal justice system (Wall, 2001b). Victims may also not realise that they have been victimised and are the subjects of a crime. The cunningness of certain ploys makes that very possible indeed.

Official statistics on cyber-crime are hard to find partly because of their trans-jurisdictional character. While this is usually a challenge for policing and law enforcement, as they are traditionally local, Wall (2001b) has pointed out the potential advantage of so-called 'forum shopping'. When a case involves more than one jurisdiction, there is sometimes a choice of which jurisdiction should handle the case. Criminal justice agents might seek to secure the law-enforcement venue that is most likely to lead to a conviction. Wall (2001b) mentions examples of investigations shifting from one US state to another for that very reason, and another instance where the investigation was passed from the US to the UK because it was believed that that would enhance the chances of successful prosecution.

Policing cyberspace

Because of its transnational nature, the law enforcement or more broadly, the governance that is required will almost by necessity be of a multi-level nature. Currently, governance of the internet can be seen to operate at five levels. First there are user groups and individual users who have taken on a policing function. These groups can be transnational, and their mandate is typically vague and non-statutory. One such a group is the Cyber Angels, who actively promote online etiquette and prevent and police cyber-crime where there are clear victims or users at risk.

The second level relates to the role and responsibilities of internet service providers (ISPs). ISPs have been warned about their possible prosecution for wrongdoing that occurs via use of their services. It is held in the UK that an ISP might be prosecuted if it fails to remove illegal material when its existence has been brought to its attention via complaints. A body called the internet Watch Foundation oversees the use of the internet and brings complaints to the attention of ISPs.

Corporate security organisations are heavily involved with policing the internet, or at least to the extent that it might affect the security of their clients. The visibility of such organisations is low, because the preference of their clientele is to operate outside of public view.

The next level comprises state-funded non-public police organisations. An example is Germany's Internet Task Force. Germany passed a law allowing police bodies in certain circumstances access to private emails in 1997. ISPs would be required to cooperate with requests to allow this to happen. Such obligations on ISPs give state law-enforcement bodies a foot in the electronic door.

Finally, there is the involvement of state-funded public police or-ganisations, often the traditional police service. At a national level in the UK, the National Criminal Intelligence Service has taken on national responsibility for the fight against internet child pornography. Several police forces up and down the country have set up specialist units to deal with internet crime as well. Meanwhile, the National Crime Squad's High Tech Crime Unit has become operational, and has a specific mandate with regard to the investigation of internet crimes involving fraud and paedophilia.

The regulation of the internet increasingly incorporates a European dimension. In its 2001 proposed strategy, the European Commission lists a number of measures. These include awareness-raising by means of public information and education campaigns. Another measure is the operation of a European warning and information system. Member states should strengthen their Computer Emergency Response Teams (CERTs) and improve the coordination among them. A further area of harmonisation relates to market-oriented standardisation and certification. European standardisation organisations work on the inter-operability of electronic signature software. Finally, the Commission aims to harmonise legal frameworks across Europe against cyber-crime, and seeks to propose legislation as well (European Commission, 2001).

The EU acknowledges the problems identified above that stem from the scarcity of data on victimisation and the difficulties in policing the internet. It is nevertheless clear that the era of freedom and lawlessness on the internet is a thing of the past, or perhaps even a myth that never corresponded too closely to reality in the first place. It is equally clear that internet security is big business. The internet was not designed with security in mind, but rather for the free flow of information. That will continue to pose challenges to users, providers and law-enforcement officials in the years ahead.

The evolution of criminal justice systems: convergence and divergence

Common enemies, such as cyber-crime and terrorism, constitute a factor that binds criminal justice systems. They serve as a driving force for convergence: common threats will invite common responses, which will increase the similarities in criminal justice systems around the world. However, common threats are not the only way in which similarities between systems can be explained. A number of mechanisms for convergence have been described by Fairchild and Dammer (2001).

The first reason is foreign domination. It explains, as we have seen, changes to criminal justice in Japan, and also explains why many colonies or former colonies have criminal justice systems not dissimilar to those of the colonial powers. Just as the inquisitorial system of justice was exported across Europe during the Napoleonic era, so has the British Empire, left a common-law legacy across the world. A second reason why systems might be similar is imitation. Many former colonies still look to the old colonial power for examples, and because the systems are often still quite similar, features from the one are often relatively easy incorporated into the other.

A further reason for convergence is simultaneous development. This is the case with regard to measures against cyber-crime and terrorism: the threats are perceived in a similar way in various countries at the same time, and measures are being developed that are similar (although by no means identical) as well. Many states, for instance, have adopted the FBI definition of terrorism.

A third reason relates to international regulation. Returning to the example of anti-terrorist legislation, international bodies such as the United Nations and the European Union specify the measures that members should take. Such specifications do not spell out exactly what needs to be done, but room for manoeuvre is often limited, and the resulting pieces of legislation are likely to be similar.

The opposing force, diversification or diversion, may arise from two mechanisms. The first is termed 'cultural persistence'. In the present context this can be defined as a tendency to resist the import of foreign programmes or structures and to persist with the arrangements that exist nationally. The stronger version of cultural persistence is indigenisation. While cultural persistence seeks to maintain a state of affairs, indigenisation seeks to change structures or processes so that they more closely resemble the 'original' or indigenous arrangements that existed in the past. This is certainly occurring in many former colonies. Under the indigenisation denominator fall certain arrangements such as the informal conflict-resolution processes that have been resurrected following the end of colonial rule. (We saw an example of this in Papua New Guinea, in Chapter 5.)

Fairchild and Dammer (2001) have argued that change in criminal justice often comes about through a mixture of such converging and diverging forces. The example quoted is that of the Japanese police force. Initially, the very idea of a police force intended to deal with crime and public order was imported from the West. After its importation, which can be said to have been an instance of convergence via a process one could call imitation, it has developed into something that truly fits the Japanese context and has thus diversified away from the Western policing blueprint. Such an indigenised process of innovation highlights the value of culturally sensitive comparative criminal justice research.

Nevertheless, the globalisation of crime and of criminal justice is likely to increase the pressure on convergence. New measures against novel forms of crime are likely to be, to an extent, directed by international regulations, which will enhance their similarities. The fact that information about foreign criminal justice systems is easier to obtain than ever before also makes it more likely that policy-makers will look abroad for examples. The variety with regard to trial procedures, sentences and judicial decision-makers might, in the future, well become less bewildering than it is today.

On one hand, this constitutes a loss. However, criminal justice systems are not like the natural world, where we should celebrate diversity for its own sake. Increased requirements for communication and harmonisation provide rewards for convergence, and criminal justice systems will, after all, be judged on their effectiveness. And one can remain sure that as long as cultures, languages, public opinions and social discourses differ, so will criminal justice systems and the way they operate.

References

Adang, O.M.J. (2001) 'Friendly But Firm: The Maintenance of Public Order', paper presented at the annual meeting of the American Political Science Association, San Francisco (29 August–2 September), unpublished.

Akdeniz, Y. (2001) 'Controlling Illegal and Harmful Content on the Internet' in D.S. Wall (ed.) *Crime and the Internet*, London: Routledge, 113–40.

Akvahan, P. (1993) 'Punishing War Crimes in the Former Yugoslavia: A Critical Juncture for the New World Order', *Human Rights Quarterly*, 15, 262–89.

Alaska Justice Reform (1996) 'Village Alaska: Community Characteristics and Public Safety', *Alaska Justice Reform*, 12(4), 1–5.

Alderson, J. (1979) *Policing Freedom*, Plymouth: Macdonald and Evans.

Amnesty International (1999) *Killing with Prejudice: Race and the Death Penalty; United States of America; Rights for All*, report (AMR 51/52/99), London: Amnesty International, International Secretariat.

Amnesty International (2001) *Death Penalty News*, 3/4 (October).

Amnesty International (2002) 'China: 13 Years on from Tiananmen: an Unresolved Human Rights Issue, press release (ASA 17/023/2002), London: Amnesty International, International Secretariat.

Anderson, M., Den Boer, M., Cullen, P., Gilmore, W.C., Raab, C.D. and Walker, N. (1995) *Policing the European Union: Theory, Law and Practice*, Oxford: Clarendon Press.

Aronowitz, A.A. (no date) 'Germany', in *The World Factbook of Criminal Justice Systems*: www.ojp.usdoj.gov/bjs/pub/ascii/wfbcjger.txt

Aronowitz, A.A. (2001) Smuggling and Trafficking in Human Beings: The Phenomena, the Markets That Drive It and the Organizations That Promote It, *European Journal of Criminal Policy and Research*, 9, 163–95.

Ashworth, A. (1997) 'Sentencing', in R. Morgan, M. Maguire and R. Reiner (eds), *Oxford Handbook of Criminology*, second edition, Oxford: Clarendon Press, 1095–135.

Ashworth, A. (1998) *The Criminal Process*, Oxford: Oxford University Press.

Auld, A. (2001) *Review of the Criminal Courts of England and Wales*, London: Lord Chancellor's Department.

Australian Bureau of Statistics (1995) *National Aboriginal and Torres Strait Islander Survey 1994: Detailed Findings* (catalogue no. 4190.0.), Canberra: Australian Bureau of Statistic.

Baldwin, J. (1985) *Pre-Trial Justice: A Study of Case Settlement in Magistrates' Courts*, Oxford: Blackwell.

Bannenberg, B. (2000) 'Victim–Offender Mediation in Germany', in *The European Forum for Victim–Offender Mediation and Restorative Justice: Victim–Offender Mediation in Europe*, Leuven, Belgium: Leuven University Press, 251–80.

Barrett, A. and Harrison, C. (1999) *Crime and Punishment in England: A Source Book*, London: UCL Press.

Bayley, D.H. (1991) *Forces of Order: Police Behaviour in Japan and the United States*, second edition, Berkeley: University of California Press.

Bayley, D.H. (1994) *Police for the Future*, Oxford: Oxford University Press.

Bedau, A.H. (1996) 'The United States', in P. Hodgkinson and A. Rutherford (eds) *Capital Punishment: Global Issues and Prospects*, Winchester: Waterside Press.

Bedau, A.H. and Ratelet, M.L. (1987) 'Miscarriages of Justice in Potentially Capital Cases', *Stanford Law Review*, 40, 21–79.

Benyon, J., Turnbull, L., Willis, A. and Woodward, R. (1993) *Police Cooperation in Europe: An Investigation*, Leicester: CSPO.

Benyon, J., Turnbull, L., Willis, A. and Woodward, R. (1994) 'Understanding Police Cooperation in Europe: Setting a Framework for Analysis', in M. Anderson and M. Den Boer (eds) *Policing across National Boundaries*, London: Pinter, 46–65.

Biles, D. (1991) 'Australia', in *The World Factbook of Criminal Justice Systems*: www.ojp.usdoj.gov/bjs/pub/ascii/wfbcjaus.txt

Black, R. (1999) 'The Lockerbie Disaster', *Edinburgh Law Review*, 3, 85–95.

Black, R. (2000) 'From Lockerbie to Zeist': www.thelockerbietrial.com/from_locker-bie_to_zeist.htm

Braithwaite, J. (1989) *Crime, Shame and Reintegration*, Cambridge: Cambridge University Press.

Brandts, C. and Field, S. (1995) 'Discretion and Accountability in Prosecution: A Comparative Perspective on Keeping Cases Out of Court', in P. Fennell, C. Harding, N. Jörg and B. Swart (eds) *Criminal Justice in Europe: A Comparative Study*, Oxford: Clarendon Press, 127–48.

Bratton, W. (1997) 'Crime is Down in New York City: Blame the Police' in N. Dennis (ed.) *Zero Tolerance: Policing a Free Society*, London: Institute of Economic Affairs, 29–43.

Bruyn, S. (1966) *The Human Perspective in Sociology: The Methodology of Participant Observation*, Englewood Cliffs, New Jersey: Prentice-Hall.

Button, M. (1999) 'Private Security and Its Contribution to Policing: Under-Researched, Under-Utilized and Underestimated', *International Journal of Police Science and Management*, 2, 103–16.

Button, M. (2002) *Private Policing*, Cullompton, Devon: Willan.

Canadian Ministry of Justice (2002) *Canada's Action against Terrorism since September 11*: www.dfait-maeci.gc.ca/anti-terrorism/canadaactions-en.asp

Canivell, J.M. (no date) 'Spain', in *The World Factbook of Criminal Justice Systems*: www.ojp.usdoj.gov/bjs/pub/ascii/wfbcjspn.txt

Carcach, C. and McDonald, D. (1997) *National Police Custody Survey*, Research and Public Policy series, no. 9, Canberra: Australian Institute of Criminology.

Cassese, A. and Röling, B.V.A. (1993) *The Tokyo Trial and Beyond*, Cambridge: Polity Press.

Castberg, A.D. (1990) *Japanese Criminal Justice*, New York: Praeger.

Chard, C. (1999) *Pleasure and Guilt on the Grand Tour*, Manchester: Manchester University Press.

Christie, N. (1994) *Crime Control as an Industry*, second edition, London: Routledge.

Clareboets, L. (1997) 'Centralization and the Control of Undercover Police Activities: The Situation in Belgium', in M.G.W. Den Boer (ed.) *Undercover Policing and Accountability from an International Perspective*, Maastricht, the Netherlands: European Institute of Public Administration, 55–58.

Clegg, I. and Whetton, J. (1995) 'In Search of a Third World Criminology', in L. Noaks, M. Levi and M. Maguire (eds) *Contemporary Issues in Criminology*, Cardiff: University of Wales Press, 26–51.

Clinard, M.B. and Abbott, D.J. (1973) *Crime in Developing Countries*, New York: Wiley.

Cohen, D. and Longtin, S. (no date) 'Canada', in *The World Factbook of Criminal Justice Systems*: www.ojp.usdoj.gov/bjs/pub/ascii/wfbcjcan.txt

Cohen, S. (1985) *Visions of Social Control*, Cambridge: Polity Press.

Cole, B.A. (1999) 'Post-Colonial Systems', in R.I. Mawby (ed.) *Policing across the World: Issues for the Twenty-First Century*, London: UCL Press, 88–108.

Cole, F., Frankowski, S.J. and Gerz, M.G. (1987) 'Comparative Criminal Justice: An Introduction', in their (eds) *Major Criminal Justice Systems: A Comparative Study*, second edition, Newbury Park: Sage, 15–26.

Corstens, G.J.M. (1999) *Het Nederlandse Strafprocesrecht*, third edition, Arnhem, the Netherlands: Gouda Quint.

Criminal Sanctions Agency (2003) *Prison Service in Finland*, Helsinki: Ministry of Justice.

Crombag, H.F.M. (2003) 'Adversarial or Inquisitorial: Do We Have a Choice?', in P.J. Van Koppen and S.D. Penrod (eds) *Adversarial versus Inquisitorial Justice*, New York: Kluwer/Plenum, 21–25.

Crystal, J. (2001) 'Criminal Justice in the Middle East', *Journal of Criminal Justice*, 29, 469–82.

Damaska, M.R. (1986) *The Faces of Justice and State Authority: A Comparative Approach to the Legal Process*, New Haven, Connecticut: Yale University Press.

Davies, M., Croall, H. and Tyrer, J. (1998) *Criminal Justice: An Introduction to the Criminal Justice System of England and Wales*, London: Longman.

De Figueiredo Dias, J. and Antunes, M.J. (1993) 'Portugal', in C. Van Den Wijngaert, C. Gane, H.H. Kühne and F. McAuley (eds) *Criminal Procedure Systems in the European Community*, London: Butterworth, 317–38.

De Keijser, J.W. (2000) *Punishment and Purpose*, Delft, the Netherlands: Thela.

De Waard, J. (1999) 'The Private Security Industry: International Perspectives', *European Journal on Criminal Policy and Research*, 7, 143–74.

Den Boer, M.C.W. (1994) 'The Quest for European Policing: Rhetoric and Justification in a Disorderly Debate', in M. Anderson and M. Den Boer (eds) *Policing across National Boundaries*, London: Pinter, 174–96.

Den Boer, M.C.W. (forthcoming) 'Torn between Two Lovers: The Dutch Police Enticed By Europe and the Region', in F.J. Pakes and I.M. McKenzie (eds) *Law, Power and Justice in the Netherlands*, Westport, Connecticut: Praeger.

Den Boer, M.C.W. and Walker, N. (1993) 'European Policing after 1992', *Journal of Common Market Studies*, 31, 3–28.

Dixon, K. (1977) 'Is Cultural Relativism Self-Refuting? *British Journal of Sociology*, 28, 75–88.

Downes, D. (1982) 'The Origins and Consequences of Dutch Penal Policy since 1945: A Preliminary Analysis', *British Journal of Criminology*, 22, 325–57.

Downes, D. (1988) *Contrasts in Tolerance: Post-War Penal Policy in the Netherlands and England and Wales*, Oxford: Clarendon Press.

Duff, P. (1993) 'The Prosecutor Fine and Social Control: The Introduction of the Fiscal Fine to Scotland', *British Journal of Criminology*, 33, 481–503.

Duff, P. (1999a) 'The Prosecution Service: Independence and Accountability', in P. Duff and N. Hutton (eds) *Criminal Justice in Scotland*, Aldershot: Ashgate, 115–30.

Duff, P. (1999b) 'The Scottish Jury: A Very Peculiar Institution, *Legal and Comtemporary Problems*, 173, 177–78.

Duff, P. (2000) 'The Defendant's Right to Trial by Jury: A Neighbour's View, *Criminal Law Review*, 85–94.

Duff, P. (2001) 'The Scottish Criminal Jury: A Very Peculiar Institution', in N. Vidmar (ed.) *World Jury Systems*, Oxford: Oxford University Press, 249–82.

Duff, P. and Hutton, N. (1999) *Criminal Justice in Scotland*, Aldershot: Ashgate.

Dwyer, F. (2001) 'Can the Police Make a Difference: The New York City Example', lecture delivered at the University of Portsmouth (May), unpublished.

Ebbe, O.N.I. (2000a) 'The Unique and Comparative Features of Criminal Justice Systems: Policing, Judiciary and Corrections', in Ebbe (ed.) *Comparative and International Criminal Justice Systems: Policing Judiciary and Corrections*, second edition, Boston: Butterworth-Heinemann, 277–89.

Ebbe, O.N.I. (2000b) 'The Judiciary and Criminal Procedure in Nigeria', in Ebbe (ed.) *Comparative and International Criminal Justice Systems: Policing Judiciary and Corrections*, second edition, Boston: Butterworth-Heinemann 183–203.

Ebbe, O.N.I. and De Olano, R.G.R. (2000) 'The Criminal Justice System in Argentina', in Ebbe (ed.) *Comparative and International Criminal Justice Systems: Policing Judiciary and Corrections*, second edition, Boston: Butterworth-Heinemann, 79–90.

Ellison, L. (2001) 'Cyberstalking: Tackling Harassment on the Internet', in D.S. Wall (ed.) *Crime and the Internet*, London: Routledge, 141–50.

European Commission (2001) *Network and Information Security: Proposal for European Policy Approach*: europa.eu.int/information_society

Europol (1999) *Annual Report 1999*, The Hague: Europol.

Fairchild, E. and Dammer, R.D. (2001) *Comparative Criminal Justice Systems*, second edition, Belmost, California: Wadsworth.

Federal Bureau of Investigation (1999), *Terrorism in the United States 1999*: www.fbi.gov/publications/terror/terror99.pdf

Feeley, M.M. and Simon, J. (1992) 'The New Penology: Notes on the Emerging Strategy of Corrections and Its Implications', *Criminology*, 30, 449–74.

Field, S. (1998) 'The Legal Framework of Covert and Proactive Policing in France', in S. Field and C. Pelser (eds) *Invading the Private: State Accountability and New Investigative Methods in Europe*, Aldershot: Ashgate, 67–82.

Field, S., Alldridge, P. and Jörg, N. (1995) 'Prosecutors, Examining Judges and Control of Police Investigations', in P. Fennell, C. Harding, N. Jörg and B. Swart (eds) *Criminal Justice in Europe: A Comparative Study*, Oxford: Clarendon Press, 227–49.

Fijnaut, C. (ed.) (1993) *The Internationalisation of Police Cooperation in Western Europe*, Deventer, the Netherlands: Kluwer.

Fijnaut, C. and Verbruggen, F. (1998) 'Proactive Investigation: A Belgian Perspective', in S. Field and C. Pelser (eds) *Invading the Private: State Accountability and New Investigative Methods in Europe*, Aldershot: Ashgate, 111–42.

Findlay, P. and Duff, P. (eds) (1988) *The Jury under Attack*, London: Butterworth

Fionda, J. (1995) *Public Prosecutors and Discretion: A Comparative Study*, Oxford: Clarendon Press.

Fitzpatrick, P. (1982) 'The Political Economy of Dispute Settlement in Papua New Guinea', in C. Sumner (ed.) *Crime, Justice and Underdevelopment*, London: Heinemann, 192–227.

Franke, H. (1990) 'Dutch Tolerance: Facts and Fables', *British Journal of Criminology*, 30, 81–93.

Foucault, M. (1979) *Discipline and Punish: The Birth of the Prison*, translated by Alan Sheridan, New York: Vintage.

Gane, C. (1993) 'Scotland', in C. Van Den Wijngaert, C. Gane, H.H. Kühne and F. McAuley (eds) *Criminal Procedure Systems in the European Community*, London: Butterworth, 339–82.

Garland, D. (1990) *Punishment and Modern Society: A Study in Social Theory*, Oxford: Clarendon Press.

Garland, D. (2001) *The Culture of Control: Crime and Order in Contemporary Society*, Chicago: University of Chicago Press.

Geertz, C. (1983) 'Local Knowledge: Fact and Law in Comparative Perspective', in Geertz (ed.) *Local Knowledge: Further Essays in Interpretative Anthropology*, New York: Basic Books, 229–45.

Geysel, F. (1990) 'Europe from the Inside', *Policing*, 6, 338–54.

Goldstein, H. (1977) *Policing a Free Society*, Cambridge, Massachusetts: Ballinger.

Greve, V. (1993) 'Denmark', in C. Van Den Wijngaert, C. Gane, H.H. Kühne and F. McAuley (eds) *Criminal Procedure Systems in the European Community*, London: Butterworth, 51–72.

Gudjonsson, G.I. (1992) *The Psychology of Interrogation, Confessions and Testimony*, Chichester: Wiley.

Hague, R., Harrop, M. and Breslin, S. (1998) *Comparative Government and Politics: An Introduction*, fourth edition, Basingstoke: Macmillan.

Halliday, F. (2002) *Two Hours That Shook the World: September 11 2001, Causes and Consequences*, London: Saqi Books.

Hatchard, J., Huber, B. and Vogler, R. (eds) (1996) *Comparative Criminal Procedure*, London: British Institute of International and Comparative Law.

Hencovska, M. (no date) 'Slovak Republic', in *The World Factbook of Criminal Justice Systems*: www.ojp.usdoj.gov/bjs/pub/ascii/wfbcjslk.txt

Hirsch, A.J. (1992) *The Rise of the Penitentiary*, New Haven, Connecticut: Yale University Press.

Hodgson, J. (2000) 'Comparing Legal Cultures: The Comparatist as Participant Observer', in D. Nelken (ed.) *Contrasting Criminal Justice*, Aldershot: Ashgate, 139–56.

Hodgson, J (2001) 'The Police, the Prosecutor and the *Juge d'Instruction*: Judicial Supervision in France, Theory and Practice', *British Journal of Criminology*, 41, 342–61.

Home Office (1996) *Judicial Statistics: England and Wales 1996*, Home Office: HMSO.

Home Office (2001) *Criminal Statistics: England and Wales 2000*, London: HMSO.

Hood, R. (1996) *The Death Penalty: A World-Wide Perspective*, second edition, Oxford: Clarendon Press.

Hopkins Burke, R. (ed.) (1998) *Zero Tolerance Policing*, Leicester: Perpetuity Press.

Horton, C. (1995) *Policing Policy in France*, London: Policy Studies Institute.

Huber, B. (1996) 'Criminal Procedure in Germany', in J. Hatchard, B. Huber and R. Vogler (eds) *Comparative Criminal Procedure*, London: British Institute of International and Comparative Law, 96–175.

Hucklesby, A. (1994) 'The Use and Abuse of Conditional Bail, *Howard Journal of Criminal Justice*, 33, 258–270.

Hucklesby, A. (2002) 'Bail in Criminal Cases', in M. McConville and G. Wilson (eds) *The Handbook of the Criminal Justice Process*, Oxford: Oxford University Press, 115–36.

Hulsman, L.H.C., Beerling, H.W.R. and Van Dijk, E. (1978) 'The Dutch Criminal Justice System from a Comparative Legal Perspective', in D.C. Fokkema (ed.) *Introduction to Dutch Law for Foreign Lawyers*, Deventer, the Netherlands: Kluwer, 19–31.

Independent Commission against Corruption (2001) *Annual Report 2000*, Hong Kong: Independent Commission against Corruption.

International Criminal Tribunal for the Former Yugoslavia [ICTY] (1993) *Statute*, The Hague: ICTY.

International Criminal Tribunal for the Former Yugoslavia [ICTY] (1998) *Fifth Annual Report of the International Tribunal for the Prosecution of Persons Responsible for Serious Violations of International Humanitarian Law Committed in the Territory of the Former Yugoslavia since 1991*, The Hague: ICTY.

International Military Tribunal (1947) *Trial of the Major War Criminals before the International Military Tribunal*, 'Blue Series', volume 1, Nuremberg: no publisher.

Interpol (2000) *Annual Report 1999*, Lyon: Interpol.

Jackson, J.D., Quinn, K. and O'Malley, T. (2001) 'The Jury System in Contemporary Ireland: In the Shadow of a Troubled Past', in N. Vidmar (ed.) *World Jury Systems*, Oxford: Oxford University Press, 281–318.

Johnson, E.H. and Heijder, D. (1983) 'The Dutch Deemphasise Imprisonment: A Sociocultural Explanation', *International Journal of Comparative and Applied Justice*, 7, 3–19.

Johnston, L. (2000) *Policing Britain: Risk, Security and Governance*, Harlow, Essex: Longman.

Jones, T. and Newburn, T. (1998) *Private Security and Public Policing*, Oxford: Clarendon Press.

Jörg, N., Field, S. and Brandts, C. (1995) 'Are Inquisitorial and Adversarial Systems Converging?', in P. Fennell, C. Harding, N. Jörg and B. Swart (eds) *Criminal Justice in Europe: A Comparative Study*, Oxford: Clarendon Press, 41–56.

Jorgensen, D.L. (1993) *Participant Observation: A Methodology for Human Studies*, Thousand Oaks, California: Sage.

Journès, C. (1998) 'Proactive Policing in France', in S. Field and C. Pelser (eds) *Invading the Private: State Accountability and New Investigative Methods in Europe*, Aldershot: Ashgate, 83–94.

Joutsen, M., Lahti, R. and Pölönen, P. (2001) *Criminal Justice Systems in Europe and North America: Finland*, Heuni report series, Helsinki: European Institute for Crime Prevention and Control.

Joyner, C.C. (1995) 'Strengthening Enforcement of Humanitarian Law: Reflections on the International Criminal Tribunal for the Former Yugoslavia', *Duke Journal of Comparative and International Law*, 6, 79–101.

Kalven, H. and Zeisel, H. (1966) *The American Jury*, Chicago: University of Chicago Press.

Kangaspunta, K., Joutsen, M. and Ollus, N. (eds) (1995) *Crime and Criminal Justice in Europe and North America*, Heuni report series, Helsinki: European Institute for Crime Prevention and Control.

Karunaratne, N.H.A. (no date) 'Sri Lanka', in *The World Factbook of Criminal Justice Systems*: www.ojp.usdoj.gov/bjs/pub/ascii/wfbcjsri.txt

Kelling, G.L., Pate, T. Dieckman, D. and Brown, C.E. (1998) 'The Kansas City Preventive Patrol Experiment: A Summary Report', in D.H. Bayley (ed.) *What Works in Policing*, New York: Oxford University Press, 30–50.

Kelk, C. (1995) 'Criminal Justice in the Netherlands', in P. Fennell, C. Harding, N. Jörg and B. Swart (eds) *Criminal Justice in Europe: A Comparative Study*, Oxford: Clarendon Press.

Kelly, L. and Regan, L. (2000) *Stopping Traffic: Exploring the Extent of and Response to Trafficking for Women for Sexual Exploitation in the UK*, Home Office Research series, no. 125, London: Home Office Policing and Reducing Crime Unit; online: www.homeoffice.gov.uk/rds/prgdfs.pdf

Kilchling, M. and Loschnig-Gspandel, M. (2000) 'Legal and Practical Perspectives on Victim/Offender Mediation in Austria and Germany', *International Review of Victimology*, 7, 305–22.

King, M. and Brearley, N. (1996) *Public Order Policing: Contemporary Perspectives on Strategy and Tactics*, Leicester: Perpetuity Press.

King, N.J. (2001) 'The American Criminal Jury', in N. Vidmar (ed.) *World Jury Systems*, Oxford: Oxford University Press, 53–91.

Komiya, N. (1999) 'A Cultural Study of the Low Crime Rate in Japan', *British Journal of Criminology*, 39, 369–90.

Kühne, H.H. (1993) 'Germany', in C. Van Den Wijngaert, C. Gane, H.H. Kühne and F. McAuley (eds) *Criminal Procedure Systems in the European Community*, London: Butterworth, 137–62.

Laqueur, W. (1999) *The New Terrorism: Fanaticism and the Arms of Mass Destruction*, London: Phoenix Press.

Leigh, L. and Zedner, L. (1992) *A Report on the Administration of Criminal Justice in the Pre-Trial Phase in France and Germany*, Royal Commission on Criminal Justice Research Study, no 1, London: HMSO.

Leishman, F. (1999) 'Policing in Japan: East Asian Archetype?' in R.I. Mawby (ed.) *Policing around the World*, London: UCL Press, 109–25.

Lipsey, M.W. (1992) 'The Treatment of Juvenile Delinquents: Results from Meta-Analysis', in F. Lösel, D. Bender and T. Bliesener (eds) *Psychology and Law: International Perspectives*, Berlin: De Gruyter, 131–43.

Lipsey, M.W. (1995) 'What Can Be Learned from 400 Studies on the Effectiveness of Treatment with Juvenile Delinquents?', in J. McGuire (ed.) *What Works: Reducing Reoffending*, Chichester: Wiley, 63–78.

Lloyd-Bostock, S. and Thomas, C. (2001) 'The Continuing Decline of the English Jury', in N. Vidmar (ed.) *World Jury Systems*, Oxford: Oxford University Press, 53–91.

Lu, H. and Miethe, T.D. (2002) 'Legal Representation and Criminal Processing in China', *British Journal of Criminology*, 42, 267–80.

McAuley, F. and O'Dowd, J. (1993) 'Ireland', in C. Van Den Wijngaert, C. Gane, H.H. Kühne and F. McAuley (eds) *Criminal Procedure Systems in the European Community*, London: Butterworth, 185–222.

McGuire, J. and Priestley, B. (1995) 'Reviewing "What Works": Past, Present and Future', in J. McGuire (ed.) *What Works: Reducing Reoffending*, Chichester: Wiley, 3–34.

McKenzie, I.M. and Gallagher, G.P. (1989) *Behind the Uniform: Policing in Britain and America*, Hemel Hempstead: Harvester Wheatsheaf.

McMahon, M. (1995) *Crime, Justice and Human Rights in the Baltics*, Heuni report series, Helsinki: European Institute for Crime Prevention and Control.

Magnarella, P.J. (2000) *Justice in Afrika: Rwanda's Genocide, Its Courts and the UN Criminal Tribunal*, Aldershot: Ashgate.

Maguire, M. and John, T. (1995) *Intelligence, Surveillance and Informants: Integrated Approaches*, Police Research Group Crime and Prevention series, paper 64, London: Home Office.

Maher, G. (1988) 'The Verdict of the Jury', in M. Findley and P. Duff (eds) *The Jury under Attack*, London: Butterworth, 40–55.

Martinson, R. (1974) 'What Works? Questions and Answers from Prison Reform', *The Public Interest*, 35, 22–54.

Matadeen (2000) *Matadeen Report*, Mauritius: Prime Minister's Office; online: www.ncb.intnet.mu/pmo/matadeen.htm

Mawby, R.I. (1990) *Comparative Policing Issues: The British and American System in International Perspective*, London: Unwin Hyman.

Mawby, R.I. (ed.) (1999a) *Policing across the World: Issues for the Twenty-First Century*, London: UCL Press.

Mawby, R.I. (1999b) 'Approaches to Comparative Analysis: The Impossibility of Becoming an Expert on Everywhere', in Mawby (ed.) *Policing across the World: Issues for the Twenty-First Century*, London: UCL Press, 13–22.

Mawby, R.I. (2000) 'Core Policing: The Seductive Myth', in F. Leishman, B. Loveday and S. Savage (eds) *Core Issues in Policing*, second edition, Harlow, Essex: Longman, 107–23.

Mead, M. (1928) *Coming of Age in Samoa: A Psychological Study of Primitive Youth for Western Civilization*, New York: Morrow.

Mead, M. (1935) *Sex and Temperament in Three Primitive Societies*, New York: Morrow.

Merrills, J.G. (2001) *Human Rights in Europe: A Study of the European Convention of Human Rights*, fourth edition, Manchester: Manchester University Press.

Miers, D. (2001) *An International Review of Restorative Justice*, Crime Reduction Research series, paper 10, London: Home Office.

Monjardet, D. (1995) 'The French Model of Policing', in J.P. Brodeur (ed.) *Comparisons in Policing: An International Perspective*, Aldershot: Ashgate, 51–68.

Monjardet, D. and Lévy, R. (1995) 'Undercover Policing in France: Elements for Description and Analysis', in C. Fijnaut and G.T. Marx (eds) *Undercover Police Surveillance in a Comparative Perspective*, The Hague: Kluwer, 29–53.

Moody, S. and Tombs, J. (1982) *Prosecution in the Public Interest*, Edinburgh: Scottish Academic Press.

Morgan, P. (1996) 'Bail in England and Wales: Understanding the Operation of Bail', in F. Paterson (ed.) *Understanding Bail in Britain*, London: HMSO.

Morgan, R. and Jones, S. (1992) 'Bail Or Jail?', in E. Stockdale and S. Casele (eds) *Criminal Justice under Stress*, London: Blackstone, 34–53.

Morris, A. and Maxwell, G. (1998) 'Restorative Justice in New Zealand: Family Group Conferences as a Case Study', *Western Criminology Review* 1(1); online: www.wcr.sonoma.edu/v1n1/morris.html

Morrow, P. (1993) 'A Sociolinguistic Mismatch: Central Alaskan Yup'iks and the Legal System', *Alaska Justice Forum*, 10(2), 1–7.

Mylonopoulos, C. (1993) 'Greece', in C. Van Den Wijngaert, C. Gane, H.H. Kühne and F. McAuley (eds) *Criminal Procedure Systems in the European Community*, London: Butterworth, 163–84.

Nakayama, K. (1987) 'Japan', in F. Cole, S.J. Frankowski and M.G. Gerz (eds) *Major Criminal Justice Systems: A Comparative Study*, second edition, London: Sage, 161–77.

Nelken, D. (1994) 'Whom Can You Trust? The Future of Comparative Criminology', in D. Nelken (ed.) *The Futures of Criminology*, London: Sage, 220–43.

Nelken, D. (1997) 'Understanding Criminal Justice Comparatively', in M. Maguire, R. Morgan and R. Reiner (eds) *The Oxford Handbook of Criminology*, second edition, Oxford: Clarendon Press, 559–73.

Newburn, T. (1999) *Understanding and Preventing Police Corruption: Lessons from the Literature*, Police Research series, paper 110, London: HMSO.

Neyroud, P. and Beckley, A. (2001) *Policing, Ethics and Human Rights*, Cullompton, Devon: Willan.

Nijboer, J.F. (1995) *Strafrechtelijk Bewijsrecht*, Nijmegen, the Netherlands: Ars Aequi Libri.

Norman, P. and Spalek, B. (2002), *Organized Crime*, Portsmouth: University of Portsmouth, Institute for Criminal Justice Studies.

O'Brien, J.C. (1993) 'The International Tribunal for Violations of International Humanitarian Law in the Former Yugoslavia', *American Journal of International Law*, 87, 639–59.

Osmancik, O. (no date) 'Czech Republic', in *The World Factbook of Criminal Justice Systems*: www.ojp.usdoj.gov/bjs/pub/ascii/wfbcjcze.txt

Packer, H. (1969) *The Limits of the Criminal Sanction*, Stanford, California: Stanford University Press.

Pakes, F.J. (1999) 'The Positioning of the Prosecution Service in England and Wales and the Netherlands: Lessons from One Extreme to Another', *Liverpool Law Review*, 21, 261–74.

Pakes, F.J. (2000a) 'League Leaders in Mid-Table: On the Major Changes in Dutch Prison Policy', *Howard Journal of Criminal Justice*, 39, 30–39.

Pakes, F.J. (2000b) 'Doing International Justice: The International Criminal Tribunal for the Former Yugoslavia, the Role of the Judge', in C.M. Breur, M.M. Kommer, J.F. Nijboer and J.M. Reijntjes (eds) *New Trends in Criminal Investigation and Evidence*, Antwerp: Intersentia, 523–33.

Pakes, F.J. (2001) 'Spiders in the Web: Public Prosecutors at Work', Ph.D dissertation, Leyden University, the Netherlands, unpublished.

Pakstaitis, L. (2002) *Crimes of Corruption in Lithuania*, lecture delivered at the Institute for Criminal Justice Studies, University of Portsmouth (April), unpublished.

Paliwala, A. (1980) 'Law and Order in the Village: Papua New Guinea's Village Courts', in C. Sumner (ed.) *Crime, Justice and Underdevelopment*, London: Heinemann, 192–227.

Parker, D.B. (1998) *Fighting Computer Crime: A New Framework for Protecting Information*, New York: Wiley.

Passas, N. (1998) 'Globalisation and Transnational Crime: Effects of Criminogenic Asymmetries', *Transnational Organised Crime*, 4, 22–56.

Philips, C. (1981) *The Royal Commission on Criminal Justice Report*, London: HMSO.

Pradel, J. (1993) 'France', in C. Van Den Wijngaert, C. Gane, H.H. Kühne and F. McAuley (eds) *Criminal Procedure Systems in the European Community*, London: Butterworth, 105–36.

Pruitt, R.C. (1997) 'Guilt By Majority in the International Criminal Tribunal for the Former Yugoslavia: Does This Meet the Standard of Proof "Beyond Reasonable Doubt"'? *Leiden Journal for International Law*, 10, 557–78.

Punch, M. (1985) *Conduct Unbecoming*, London: Tavistock.

Punch, M. (1997) 'The Dutch Criminal Justice System: A Crisis of Identity', *Security Journal*, 9, 177–84.

187

Reichel, P.L. (1999) *Comparative Criminal Justice Systems: A Topical Approach*, second edition, Upper Saddle River, New Jersey: Prentice Hall.

Reiner, R. (2000a) *The Politics of the Police*, third edition, Hemel Hempstead: Harvester Wheatsheaf.

Reiner, R. (2000b) 'Romantic Realism: Policing and the Media', in F. Leishman, B. Loveday and S. Savage (eds) *Core Issues in Policing*, second edition, Harlow, Essex: Longman, 523–66.

Richmond, D.C. (2000) 'The Changing Boundaries between Federal and Local Law Enforcement', in P. MacDonald and J. Munsterman (eds) *Boundary Changes in Criminal Justice Organizations*, Washington, D.C.: US Department of Justice, 81–111.

Robinson, G. (1999) *Crimes against Humanity: The Struggle for Global Justice*, London: Penguin.

Rosenthal, R. (1991) *Meta-Analytic Procedures for Social Research*, Newbury Park, California: Sage.

Rothman, D.J. (1990) *The Discovery of the Asylum: Social Order and Disorder in the New Republic*, second edition, Boston: Little Brown.

Ruiz Vadillo, E. (1993) 'Spain', in C. Van Den Wijngaert, C. Gane, H.H. Kühne and F. McAuley (eds) *Criminal Procedure Systems in the European Community*, London: Butterworth, 383–400.

Salas, L. (no date) 'Venezuela', in *The World Factbook of Criminal Justice Systems*: www.ojp.usdoj.gov/bjs/pub/ascii/wfbcjven.txt

Sanders, A. (2002) 'Prosecution Systems', in M. McConville and G. Wilson (eds) *The Handbook of the Criminal Justice Process*, Oxford: Oxford University Press, 149–65.

Savitt, D.N. and Gottlieb, B. (1983) *Pennsylvania Grand Jury Practice*, Harrisburg, Pennsylvania: Banks-Baldwin.

Schmalleger, F. (1997) *Criminal Justice: A Brief Introduction*, second edition, Englewood Cliffs, New Jersey: Prentice Hall.

Selih, A. and Maver, D. (no date) 'Slovenia', in *The World Factbook of Criminal Justice Systems*: www.ojp.usdoj.gov/bjs/pub/ascii/wfbcjslv.txt

Shafer, N.E. and Curtis, R. (1997) 'Alaska Supreme Court: Fairness and Access Problems and Recommendations', *Alaska Justice Forum*, 14(3), 1–8.

Shelley, L.I. (1999) 'Post-Socialist Policing: Limitations on Institutional Change', in R.I. Mawby (ed.) *Policing around the World: Issues for the Twenty-First Century*, London: UCL Press, 75–87.

Sheptycki, J.W.E. (ed.) (2000) *Issues in Transnational Policing*, London: Routledge.

Sheehan, A.V. (1975) *Criminal Procedure in Scotland and France*, Edinburgh: HMSO.

Simon. R.J. (1977) *The Jury: Its Role in American Society*, Lexington, Massachusetts: Lexington Books.

Skogan, W. (1995) 'Community Policing in the United States', in J.P. Brodeur (ed.) *Comparisons in Policing: An International Perspective*, Aldershot: Ashgate, 86–111.

Skogan, W., Hartnett, S.M., Dubois, J., Comey, J.T., Kaiser, M. and Lovig, J.H. (1999) *On the Beat: Police and Community Problem Solving*, Boulder, Colorado: Westview Press.

Skolnick, J. and Bayley, D. (1988) *The New Blue Line*, New York: Free Press.

Smelser, N.J. (1962) *Theory of Collective Behaviour*, New York: Free Press.

Souryal, S.S. (1987) 'The Religionization of a Society: The Continuing Application of Shariah Law in Saudi Arabia', *Journal for the Scientific Study of Religion*, 26, 429–49.

Souryal, S.S., Potts, D.W. and Alobied, A.I. (1994) 'The Penalty of Hand Amputation for Theft in Islamic Justice, *Journal of Criminal Justice*, 22, 249–65.

Spielmann, A. and Spielmann, D. (1993) 'Luxembourg', in C. Van Den Wijngaert, C. Gane, H.H. Kühne and F. McAuley (eds) *Criminal Procedure Systems in the European Community*, London: Butterworth, 261–78.

Swart, A.H.J. (1993) 'The Netherlands', in C. Van Den Wijngaert, C. Gane, H.H. Kühne and F. McAuley (eds) *Criminal Procedure Systems in the European Community*, London: Butterworth, 279–316.

Tak, P.J.P. (1986) *The Legal Scope of Non-Prosecution in Europe*, Heini Publication series, no. 8, Helsinki: Institute for Crime Prevention and Control.

Tak, P.J.P. (1999) *The Dutch Criminal Justice System: Organization and Operation*, The Hague: Wetenschappelijk Onderzoek- en Documentatiecentrum [WODC].

Takayanagi, K. (1963) 'A Century of Innovation: The Development of Japanese Law 1868–1961', in R. von Mehren (ed.) *Law in Japan: Legal Order in a Changing Society*, Cambridge, Massachusetts: Harvard University Press, 14–40.

Taylor, P.A. (1999) *Hackers: Crime in the Digital Sublime*, London: Routledge.

Thaman, S.C. (2001) 'Europe's New Jury Systems: The Cases of Spain and Russia', in N. Vidmar (ed.) *World Jury Systems*, Oxford: Oxford University Press, 319–51.

Tochilovski, V. (1998) 'Trial in International Criminal Jurisdictions: Battle or Scrutiny?', *European Journal of Crime, Criminal Law and Criminal Justice*, 6, 55–60.

Törnudd, P. (1993) *Fifteen Years of Decreasing Prisoner Rates in Finland*, (Research Communication 8/93), Helsinki: National Research Institute of Legal Policy.

Uglow, S. (2002) *Criminal Justice*, second edition, London: Sweet and Maxwell.

Umbreit, M. and Coates, R. (1992) *Victim Offender Mediation: An Analysis of Programs in Four States in the US*, Minneapolis: University of Minnesota, Center for Restorative Justice and Peacemaking.

Umbreit, M. and Greenwood, J. (1998) *National Survey of Victim Offender Mediation Programs in the US*, Minneapolis: University of Minnesota, Center for Restorative Justice and Peacemaking.

United Nations (2001) *Resolution 1368* (12 September), New York: United Nations.

Upham, F.K. (1987) *Law and Social Change in Postwar Japan*, Cambridge, Massachusetts: Harvard University Press.

Urquhart, P.D. (1998) *The Police Integrity Commission in New South Wales*, paper presented to the 13th World Conference of the International Association for Civilian Oversight of Law Enforcement, Seattle, Washington (October 1998), unpublished.

Vaitiekus, S. (2001) *National Integrity Report: Lithuania*, Transparancy International: www.transparancy.org.

Van Den Wijngaert, C. (1993) 'Belgium', in C. Van Den Wijngaert, C. Gane, H.H. Kühne and F. McAuley (eds) *Criminal Procedure Systems in the European Community*, London: Butterworth, 1–50.

Van Den Wijngaert, C., Gane, C., Kühne, H.H. and McAuley, F. (eds) (1993) *Criminal Procedure Systems in the European Community*, London: Butterworth.

Van Kesteren, J., Mayhew, P. and Nieuwbeerta, P. (2001) *Criminal Victimisation in Seventeen Industrialised Countries: Key Findings from the 2000 International Crime Survey*, The Hague: Scientific Research and Development Centre.

Van Traa, M. (1997) 'The Findings of the Parliamentary Inquiry Viewed from an International Perspective', in M.G.W. Den Boer (ed.) *Undercover Policing and Accountability from an International Perspective*, Maastricht, the Netherlands: European Institute of Public Administration, 15–25.

Vidmar, N. (2001a) 'A Historical and Comparative Perspective on the Common Law Jury', in N. Vidmar (ed.) *World Jury Systems*, Oxford: Oxford University Press, 1–52.

Vidmar, N. (2001b) 'The Jury Elsewhere in the World', in N. Vidmar (ed.) *World Jury Systems*, Oxford: Oxford University Press, 421–47.

Vogler, R. (1996) 'Criminal Procedure in France', in J. Hatchard, B. Huber and R. Vogler (eds) *Comparative Criminal Procedure*, London: British Institute of International and Comparative Law, 14–95.

Waddington, P.A.J. (1999) *Policing Citizens*, London: UCL Press.

Waddington, P.A.J. (2000) 'Public Order Policing: Citizenship and Moral Ambiguity', in F. Leishman, B. Loveday and S. Savage (eds) *Core Issues in Policing*, second edition, Harlow, Essex: Longman, 156–75.

Wadham, J. (1998) 'Zero Tolerance Policing: Striking the Balance, Rights and Liberties', in R. Hopkins Burke (ed.) *Zero Tolerance Policing*, Leicester: Perpetuity Press, 49–56.

Wagenaar, W.A., Van Koppen, P.J. and Crombag, H.F.M. (1993) *Anchored Narratives: The Psychology of Criminal Evidence*, Hemel Hempstead: Harvester Wheatsheaf.

Walker, N. (1991) *Why Punish?* Oxford: Oxford University Press.

Wall, D.S. (2001a) 'Cybercrimes and the Internet', in Wall (ed.) *Crime and the Internet*, London: Routledge, 1–18.

Wall, D.S. (2001b) 'Maintaining Law and Order on the Internet', in Wall (ed.) *Crime and the Internet*, London: Routledge, 167–83.

Walmsley, R. (2002) *World Prison List*, third edition, London: HMSO.

Wilson and Kelling (1982) 'Broken Windows: The Police and Neighborhood Safety', *Atlantic Monthly* (March).

Wing Lo, T. (2000) 'An Overview of The Criminal Justice System in Hong Kong', in O.N.I. Ebbe (ed.) *Comparative and International Criminal Justice Systems*, Boston: Butterworth-Heinemann, 113–27.

Wootten, H. (1991) *Regional Report of Inquiry in New South Wales, Victoria and Tasmania*, Royal Commission into Aboriginal Deaths in Custody, Canberra: Australian Government Publishing Service.

Wright, A. (2002a) *Policing: An Introduction to Concepts and Practice*, Cullompton, Devon: Willan.

Wright, A. (2002b) *Human Rights and Police Ethics*, Portsmouth: University of Portsmouth, Institute for Criminal Justice Studies.

Young, L.F. (1995) 'United States Computer Crime Laws, Criminals and Deterrence, *International Yearbook of Law, Computers and Technology*, 9, 1–16.

Zedner, L. (1995) 'Comparative Research in Criminal Justice', in L. Noaks, M. Levi and M. Maguire (eds) *Contemporary Issues in Criminology*, Cardiff: University of Wales Press, 8–25.

Zedner, L. (1997) 'Victims', in M. Maguire, R. Morgan and R. Reiner (eds) *Oxford Handbook of Criminology*, second edition, Oxford: Oxford University Press, 577–612.

Index